Symbiotic Wisdom: Exploring Ethnoecological Paradigms within Indigenous Environmental Law Narratives

Tulishree Pradhan · Chinmayee Nanda ·
Binita Behera

Symbiotic Wisdom: Exploring Ethnoecological Paradigms within Indigenous Environmental Law Narratives

Springer

Tulishree Pradhan
School of Law
KIIT Deemed University
Bhubaneswar, Odisha, India

Chinmayee Nanda
Department of Liberal Arts
XIM University
Bhubaneswar, Odisha, India

Binita Behera
School of Law
KIIT Deemed University
Bhubaneswar, Odisha, India

ISBN 978-981-95-1041-2 ISBN 978-981-95-1042-9 (eBook)
https://doi.org/10.1007/978-981-95-1042-9

This Springer imprint is published by the registered company Springer Nature Singapore Pte Ltd.
The registered company address is: 152 Beach Road, #21-01/04 Gateway East, Singapore 189721, Singapore

Beneath the canopy, where wisdom flows,
In songs of rivers, the spirit grows.
Drums of the Earth, hearts intertwine,
Echoes of the past, forever shine.

~Inspired from a recurring theme in Ricky Kej's musical journey

Foreword

Static concept of environment with its resources has made way for the dynamic of climate change and climate justice with the post-Rio conference realization of the scientific data and life of ecosystem people. The emergent wisdom is symbiotic, drawing from experiences across different continents and ecosystems of the world. Ethnic and indigenous ways of life had nature and its conservation in the core, thus made its way in knowledge and regulation. There was a discovery of parallels, common strengths, common fears and common determination to protect the earth. These are still being documented in the various initiatives of the conference of parties in last three decades, which recently coincided with the Sustainable Development Goals held in primacy by the UN and the member nations.

Against this backdrop, this work assumes importance. It weaves together the three strains of concepts, legal framework and their global resonances. In its three sections spreading over large number of chapters, it brings together experiences from all continents and all ethnic groups alongside global legal framework, national legal narratives and resonances in case-based experiences. Over the last several decades, the international framework for environmental law has seen tremendous change, with global sustainability initiatives being shaped by treaties and accords including the Paris Agreement, the Convention on Biological Diversity and the United Nations Sustainable Development Goals. Yet, national implementation and compliance are necessary for these structures to be successful. The work demonstrates the difficulties of converting international environmental requirements into local action by highlighting the discrepancies between national compliance and global commitments. The function of indigenous communities and ethnoecological knowledge in environmental governance is another important aspect that this work addresses. Though their opinions are sometimes ignored throughout the policymaking process, Indigenous people have long been the guardians of biodiversity and natural resources. By acknowledging the priceless contributions of traditional ecological knowledge to sustainable practices, this book broadens their viewpoints. To promote inclusive and efficient environmental governance, legislative frameworks must include indigenous rights. This book questions popular environmental rhetoric and promotes a more comprehensive approach to environmental sustainability by including ethnoecological viewpoints.

Thus the work responds to the need for unifying and harmonizing otherwise remotely located situations of Amazon, Alaska, Africa, India and New Zealand—to mention a few. It echoes the interdisciplinary and multidisciplinary underpinning of the environmental law and policy as well as reform approaches. It spells out the crucial role of administration, policies and legislation in tackling these issues is crucial in the context of growing effects of climate change, biodiversity loss and environmental degradation. Thus this book strongly and successfully integrates critical issues and views on societal structures, legislation, global ideologies and ethnoecological views with a thorough grasp of how laws affect, how the environmental problems surface and explores the viability of various remedies including the judicial and alternative remedies rooted in native practices.

Environmental stewardship by people was seen in my personal research and movement engagement. The course of sustainability in the environment is determined by the interaction of indigenous knowledge systems, neoliberal policies and regulatory procedures. This work clarifies the crucial role that environmental laws play in attaining sustainability, going beyond the typical environmental discourse that overstresses scientific and geographical issues, what some scholars loathe. This work addresses the need for a groundbreaking addition to the subject since it presents an interplay of legal, political, social and cultural variables.

This work features the exploration of Indigenous leadership and how it affects environmental policy. Environmental decision-making processes have been greatly influenced by the rise of commercial agendas and the increasing globalization of trade. Policymakers and legal professionals need to be aware of how economic liberalization affects environmental preservation initiatives. This book highlights the pressing requirement for legal frameworks that strike an equilibrium between economic desires and environmental obligations by seriously investigating how neoliberal policies intersect with environmental regulations, frequently resulting in disputes between sustainability and prosperity. Predominance of profit logic is challenged with a perceptive examination of national and international legal systems.

This Book will be a huge gain to a variety of readers as rich as the subjects it examines. The multidisciplinary character of environmental concerns will be appreciated by scholars and researchers in the fields of law, anthropology, environmental studies, sociology, and political science courtesy of this work. Evidence-based approaches that cross-cultural, political and legal factors will be a boon for policymakers. The in-depth talks on mobilization tactics and ecological justice will be valued by activists. This work will be a stimulating and informative study for people worldwide who are concerned about environmental issues.

This book is more of a call for change rather than just an intellectual examination of the status quo. The book emphasizes the value of inclusion and calls on civil society, legal experts and governments to cooperate to create a more sustainable future. It opens the door to a more resilient and egalitarian form of governance for the environment by acknowledging the interaction underlying ideology, legislation and indigenous leadership.

I commend the editors and authors for the groundbreaking work *Symbiotic Wisdom: Exploring Ethnoecological Paradigms within Indigenous Environmental*

Law Narratives. It certainly enhances the knowledge of sustainability in ecology from an integrative legal standpoint. It questions received knowledge, encourages critical thinking and motivates action. I applaud the w thorough investigation and dedication in this contribution towards improving environmental governance.

It is a must-read for everyone interested in using law, policy and inclusive governance to shape a sustainable future !!!!

Bhubaneswar, India

Dr Shashikala Gurpur
Fulbright Scholar and Jean-Monnet
Chair Professor—European Union
Climate Change Law Policy
Governance Management,
Professor of Law and Director,
Symbiosis Law School, Pune, Dean,
Faculty of Law, Symbiosis
International Deemed University

Preface

This book integrates ethnoecological perspectives, legal frameworks, political systems and global ideologies to offer a cohesive insightful exploration of the challenges and opportunities in achieving environmental sustainability. While discussions on environmental issues often focus on scientific and spatial aspects, this book aimed to highlight the significance of environmental laws in shaping our approach to environmental sustainability. By examining the intersection of neoliberalism, international and national legal and political frameworks and other influential factors, the book aims to uncover how these elements collectively impact our perception of environmental challenges and influence our ability to implement effective solutions. This book is for a wide-ranging audience, Academics and Researchers: Scholars in the fields of law, anthropology, environmental studies, sociology and political science will find this book a valuable resource for understanding the interdisciplinary nature of environmental challenges, Policymakers and Activists: Policymakers seeking evidence-based solutions and activists advocating for sustainable practices, will gain insights into the legal, cultural and political dynamics that shape environmental policies, Global Citizens: Anyone concerned about the future of our planet and interested in the unique perspectives and experiences of indigenous communities and the environmental laws worldwide, will find this book enlightening and thought-provoking. It is a pioneering work that not only illuminates the critical issues surrounding environmental sustainability but also offers a path forward by emphasizing the importance of environmental laws in shaping our approach to these challenges. This book serves as a call to action, urging us to embrace a more comprehensive and inclusive perspective in our quest for a sustainable future.

Bhubaneswar, India

Tulishree Pradhan
Chinmayee Nanda
Binita Behera

Acknowledgments Embarking on the scholarly journey that culminates in *Symbiotic Wisdom: Exploring Ethnoecological Paradigms within Indigenous Environmental Law Narratives* has been enriched by the unwavering support, inspiration and guidance of numerous esteemed institutions and individuals. It is with profound gratitude and heartfelt appreciation that we extend our acknowledgements to those who have been instrumental in bringing this work to fruition.

First and foremost, we extend our deepest thanks to the School of Law, KIIT Deemed University, Bhubaneswar, Odisha. This venerable institution provided a nurturing platform that fostered multidisciplinary research, allowing us to delve deeply into the intricate intersections of ethnoecology and indigenous environmental law. The academic rigor and intellectual environment at KIIT have been pivotal in shaping the contours of our exploration, enabling us to weave together diverse threads of knowledge into a coherent and compelling narrative. Our sincere appreciation also goes to KISS Deemed University, Bhubaneswar, Odisha, India, the sister university of KIIT, both visionary establishments founded by the illustrious Dr Achyuta Samanta. KISS Deemed University's remarkable commitment to education, demonstrated by its free education to over 50,000 Indigenous students from Kindergarten through to PhD, serves as a beacon of hope and an exemplar of inclusive educational excellence. The symbiotic existence of these institutions, fostering an environment where marginalized communities can thrive, has been a profound source of inspiration for our work. The harmonious collaboration and shared ethos between KIIT and KISS embody the very principles of symbiosis that our book seeks to illuminate. We are especially indebted to Dr Amareswar Galla, Pro-Chancellor of KIIT Deemed University, whose clarion call for an inclusive environment resonated deeply with our mission. His visionary leadership and steadfast dedication to creating spaces where every voice is heard and valued have been instrumental in shaping our research trajectory. Dr Galla's commitment to inclusivity underscores the importance of equitable representation, a theme that is intricately woven into the fabric of our narrative. Our heartfelt thanks also extend to Dr Deepak Kumar Behera, whose impassioned advocacy for creating a level playing field for each marginalized community has been a cornerstone of our motivation. Dr Behera's unwavering support and insightful guidance have empowered us to navigate the complexities of Indigenous environmental law with confidence and clarity. His dedication to fostering equity and justice within academic and legal frameworks has profoundly influenced our approach and enriched our scholarly pursuits.

We gratefully acknowledge the Indian Council of Social Science Research (ICSSR), Ministry of Education, Government of India, for bestowing upon us the honor of being granted a project under its special Call for Studies. The ICSSR's recognition and support for our research on the culture, history and geography of the Scheduled Tribes of India for the year 2022–23 have been indispensable. This prestigious endorsement not only validated the significance of our work but also provided the necessary resources and impetus to undertake this comprehensive study. The ICSSR's commitment to advancing social science research has been a guiding light, enabling us to contribute meaningfully to the discourse on indigenous environmental law and ethnoecological paradigms.

We also extend our gratitude to the myriad of faculty members, researchers and administrative staff at both KIIT and KISS Deemed Universities whose collective wisdom, encouragement and collaborative spirit have been invaluable. With heartfelt gratitude, we also acknowledge the steadfast dedication of the Tribal Affairs Research and Advocacy (TARA) Centre, School of Law, KIIT Deemed University. Their tireless efforts in advancing Indigenous research illuminate pathways of justice and inclusion, fostering a profound understanding of tribal narratives and their rightful place in the fabric of law. Their dedication to fostering an environment of intellectual curiosity and scholarly excellence has greatly enriched our research experience. Lastly, we wish to acknowledge the indigenous communities whose resilience, knowledge and harmonious relationship with their natural environment form the very essence of our study. Their lived experiences and traditional wisdom have provided the foundational insights that animate our exploration of symbiotic wisdom within environmental law narratives. This book stands as a testament to the collective efforts and unwavering support of all those who have contributed to its creation. To the School of Law KIIT Deemed University, KISS Deemed University, Dr Achyuta Samanta, Dr Amareswar Galla, Dr Deepak Kumar Behera, the Indian Council of Social Science Research and the countless individuals who have walked this path with us, we offer our deepest gratitude. May this work honor every contribution and further the quest for knowledge, equity and sustainable symbiosis between humanity and the natural world.

Competing Interests The authors have no competing interests to declare that are relevant to the content of this manuscript.

Contents

1 Ecological Resilience and Human Adaptation 1
1.1 Indigenous Knowledge as a Blueprint for Sustainability 3
1.2 International Conventions, Protocols and SDG Goals 3
1.2.1 Convention on Biological Diversity (CBD) 3
1.2.2 Paris Agreement on Climate Change 4
1.2.3 United Nations Declaration on the Rights of Indigenous Peoples (UNDRIP) 4
1.2.4 Sustainable Development Goals (SDGs) 4
1.3 Bridging the Gap Between Tradition and Modernity 5
1.3.1 Integrated Agroforestry Systems 5
1.3.2 Community-Led Technology Adoption 6
1.3.3 Traditional Healing and Biodiversity Conservation 6
1.4 Alignment with International Conventions, Protocols and SDG Goals 7
1.4.1 United Nations Declaration on the Rights of Indigenous Peoples (UNDRIP) 7
1.4.2 Convention on Biological Diversity (CBD) 7
1.4.3 Paris Agreement 7
1.4.4 Sustainable Development Goals (SDGs) 7
1.5 Emphasizing the Role of Cultural and Spiritual Beliefs in Ecological Practices 8
1.5.1 Sacred Natural Sites as Conservation Tools 9
1.5.2 Cultural Taboos Supporting Biodiversity 9
1.5.3 Eco-Spiritual Festivals 9
1.6 Alignment with International Conventions, Protocols and SDG Goals 10
1.6.1 Convention on Biological Diversity (CBD) 10
1.6.2 UNESCO Convention for the Safeguarding of Intangible Cultural Heritage (ICH) 10
1.6.3 United Nations Declaration on the Rights of Indigenous Peoples (UNDRIP) 10

1.6.4 Sustainable Development Goals (SDGs) 10
1.7 Addressing Contemporary Challenges Through Indigenous Lenses 11
1.7.1 Climate Change Resilience 11
1.7.2 Biodiversity Conservation 11
1.7.3 Water Resource Management 12
1.7.4 Sustainable Agriculture 12
1.8 Alignment with International Conventions, Protocols and SDG Goals 12
1.8.1 United Nations Declaration on the Rights of Indigenous Peoples (UNDRIP) 12
1.8.2 Convention on Biological Diversity (CBD) 12
1.8.3 Paris Agreement on Climate Change 13
1.8.4 Sustainable Development Goals (SDGs) 13
1.9 Advocating for Policy Integration and Legal Recognition 13
1.9.1 Policy Integration in Land Rights 14
1.9.2 Indigenous Practices in Climate Policy 14
1.9.3 Legal Recognition of Traditional Knowledge 15
1.10 Community-Led Co-Management Models 16
1.11 International Conventions, Protocols and SDG Goals 17
1.11.1 United Nations Declaration on the Rights of Indigenous Peoples (UNDRIP) 17
1.11.2 Convention on Biological Diversity (CBD) 17
1.11.3 Paris Agreement on Climate Change 17
1.11.4 Sustainable Development Goals (SDGs) 17
1.12 Five Sociological Models to Explore 18
1.12.1 Cultural Ecology Model 18
1.12.2 Conflict Theory Model 20
1.12.3 Symbolic Interactionism Model 22
1.12.4 Systems Theory Model 28
1.12.5 Critical Theory Model 30
1.13 Ecological Resilience and Human Adaptation 34
1.14 Ethnoecological Paradigms 34
1.15 The Role of Religious Beliefs in Customary Laws 35
1.16 Symbiosis in Indigenous Environmental Law 35
1.17 Navigating the Barriers 36
References: 36

2 Environmental Justice and Indigenous Perspectives ... 41
2.1 Overview ... 41
2.2 Origins and Historical Contexts ... 42
2.3 Key Concepts of Environmental Justice ... 43
2.4 Environmental Justice and Climate Change ... 44
2.5 Key Issues in Environmental Justice ... 44
2.6 Strategies and Remedies for Environmental Justice ... 45
2.7 History and Evolution of Environmental Justice ... 46
2.8 Traditional Ecological Knowledge (TEK) ... 47
2.9 Sacredness of the Environment ... 47
2.10 Stewardship and Conservation Practices ... 47
2.11 Colonialism, Land Dispossession and Environmental Racism ... 47
2.12 Colonialism and Land Dispossession ... 48
2.13 Environmental Racism ... 49
2.14 The Intersection of Colonialism, Land Dispossession and Environmental Racism ... 49
2.15 Contemporary Struggles and Resistance ... 50
2.15.1 Resource Extraction (Mining, Oil Drilling, Logging, Etc.) ... 50
2.15.2 Pollution and Toxic Waste Sites ... 51
2.15.3 Deforestation and Habitat Destruction ... 51
2.15.4 Climate Change Impacts on Indigenous Lands and Cultures ... 52
2.15.5 Water Rights and Contamination ... 52
2.16 Movements for Environmental Justice: Indigenous Activism and Leadership ... 53
2.17 Legislative and Policy Frameworks for Indigenous Environmental Rights ... 54
2.18 Indigenous Solutions to Environmental Justice: A Path Forward ... 55
2.18.1 Reviving Ecological Knowledge and Indigenous Governance ... 55
2.18.2 Collaborative Models of Environmental Justice: Indigenous-Led Conservation ... 56
2.18.3 Sustainable Livelihoods and Eco-Tourism as Indigenous Economic Alternatives ... 56
2.18.4 Using Cultural Revival to Advance Environmental Justice ... 57
2.18.5 The Promotion of Environmental Justice Through Cultural Revival ... 57
2.19 Case Studies in Indigenous Environmental Justice ... 58
2.19.1 The Dakota Access Pipeline and the Standing Rock Sioux (DAPL) ... 58
2.19.2 The Battle Against Deforestation and the Amazon ... 58
2.19.3 The Fight Against the Pebble Mine in Alaska ... 59

2.19.4 The Battle Against Wind Turbine Projects and the Sámi 60
2.19.5 The Maasai and Conservation in East Africa 60
2.20 The Save the Narmada Movement, also Known as the Narmada Bachao Andolan 62
2.21 The Chipko Movement 63
2.21.1 Activism and Resistance 64
2.22 The Struggle Against Mining in the Niyamgiri Hills (Dongria Kondh Tribe) 65
2.23 Environmental Injustice 65
2.24 Fishermen's and Indigenous Peoples' Opposition to the Koodankulam Nuclear Power Plant Protest 66
2.25 Environmental Justice and Indigenous Perspective as Reflected in Film and Literature 68
2.25.1 Documentary Works that Show Indigenous Environmental Justice 68
2.25.2 Indigenous Environmental Justice in Literature 69
2.26 Native American Environmental Stories 74
2.26.1 Ecological Knowledge and Stewardship 74
2.26.2 Sacred Landscapes and Place-Based Knowledge 75
2.26.3 Sustainability and Life Cycles 75
2.26.4 Spiritual Bond with Nature 75
2.27 The Relationship Between World Music and Indigenous Environmental Stories 75
2.28 The Relationship Between World Music and Indigenous Environmental Soundscapes and Nature 76
2.28.1 Rhythm and Cycles 76
2.28.2 Ceremonial Music and Rituals 76
2.28.3 Transmission of Ecological Knowledge 77
2.28.4 Healing and Environmental Restoration 77
2.28.5 Examples of Indigenous Music from Around the World: 77
2.29 Indigenous Women and Environmental Justice: A Crucial Intersection 79
2.30 The Confluence of Indigenous Rights and Environmental Justice 79
2.31 Gender and the Environment: The Role of Indigenous Women 80
2.32 The Effects of Environmental Injustice on Indigenous Women 80
2.32.1 Climate Change 81
2.32.2 The Leadership of Indigenous Women in Environmental Justice 81

2.32.3 Gender's Significance in Environmental Justice Campaigns 82
2.33 Environmental Justice and Indigenous Perspectives 83
2.33.1 United States: Environmental Racism and Sacred Land Protection 84
2.33.2 Brazil: Deforestation and Amazonian Tribes 84
2.33.3 Australia: Aboriginal Land Rights and Mining 84
2.33.4 India: Tribal Resistance to Industrial Projects 84
2.33.5 Canada: Land and Water Defenders 85
2.33.6 Global Perspectives: Amplifying Marginalized Voices 85
References 86

3 Legal Dimensions of Conservation Practices 93
3.1 Historical Evolution of Conservation Laws with Indigenous Contributions 93
3.2 Indigenous Roots of Conservation Laws 94
3.2.1 Bishnoi Community: A Model for Legal Wildlife Protection in India 94
3.2.2 The Māori's Kaitiakitanga and Its Legal Integration in New Zealand 95
3.3 Bridging Customary Practices and Formal Legal Systems 96
3.4 Contemporary Legal Relevance and Challenges 96
3.5 International Legal Instruments Supporting Indigenous Contributions 96
3.6 A Path Forward for Conservation Laws 97
3.7 Indigenous Sovereignty in Conservation Law 97
3.8 Legal Personhood of the Whanganui River: A Case Study in Māori Sovereignty 98
3.9 Indigenous Protected and Conserved Areas (IPCAs) in Canada: A Collaborative Governance Model 98
3.10 Participatory Governance Models: Empowering Indigenous Communities in Conservation 99
3.11 Legal Recognition of Indigenous Sovereignty: A Global Trend 100
3.12 The Future of Indigenous Sovereignty in Conservation Law 100
3.13 Intersection of Cultural Beliefs and Legal Frameworks 101
3.14 Uluru-Kata Tjuta National Park: Protecting Sacred Sites Through Legal Measures 101
3.15 Bolivia's Recognition of Pachamama (Mother Earth) as a Legal Entity 102
3.16 Cultural Beliefs as Tools for Effective Environmental Governance 102
3.17 The Global Relevance of Cultural and Legal Integration 103
3.18 A Holistic Approach to Conservation Law 104

3.18.1 Addressing Global Challenges Through Legal Innovations 104
3.19 Legal Recognition of Indigenous Knowledge in Global Environmental Governance 106
3.20 The Role of Indigenous-Led Legal Mechanisms in Climate Change Mitigation 106
3.21 Alignment with International Protocols and SDGs 107
3.21.1 SDG 13: Climate Action and Indigenous Knowledge 108
3.21.2 SDG 15: Life on Land and Biodiversity Conservation 109
3.21.3 SDG 16: Peace, Justice and Strong Institutions 109
3.21.4 Convention on Biological Diversity (CBD) and Indigenous Contributions 110
3.21.5 The Paris Agreement and Indigenous Climate Solutions 110
3.21.6 Harmonizing Local Traditions with Global Legal Frameworks 111
3.22 Cultural Beliefs and the Environment: Rituals as Conservation Catalysts 112
3.23 Folklore as Environmental Stewardship 112
3.24 Indigenous Cosmologies and Legal Innovations 113
3.25 Biodiversity Conservation Through Cultural-Legal Synthesis 113
3.26 Sustainable Resource Use and Ecosystem Protection 113
3.27 Harmonizing Culture and Law 114
3.28 Legislative Protection for Indigenous Populations in India: A Detailed Analysis 114
3.28.1 Constitutional Provisions 114
3.28.2 The Forest Rights Act (FRA), 2006 in Brief 114
3.28.3 Biological Diversity Act, 2002 116
3.28.4 The Panchayats (Extension to Scheduled Areas) Act (PESA), 1996 116
3.28.5 The Environment Protection Act, 1986 116
3.28.6 The Scheduled Tribes and Other Traditional Forest Dwellers (Recognition of Forest Rights) Act, 2006 117
3.29 Case Studies 117
3.29.1 Niyamgiri Hills, Odisha 117
3.29.2 Sacred Groves in Meghalaya 117
3.30 Recommendations for Strengthening Legal Protections 118
3.30.1 Enhanced Implementation 118
3.30.2 Stronger EIA Mechanisms 118
3.30.3 Capacity-Building 118
3.30.4 International Collaboration 119
3.31 Legislative Protection for Indigenous Populations in Australia: A Detailed Analysis 119

3.31.1 Constitutional Recognition and Challenges 119
3.31.2 Native Title Act, 1993 119
3.31.3 Environment Protection and Biodiversity Conservation Act, 1999 (EPBC Act) [41] 121
3.31.4 Aboriginal Land Rights (Northern Territory) Act, 1976 122
3.31.5 Water Rights and Natural Resource Management 122
3.31.6 Cultural Heritage Protection Laws 122
3.31.7 Strengths of Australia's Legal Framework 123
3.32 Case Studies 123
3.32.1 A Joint Management Model of Cultural and Ecological Conservation 123
3.32.2 Historical Context and Traditional Knowledge of the Mirarr People 124
3.32.3 The Establishment of Joint Management 124
3.32.4 Cultural and Ecological Conservation: The Intersection 124
3.32.5 Successes and Challenges of Joint Management 125
3.32.6 A Model for the Future 125
3.33 Rangers Programs 126
3.33.1 Indigenous Ranger Programs in Australia: Traditional Fire Management and Biodiversity Protection 126
3.33.2 Traditional Fire Management as a Conservation Tool 126
3.33.3 The Role of Indigenous Knowledge in Biodiversity Protection 127
3.33.4 Integration of Traditional Practices with Modern Conservation Approaches 127
3.33.5 Cultural and Economic Benefits 128
3.33.6 Impact on the Kimberley Region's Biodiversity and Future Prospects 128
3.34 Recommendations for Strengthening Indigenous Protections 129
3.34.1 Enhance Legal Frameworks 129
3.34.2 Constitutional Recognition 129
3.34.3 Expand Indigenous Protected Areas 129
3.34.4 Improve Consultation Processes 129
3.35 Australia: Aboriginal Cosmologies and Native Title 130
3.36 Legislative Protection for Indigenous Populations in the United States: A Detailed Analysis 130
3.37 Tribal Sovereignty: Foundations and Framework 130
3.38 Key Federal Legislation Supporting Indigenous Rights 130
3.38.1 Indian Self-Determination and Education Assistance Act (ISDEAA), 1975 131
3.38.2 National Historic Preservation Act (NHPA), 1966 132

3.38.3 Native American Graves Protection and Repatriation Act (NAGPRA), 1990 132
3.38.4 Clean Water Act (CWA), 1972 & Clean Air Act (CAA), 1963 132
3.39 Co-management of Natural Resources 133
3.39.1 Yellowstone National Park (and Other Federal Lands) 133
3.39.2 Alaska Native Claims Settlement Act (ANCSA), 1971 133
3.40 Sacred Lands and Environmental Justice 133
3.40.1 Bears Ears National Monument 133
3.40.2 Environmental Justice Framework 133
3.41 Integration of Traditional Ecological Knowledge (TEK) 134
3.42 Case Studies: Success and Challenges 134
3.42.1 Success Stories 134
3.42.2 Ongoing Challenges 134
3.43 Strengths of U.S. Legislative Framework 135
3.43.1 Recognition of Sovereignty 135
3.43.2 Incorporation of TEK 135
3.43.3 Environmental Justice 135
3.44 Recommendations for Strengthening Protections 135
3.44.1 Stronger Enforcement Mechanisms 135
3.44.2 Expanded Funding 135
3.44.3 Enhanced Co-management 135
3.44.4 Climate Change Adaptation 136
3.45 United States: Tribal Sovereignty and Environmental Management 136
3.46 Legislative Protection for Indigenous Populations in Brazil: A Detailed Analysis 136
3.46.1 Legal Framework for Indigenous Rights in Brazil 137
3.46.2 Role of Indigenous Territories in Conservation 138
3.46.3 Challenges in Enforcement 138
3.46.4 Judicial Interventions and Advocacy 139
3.46.5 International Recognition and Support 139
3.46.6 Recommendations for Strengthening Indigenous Rights 140
3.46.7 Brazil: Indigenous Land Rights and the Amazon 141
3.47 Legislative Protection for Indigenous Populations in New Zealand: A Detailed Analysis 141
3.47.1 Māori Cosmology and Environmental Stewardship 141
3.47.2 Key Legislation Protecting Māori Interests and Recognizing the Legal Personhood of Nature 142
3.47.3 Impact and Global Implications of Legal Personhood for Nature 143

3.47.4 Broader Implications for Conservation and Indigenous Rights ... 144
3.47.5 New Zealand: Māori Cosmology and Legal Personhood of Nature ... 145
3.48 Legislative Protection for Indigenous Populations in Africa: A Detailed Analysis ... 145
3.48.1 Cultural Practices and Folklore in African Conservation ... 146
3.48.2 Legislative Protection and Community-Based Conservation (CBC) ... 146
3.48.3 Challenges and Opportunities ... 148
3.48.4 Africa: Folklore and Community-Based Conservation ... 149
3.49 Detailed Analysis of Global Legislative Protection for Indigenous Populations in Conservation ... 150
3.49.1 Convention on Biological Diversity (CBD) ... 150
3.49.2 UNESCO World Heritage Convention ... 151
3.49.3 International Labour Organization (ILO) Convention No. 169 ... 152
3.49.4 UN Declaration on the Rights of Indigenous Peoples (UNDRIP) ... 152
3.49.5 Convention on International Trade in Endangered Species of Wild Fauna and Flora (CITES) ... 153
3.50 Global Initiatives: Cultural Integration in Conservation Treaties ... 154
3.50.1 Challenges and Opportunities ... 154
References ... 158

About the Authors

Dr Tulishree Pradhan, Associate Professor-I at the School of Law, KIIT Deemed University, Odisha, India, is a distinguished academic and legal scholar. With a PhD in Media and Law, her journey spans diverse educational landscapes, fostering deep societal empathy. Renowned for her expertise in Constitution and Administrative Law, she has presented at global platforms like the University of Warsaw, Poland, the University of Coimbra, Portugal, and NOVA University, Portugal. Recipient of the ICSSR doctoral fellowship and the prestigious Bharat Vikas Award, Dr Pradhan leads key research centers and has spearheaded ICSSR-funded projects on water laws and justice for Scheduled Tribes. A legal consultant for NGOs viz. Save Elephant Foundation Trust, Justice & Liberty Foundation, and Corruption Free Odisha, she champions justice, conservation and empowerment while embracing nature, literature and meditation.

Dr Chinmayee Nanda is an Assistant Professor, currently serving in the Department of Liberal Arts, XIM University, Odisha, India. She has completed her PhD thesis in the area of Comparative Literature and Feminism. Enthusiastic about interdisciplinary areas of studies she has an EMBA and PGJMC degree to her credit. Her areas of interest include Feminism, Gender Studies, Tribal Literature, Translation, Cross-Cultural Communication, Law and Language, and Partition Literature. She has published papers in journals of repute and in the form of book chapters, also presented in various conferences in forums like IITs and IIMs. She has the opportunity of presenting her research at the University of Oxford in July 2023. She is currently working on a collaborative project on the Rights of Women Prisoners.

Dr Binita Behera, Assistant Professor-II at the School of Law, KIIT Deemed University, Odisha, India, with a PhD in Sociology and 20+ Post PhD years of experience. She has authored several papers on gender issues, equity, culture, ecological resilience and public policy. Passionate about equitable and sustainable development, Dr Behera actively engages in interdisciplinary research and policy discourse, driving innovative strategies to address global environmental and socioeconomic challenges. At present, she is working as Assistant Professor in the School of Law, KIIT Deemed University, Odisha, India, and is passionately pursuing socio-legal research.

Abbreviations

ABS	Access and Benefit-Sharing
Adivasi	Indigenous people in India (often used interchangeably with tribal communities)
ANCSA	Alaska Native Claims Settlement Act
APIB	Articulation of Indigenous Peoples of Brazil
BIA	Bureau of Indian Affairs
BIPOC	Black, Indigenous, and People of Color
BMCs	Biodiversity Management Committees
CAA	Clean Air Act
CBA	Community-Based Adaptation
CBC	Community-Based Conservation
CBD	Convention on Biological Diversity
CBNRM	Community-Based Natural Resource Management
CWA	Clean Water Act
DAPL	Dakota Access Pipeline
DDT	Dichlorodiphenyltrichloroethane (a pesticide)
EC	Environment Conservation
EIAs	Environmental Impact Assessments
EJ	Environmental Justice
EPBC	Environment Protection and Biodiversity Conservation
FPIC	Free, Prior, and Informed Consent
FRA	Forest Rights Act
FUNAI	National Foundation for Indigenous Peoples
HEC	Human-Elephant Conflict
IBAMA	Brazilian Institute of Environment and Renewable Natural Resources
IBI	Indigenous Biodiversity Initiative
ICF	Indigenous Conservation Foundation
IFS	Indian Forest Service
IHL	International Humanitarian Law
ILO	International Labour Organization

IPA	Indigenous Protected Areas
IPCAs	Indigenous Protected and Conserved Areas
ISDEAA	Indian Self-Determination and Education Assistance Act
kaitiakitanga	Guardianship or Environmental Stewardship
KKNPP	Koodankulam Nuclear Power Plant
NBA	Narmada Bachao Andolan
NEMA	National Environmental Management Act
NEPA	National Environmental Policy Act
NHPA	National Historic Preservation Act
NT	Native Title
NT	Northern Territory
PBRs	People's Biodiversity Registers
PESA	Panchayats (Extension to Scheduled Areas) Act
PMANE	People's Movement Against Nuclear Energy
PWD	Persons with Disabilities
SDG	Sustainable Development Goals
TCO	Tierra Comunitaria de Origen
TEK	Traditional Ecological Knowledge
UNDRIP	United Nations Declaration on the Rights of Indigenous Peoples
UNESCO	United Nations Educational, Scientific and Cultural Organization
USA	United States of America
Wangari Maathai	The name of the author, not an abbreviation, but referenced as a key figure
Wunambal Gaambera	An Indigenous group from the Kimberley region of Australia
Zampoña	A type of traditional pan flute used in Andean music

Chapter 1
Ecological Resilience and Human Adaptation

Abstract This chapter examines the symbiotic relationship between ecological resilience and human adaptation, focusing on how indigenous communities worldwide have developed sustainable practices to thrive in diverse ecosystems. Indigenous knowledge systems, often interwoven with cultural and spiritual beliefs, have fostered adaptive strategies that enhance ecological resilience and mitigate environmental challenges. The chapter explores these practices in both historical and contemporary contexts, shedding light on the critical role indigenous populations play in maintaining ecological balance. Environmental sustainability is at the forefront of global discourse, necessitating a nuanced understanding that transcends scientific, legal and cultural boundaries. While much of the focus on environmental challenges has historically centered on scientific and spatial analyses, the role of environmental laws in shaping and steering sustainable practices often remains understated. *Ecological Resilience and Human Adaptation* aims to fill this critical gap, offering a comprehensive exploration of how legal frameworks, political systems and indigenous knowledge converge to address pressing ecological concerns. This chapter delves into the intersection of diverse elements such as neoliberal ideologies, international and national legal systems and ethnoecological practices to provide a holistic perspective on environmental governance. By doing so, it underscores the indispensable role of environmental laws in fostering a sustainable future while bringing to light the cultural narratives and ethical wisdom of Indigenous communities worldwide.

Keywords Ethnoecology · Spatial aspects · Indigeneity · Sustainable development · Mitigating measures

See Fig. 1.1.

Indigenous communities have long lived in harmony with their surroundings, cultivating intricate understandings of natural systems. In India, practices such as agroforestry and the protection of sacred groves showcase a deep-seated commitment to biodiversity. For instance, sacred groves serve as reservoirs of genetic diversity and microhabitats for threatened species, reflecting the interplay between spiritual beliefs and conservation. Similarly, Aboriginal Australians have practiced traditional

T. Pradhan et al., *Symbiotic Wisdom: Exploring Ethnoecological Paradigms within Indigenous Environmental Law Narratives*,
https://doi.org/10.1007/978-981-95-1042-9_1

Fig. 1.1 The transition from Ancient to New

fire management, using controlled burns to maintain healthy landscapes and prevent wildfires, a method now recognized for its modern applicability [1].

The chapter also explores the resilience of Amazonian tribes in Brazil, whose intricate agro-ecological systems, such as forest gardening, support sustainable livelihoods while preserving the rainforest's biodiversity. In New Zealand, the Māori worldview, centered on kaitiakitanga (guardianship), emphasizes stewardship of natural resources as a communal responsibility, embodying principles of sustainability and adaptation.

In Africa, indigenous pastoralist communities like the Maasai of Kenya and Tanzania have demonstrated remarkable adaptability through rotational grazing systems, ensuring sustainable use of grasslands and water resources. North America's Native American tribes have relied on traditional ecological knowledge to manage wildlife populations and maintain soil fertility through rotational farming practices. It also highlights the threats indigenous communities face due to climate change, industrial development and policy exclusion, which disrupt their adaptive strategies and compromise ecological resilience. By analyzing these global examples, the chapter underscores the necessity of integrating indigenous knowledge systems into contemporary environmental policies and practices (Fig. 1.1). Ultimately, this chapter advocates for recognizing indigenous wisdom as a cornerstone of ecological resilience, calling for inclusive approaches that respect and amplify the voices of indigenous populations in shaping sustainable futures (Fig. 1.1).

1.1 Indigenous Knowledge as a Blueprint for Sustainability

This chapter highlights how Indigenous communities have historically harmonized with their environments, offering valuable lessons for modern ecological challenges. Practices like rotational farming, water conservation and forest management by communities such as the Zuni in North America and the Ifugao in the Philippines demonstrate sustainable techniques that enhance ecological resilience. These time-tested strategies are increasingly recognized as blueprints for addressing issues like soil degradation, water scarcity and biodiversity loss [2]. By presenting these examples, the chapter emphasizes the relevance of Indigenous knowledge systems in contemporary environmental discourse.

Indigenous knowledge systems are not merely cultural artifacts but pragmatic frameworks rooted in centuries of environmental observation and adaptation. These systems encompass practices like sustainable land management, biodiversity conservation and water resource optimization, all of which have proven their efficacy in maintaining ecological balance. For instance, the *Zuni Waffle Gardens* in North America use intricate soil and water conservation techniques to maximize agricultural yield in arid environments. Similarly, the *Qhapaq Ñan* (Andean road system) demonstrates how Indigenous infrastructure can harmonize with mountainous ecosystems without disrupting their integrity. By adopting such methods, modern environmental management can avoid the pitfalls of over-reliance on technology and exploitative resource extraction. These practices are scalable and adaptable to various ecosystems, offering an effective response to challenges like soil erosion, deforestation and climate change (Fig. 1.2). Governments and organizations integrating Indigenous practices into local and regional development initiatives have reported improved outcomes in sustainability and resource efficiency, demonstrating their practical utility.

1.2 International Conventions, Protocols and SDG Goals

1.2.1 Convention on Biological Diversity (CBD)

The CBD explicitly recognizes the role of Indigenous communities in conserving biodiversity. Articles 8(j) and 10(c) of the CBD call for the preservation and promotion of Indigenous knowledge systems [3]. Practices such as rotational farming and sacred forest conservation by the Khasi tribes in India align with this mandate, preserving biodiversity while ensuring sustainable livelihoods.

Fig. 1.2 The interconnectedness of indigenous traditions, natural landscapes and ecological harmony, through vibrant and symbolic imagery

1.2.2 Paris Agreement on Climate Change

Indigenous knowledge, particularly in monitoring ecological changes, complements scientific methods. For instance, Inuit observations of shifting ice patterns have informed climate adaptation strategies [4]. These contributions support the Paris Agreement's goal of strengthening resilience to climate impacts while promoting low-carbon solutions.

1.2.3 United Nations Declaration on the Rights of Indigenous Peoples (UNDRIP)

UNDRIP underscores the importance of Indigenous peoples' participation in environmental decision-making. Showcasing their knowledge as a sustainability blueprint directly fulfills Articles 25 and 29, which emphasize their role in maintaining ecological health and utilizing resources sustainably [5].

1.2.4 Sustainable Development Goals (SDGs)

- **SDG 13 (Climate Action)**: Indigenous adaptation strategies, like water conservation in arid regions, are critical to mitigating the effects of climate change.

- **SDG 15 (Life on Land)**: Indigenous practices in afforestation and biodiversity conservation, such as the Bishnoi community's efforts in Rajasthan, India, directly contribute to this goal.
- **SDG 6 (Clean Water and Sanitation)**: Traditional water harvesting systems, like *baolis* (stepwells) in India, exemplify sustainable water resource management.
- **SDG 12 (Responsible Consumption and Production)**: Indigenous approaches to resource use, such as the Sámi people's sustainable herding, promote balance between consumption and ecosystem health.

By highlighting Indigenous knowledge as a practical, sustainable blueprint, we not only enrich modern environmental strategies but also fulfill global commitments under international conventions and SDGs. Recognizing and institutionalizing these practices ensures a harmonious blend of tradition and innovation, creating resilient ecosystems and communities worldwide [6]. This pragmatic integration is essential for achieving sustainability at local and global scales.

1.3 Bridging the Gap Between Tradition and Modernity

A unique aspect of this chapter is its focus on the interplay between traditional ecological practices and modern science. It examines how Indigenous methods, such as agroforestry among the Kayapo in the Amazon or the Māori's *rahui* (temporary restrictions on resource use), align with scientific principles of ecosystem management [7]. By bridging the gap between Indigenous wisdom and modern technology, the chapter underscores the potential for integrative approaches to environmental resilience and human adaptation.

Bridging the gap between traditional Indigenous practices and modern environmental management involves integrating time-tested knowledge systems with scientific advancements. This approach respects cultural heritage while addressing contemporary environmental challenges. For example:

1.3.1 Integrated Agroforestry Systems

The Kayapo people of the Amazon combine traditional forest farming with modern agroforestry techniques. Their methods, which mimic natural ecosystems, enhance biodiversity, sequester carbon and sustain livelihoods [7].

1.3.2 Community-Led Technology Adoption

The Maasai in East Africa use traditional rotational grazing methods, now supported by modern satellite mapping, to monitor grazing lands and manage livestock sustainably. This integration enhances resilience against climate variability [8].

1.3.3 Traditional Healing and Biodiversity Conservation

The use of medicinal plants by Indigenous communities, like the Kani tribe in India, is now being researched and commercialized responsibly through partnerships with scientific institutions, ensuring biodiversity conservation and fair benefit-sharing [9]. Such practical applications not only solve pressing ecological issues but also create a shared platform where tradition informs innovation, fostering inclusive environmental governance (Fig. 1.3).

The illustration captures the integration of ecological wisdom with technological advancements, emphasizing biodiversity, sustainability and inclusive environmental governance.

Fig. 1.3 The illustration captures the integration of ecological wisdom with technological advancements, emphasizing biodiversity, sustainability and inclusive environmental governance

1.4 Alignment with International Conventions, Protocols and SDG Goals

1.4.1 United Nations Declaration on the Rights of Indigenous Peoples (UNDRIP)

UNDRIP encourages the protection and promotion of Indigenous cultural heritage. Bridging tradition and modernity respects Article 31, which acknowledges Indigenous peoples' right to maintain and develop their knowledge systems [10].

1.4.2 Convention on Biological Diversity (CBD)

Article 10(c) promotes sustainable use of biological resources based on Indigenous knowledge, while Article 8(j) encourages equitable benefit-sharing from the use of traditional practices. By merging traditional systems with modern methods, projects like Peru's quinoa farming initiatives fulfill these obligations, conserving biodiversity while enhancing agricultural productivity [11].

1.4.3 Paris Agreement

Indigenous knowledge provides vital inputs for climate adaptation and mitigation strategies. Combining traditional ecological knowledge with climate science, such as in the Inuit's ice mapping and climate monitoring in the Arctic, supports the Paris Agreement's goal of strengthening adaptive capacity [12].

1.4.4 Sustainable Development Goals (SDGs)

Integrating Indigenous Practices with Sustainable Development Goals (SDGs)
See Table 1.1.

- **SDG 13 (Climate Action)**: Integrating Indigenous and modern practices strengthens resilience to climate impacts. For instance, traditional water conservation techniques in India's desert regions combined with modern hydrological studies improve water security.
- **SDG 15 (Life on Land)**: By promoting sustainable land management, practices like the Sámi's reindeer herding enhance biodiversity conservation and ensure sustainable livelihoods.

Table 1.1 Indigenous knowledge and sustainable development goals

SDG	Focus area	Indigenous practice	Modern integration	Outcome
SDG 13: Climate Action	Strengthening resilience to climate impacts	Traditional water conservation techniques (e.g., step wells and Johads in India)	Modern hydrological studies and modeling	Improved water security and climate adaptation strategies
SDG 15: Life on Land	Sustainable land management and biodiversity conservation	Sámi reindeer herding practices	Advanced monitoring systems and ecological studies	Enhanced biodiversity, sustainable livelihoods and conservation of fragile ecosystems
SDG 17: Partnerships for the Goals	Collaborative efforts between Indigenous and modern institutions	Co-management of Yasuni National Park by Ecuadorian Indigenous communities	Joint decision-making frameworks, policy support	Effective partnerships that balance conservation with socioeconomic needs

- **SDG 17 (Partnerships for the Goals)**: Collaborative efforts between Indigenous communities and modern institutions, such as Ecuador's co-management of Yasuni National Park, embody effective partnerships for sustainable development.

Bridging the gap between tradition and modernity pragmatically integrates cultural wisdom with technological advancements, enabling innovative solutions to global environmental challenges. This approach not only fulfills commitments under international conventions and SDGs but also reinforces the value of inclusive, cross-cultural collaboration in achieving sustainable futures. It exemplifies how respecting Indigenous heritage while embracing innovation can drive progress toward resilient ecosystems and equitable development.

1.5 Emphasizing the Role of Cultural and Spiritual Beliefs in Ecological Practices

Cultural and spiritual beliefs are inseparable from Indigenous environmental practices, often guiding how communities interact with their ecosystems. The chapter delves into examples like the Bishnoi community in India, whose conservation ethics stem from their religious reverence for nature and the Yupik people in Alaska, whose seasonal subsistence practices reflect deep ecological understanding [13]. These examples illuminate the profound connection between culture, spirituality and sustainability, offering insights into how respect for nature can be institutionalized in environmental governance. Cultural and spiritual beliefs are intrinsic to many Indigenous ecological practices, offering a framework for sustainable resource management and environmental stewardship. These beliefs are not abstract ideals but practical systems guiding land use, biodiversity conservation and community well-being. Examples include:

1.5.1 Sacred Natural Sites as Conservation Tools

The Chagga people of Tanzania maintain sacred forests on Mount Kilimanjaro, which act as critical water catchment areas [14]. These forests are protected through spiritual reverence, ensuring sustainable water supplies for agriculture and domestic use.

1.5.2 Cultural Taboos Supporting Biodiversity

In Madagascar, *fady* (cultural taboos) prohibit hunting certain species or exploiting specific forests, effectively safeguarding biodiversity and maintaining ecological balance [15].

1.5.3 Eco-Spiritual Festivals

India's Bishnoi community conducts rituals to protect wildlife and trees, often risking their lives to prevent illegal logging or hunting. Such practices contribute to ecosystem preservation while reinforcing community identity [16].

By emphasizing these cultural and spiritual dimensions, this approach integrates ethical and practical aspects of environmental conservation, offering scalable models for ecological resilience.

1.6 Alignment with International Conventions, Protocols and SDG Goals

1.6.1 Convention on Biological Diversity (CBD)

Articles 8(j) and 10(c) advocate for the recognition of Indigenous practices and traditional knowledge in biodiversity conservation. Cultural beliefs like sacred groves in India or the Australian Aboriginal Dreamtime narratives align with this directive, ensuring biodiversity conservation through cultural stewardship [17].

1.6.2 UNESCO Convention for the Safeguarding of Intangible Cultural Heritage (ICH)

This convention recognizes the interconnection between cultural heritage and sustainable development. Practices such as Māori conservation rituals in New Zealand fulfill its objectives, safeguarding intangible heritage while promoting environmental resilience [18].

1.6.3 United Nations Declaration on the Rights of Indigenous Peoples (UNDRIP)

Articles 12 and 25 affirm the right of Indigenous communities to maintain their spiritual practices and traditional relationships with their lands. Initiatives like the Sámi people's seasonal reindeer herding, intertwined with their spiritual calendar, embody this principle [19].

1.6.4 Sustainable Development Goals (SDGs)

- **SDG 15 (Life on Land)**: Cultural and spiritual practices directly contribute to the sustainable management of forests, deserts and biodiversity conservation.
- **SDG 11 (Sustainable Cities and Communities)**: Sacred natural sites and community-led conservation initiatives ensure the preservation of cultural and natural heritage.
- **SDG 13 (Climate Action)**: Practices rooted in eco-spirituality, such as the Andean peoples' rituals to honor *Pachamama* (Mother Earth), promote climate-resilient behaviors and sustainable resource use.

By emphasizing cultural and spiritual beliefs in ecological practices, this approach pragmatically integrates ethical, cultural and practical conservation methods. It aligns with international frameworks like the CBD and ICH while contributing significantly to SDGs, particularly those focusing on biodiversity, cultural heritage and climate action [20]. Recognizing and scaling these practices foster inclusive environmental governance and sustainable development, ensuring that ecological solutions honor both nature and the communities that depend on it.

1.7 Addressing Contemporary Challenges Through Indigenous Lenses

This chapter uniquely tackles how Indigenous communities adapt to modern environmental challenges such as climate change and globalization. For instance, the Inuit in Canada are employing traditional knowledge alongside modern tools to monitor and adapt to changes in Arctic ecosystems. Similarly, the Sami people in Scandinavia are integrating Indigenous practices with state policies to safeguard reindeer herding in the face of industrialization and climate shifts [21]. These case studies showcase the resilience of Indigenous populations in navigating contemporary challenges while maintaining ecological balance. Indigenous perspectives offer invaluable tools for addressing contemporary global challenges such as climate change, biodiversity loss, water scarcity and food insecurity. These lenses combine traditional ecological knowledge with adaptive strategies honed over generations. By integrating Indigenous approaches into modern frameworks, we can find innovative solutions to pressing issues.

1.7.1 Climate Change Resilience

Indigenous communities like the Inuit in the Arctic possess deep knowledge of changing weather patterns and ice conditions, which they have adapted to for centuries [22]. Their observations are now complementing modern climate models, offering insights into climate resilience and adaptive responses.

1.7.2 Biodiversity Conservation

The Kayapo people in Brazil's Amazon rainforest protect over 10 million hectares of tropical forest using traditional land management practices [23]. By merging these methods with modern technology, such as satellite monitoring, they are combating illegal logging and deforestation, preserving crucial carbon sinks.

1.7.3 Water Resource Management

Indigenous water management techniques, such as Peru's *amunas* (ancient water channels), are being revitalized to address contemporary water scarcity [24]. These systems capture and store rainwater, ensuring year-round availability and enhancing agricultural productivity.

1.7.4 Sustainable Agriculture

The *milpa* system, practiced by Indigenous farmers in Mexico, involves rotating crops like maize, beans and squash to enhance soil fertility and reduce pests [25]. This practice is a sustainable alternative to monoculture farming, offering solutions to food security challenges.

By addressing these challenges through Indigenous lenses, we enhance resilience, reduce ecological degradation and build sustainable systems tailored to diverse ecosystems and communities.

1.8 Alignment with International Conventions, Protocols and SDG Goals

1.8.1 United Nations Declaration on the Rights of Indigenous Peoples (UNDRIP)

Article 29 calls for the sustainable development of Indigenous territories, ensuring environmental health and community well-being [26]. Incorporating Indigenous strategies aligns with this mandate by leveraging local knowledge for sustainable development.

1.8.2 Convention on Biological Diversity (CBD)

Articles 8(j) and 10(c) emphasize the role of traditional knowledge in conserving biodiversity and ensuring its sustainable use [27]. Initiatives like co-management of protected areas in Canada with Indigenous nations fulfill these objectives, combining Indigenous stewardship with conservation science.

1.8.3 Paris Agreement on Climate Change

Indigenous knowledge complements global efforts to enhance climate resilience. For example, Indigenous fire management practices in Australia reduce the intensity of wildfires, supporting the Agreement's adaptation goals.

1.8.4 Sustainable Development Goals (SDGs)

- **SDG 13 (Climate Action)**: Indigenous adaptation strategies offer scalable solutions for mitigating and adapting to climate impacts.
- **SDG 15 (Life on Land)**: Indigenous practices safeguard terrestrial ecosystems, promoting sustainable land management and biodiversity conservation.
- **SDG 6 (Clean Water and Sanitation)**: Traditional water management techniques ensure equitable access to water resources, supporting sustainable water use.
- **SDG 2 (Zero Hunger)**: Sustainable farming practices like agroforestry and crop rotation address food security while maintaining soil health.

Addressing contemporary challenges through Indigenous lenses provides practical, time-tested solutions that are adaptable to modern contexts. This approach fulfills global commitments under conventions like the CBD and UNDRIP and advances SDGs, particularly those addressing climate action, biodiversity and sustainable development. By respecting and integrating Indigenous perspectives, we not only address urgent global issues but also honor the cultural and ecological wisdom that has sustained these communities for centuries.

1.9 Advocating for Policy Integration and Legal Recognition

The chapter emphasizes the critical role of Indigenous populations in global environmental governance. It argues for the integration of Indigenous practices into national and international policies, as seen in New Zealand's co-management of resources with the Māori or Ecuador's recognition of the Rights of Nature. By advocating for legal frameworks that respect Indigenous contributions, the content positions Indigenous communities not as passive stakeholders but as active architects of sustainable futures. Policy integration and legal recognition of Indigenous knowledge systems are essential for inclusive and sustainable governance [28]. Indigenous communities often steward critical ecosystems but lack formal recognition in policymaking processes. Advocating for their inclusion ensures that their time-tested practices inform environmental governance and contribute to global sustainability goals.

1.9.1 Policy Integration in Land Rights

Legal recognition of land ownership and stewardship by Indigenous communities, such as in Bolivia's *Tierra Comunitaria de Origen* framework, empowers communities to sustainably manage natural resources [29]. Such policies prevent deforestation, promote biodiversity and ensure equitable resource distribution.

Legal recognition of land ownership and stewardship by Indigenous communities is a cornerstone for achieving sustainable resource management. Bolivia's Tierra Comunitaria de Origen (TCO) framework exemplifies this principle by granting Indigenous groups legal rights to ancestral lands. This policy allows Indigenous communities to exercise sovereignty over millions of hectares, preserving ecosystems and combating environmental degradation. By managing these lands according to traditional ecological knowledge, Indigenous groups have successfully prevented large-scale deforestation and fostered biodiversity. The TCO model not only strengthens environmental governance but also promotes equitable resource distribution by prioritizing the needs of local communities over extractive industries. However, challenges remain, including enforcement gaps and external pressures from commercial interests. Strengthening legal protections and incorporating community-driven monitoring systems can enhance the effectiveness of such frameworks. Globally, this approach aligns with international agreements like UNDRIP, which emphasizes the recognition of Indigenous land rights and the CBD, which advocates for sustainable land management practices. Empowering Indigenous stewardship through land rights integration serves as a scalable model for balancing ecological conservation and human development, particularly in regions where Indigenous territories overlap with biodiversity hotspots.

1.9.2 Indigenous Practices in Climate Policy

Countries like Australia have integrated Indigenous fire management practices into national bushfire mitigation strategies. These practices, based on low-intensity controlled burns, reduce wildfire severity, protect biodiversity and contribute to national climate adaptation efforts. Indigenous fire management practices offer pragmatic solutions for mitigating the impacts of climate change, particularly in fire-prone regions. Australia has successfully integrated these practices into its national bushfire mitigation strategies, showcasing the value of traditional ecological knowledge. Indigenous fire management, often referred to as "cultural burning," involves low-intensity controlled burns conducted during specific seasons to reduce fuel loads and minimize the risk of catastrophic wildfires [30]. These methods, refined over millennia, not only protect biodiversity but also enhance soil fertility and promote the regeneration of native vegetation. For instance, Indigenous-led programs in Northern Australia have reduced greenhouse gas emissions by preventing large-scale wildfires, contributing to the country's climate mitigation goals. Moreover, cultural burning respects the interconnectedness of ecosystems and traditional land use practices, fostering ecological resilience. Integrating these methods into national policies requires ongoing collaboration with Indigenous communities and adequate funding for capacity building. It also aligns with the Paris Agreement, which underscores the importance of Indigenous knowledge in climate adaptation and mitigation efforts. By scaling such initiatives, other countries can adopt culturally sensitive and environmentally effective approaches to wildfire management, addressing one of the most pressing challenges posed by climate change.

1.9.3 Legal Recognition of Traditional Knowledge

Nations such as New Zealand legally recognize the Māori worldview, or *Te Ao Māori*, in environmental law. For instance, the Whanganui River has been granted legal personhood, ensuring its protection through both Indigenous and state-led governance (Fig. 1.4).

Legal recognition of traditional knowledge represents a transformative step toward inclusive environmental governance. New Zealand's recognition of the Māori worldview, *Te Ao Māori*, serves as a pioneering example. In 2017, the Whanganui River was granted legal personhood, affirming its status as a living entity with intrinsic rights [31]. This landmark decision acknowledges the spiritual and cultural significance of the river to the Māori people while ensuring its protection through co-management

Fig. 1.4 A realistic portrayal of the Whanganui River in New Zealand, reflecting its cultural and environmental significance under the Māori worldview and its legal recognition as a living entity. The collaboration between Indigenous traditions and modern governance in protecting sacred natural resource

by Māori and government-appointed guardians. By blending Indigenous values with modern legal systems, the policy establishes a framework for preserving ecosystems in culturally resonant ways. This recognition not only enhances biodiversity conservation but also fosters a deeper respect for Indigenous philosophies, which view humans as interconnected with nature rather than separate from it. Furthermore, it sets a precedent for other nations to integrate Indigenous perspectives into their legal systems, bridging the gap between traditional and state-centric governance. Legal personhood for natural entities is also aligned with global commitments like the CBD and SDGs, particularly SDG 15, which emphasizes sustainable management of ecosystems. As more countries explore this approach, they can foster harmonious relationships between Indigenous communities, environmental stewardship and state governance.

1.10 Community-Led Co-Management Models

Canada's establishment of Indigenous Protected and Conserved Areas (IPCAs) empowers Indigenous communities to manage protected lands collaboratively. These models blend traditional ecological knowledge with scientific approaches, ensuring ecosystem preservation and community well-being. Community-led co-management models provide a practical framework for harmonizing traditional ecological knowledge with modern conservation strategies. Canada's Indigenous Protected and Conserved Areas (IPCAs) are a testament to this approach, empowering Indigenous communities to co-manage protected lands in collaboration with government agencies [32]. IPCAs prioritize Indigenous leadership in decision-making processes, ensuring that conservation strategies respect traditional knowledge, cultural practices and community needs. These areas often overlap with regions of high biodiversity, making them critical for global conservation efforts. For example, the Thaidene Nëné National Park Reserve, co-managed by the Łutsël K'é Dene First Nation and Parks Canada, protects a vast expanse of boreal forest and freshwater ecosystems while supporting the cultural and economic aspirations of the local community [33]. Such models demonstrate how Indigenous stewardship enhances ecosystem resilience, as traditional land management practices are often more sustainable and adaptive to local conditions than purely scientific approaches. Community-led models align with global goals such as UNDRIP, which calls for the active involvement of Indigenous peoples in governance and SDG 16, which advocates for inclusive institutions. By expanding these co-management frameworks, nations can achieve equitable and sustainable environmental governance while honoring the contributions of Indigenous communities. By formalizing Indigenous contributions in legal frameworks, policy integration bridges the gap between traditional knowledge and contemporary governance, fostering sustainable solutions.

1.11 International Conventions, Protocols and SDG Goals

1.11.1 United Nations Declaration on the Rights of Indigenous Peoples (UNDRIP)

Articles 26 and 27 advocate for the recognition of Indigenous land rights and the inclusion of their governance systems in national policies. Integrating Indigenous knowledge into environmental policy directly fulfills this mandate [34].

1.11.2 Convention on Biological Diversity (CBD)

Articles 8(j) and 10(c) emphasize the role of Indigenous knowledge in biodiversity conservation and sustainable use. Legal recognition of Indigenous practices, such as in Ecuador's Yasuni Biosphere Reserve, aligns with CBD goals [35].

1.11.3 Paris Agreement on Climate Change

The Agreement highlights the importance of incorporating local and Indigenous knowledge into climate adaptation and mitigation strategies. Australia's use of Indigenous fire management in its climate policies exemplifies this integration.

1.11.4 Sustainable Development Goals (SDGs)

- **SDG 16 (Peace, Justice and Strong Institutions)**: Legal recognition fosters inclusive institutions by ensuring Indigenous participation in governance.
- **SDG 15 (Life on Land)**: Policies recognizing Indigenous stewardship promote sustainable management of ecosystems and biodiversity conservation.
- **SDG 13 (Climate Action)**: Integrating Indigenous practices enhances resilience to climate impacts and mitigates greenhouse gas emissions.
- **SDG 10 (Reduced Inequalities)**: Legal recognition reduces disparities by empowering Indigenous communities in decision-making processes.

Advocating for policy integration and legal recognition of Indigenous knowledge systems is a pragmatic approach to addressing global environmental and social challenges. It aligns with international frameworks like UNDRIP, CBD and the Paris Agreement while advancing SDGs focused on equity, sustainability and environmental stewardship. By embedding Indigenous perspectives into legal and policy frameworks, we not only strengthen ecological resilience but also honor and uphold the rights of Indigenous communities as equal partners in sustainable development.

1.12 Five Sociological Models to Explore

See Fig. 1.5.

1.12.1 Cultural Ecology Model

- **Core Idea**: Examines the reciprocal relationship between Indigenous communities and their environment, emphasizing how traditional knowledge systems are adapted to ecological constraints [36].
- **Approach**:
  - Map traditional practices that align with conservation efforts.
  - Highlight laws embedded in oral traditions or folklore to ensure sustainability.
  - Analyze how modern environmental challenges are addressed using these practices.
- **Outcome**: A framework for integrating Indigenous ecological wisdom into mainstream legal and policymaking processes.

A Real-World Application

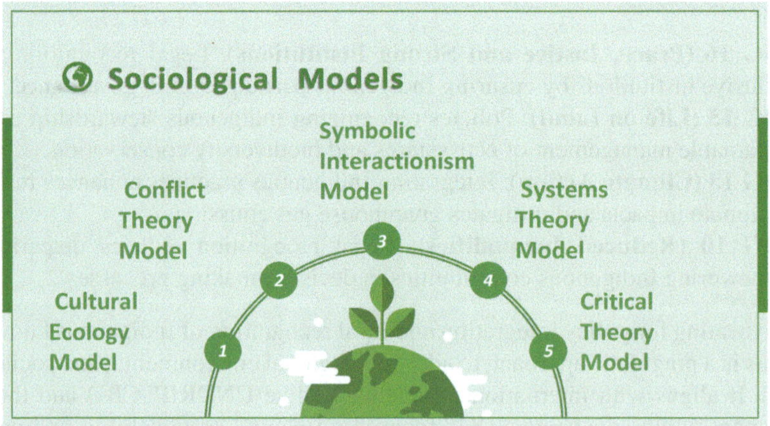

Fig. 1.5 Sociological models

Reciprocal Relationship Between Communities and the Environment

The Cultural Ecology Model emphasizes the symbiotic relationship Indigenous communities maintain with their environment. This model illustrates how traditional knowledge systems, shaped over generations respond to ecological constraints. Such systems are deeply rooted in practices, folklore and spiritual beliefs, forming the basis for Indigenous environmental laws and conservation strategies.

An example of this can be observed among the **Maasai community in East Africa (Kenya and Tanzania)**. The Maasai have traditionally relied on transhumance, a method of seasonal livestock grazing to prevent overgrazing and maintain ecological balance. Their practices not only conserve grasslands but also foster biodiversity, showcasing a sustainable relationship between humans and their environment [37].

Mapping Traditional Practices that Align with Conservation Efforts

The model begins by documenting practices that inherently align with conservation. For instance, in **Australia**, the Indigenous **Martu people** practice "fire-stick farming," a method of controlled burning that reduces wildfire risks while promoting the growth of certain plant species [38]. This method, embedded in their cultural knowledge, sustains local ecosystems and enhances wildlife habitats. Similarly, the **Tlingit people of Alaska** manage salmon populations by observing strict seasonal fishing patterns, ensuring long-term sustainability of this critical resource [39]. These examples demonstrate that traditional ecological practices, often seen as antiquated, are not only relevant but also necessary for contemporary conservation efforts.

Highlighting Laws Embedded in Oral Traditions or Folklore

Indigenous environmental laws are often unwritten but profoundly embedded in oral traditions and folklore. For example, the **Guna Yala people of Panama** use myths to emphasize the sanctity of the coral reefs and mangroves they inhabit [40]. Such narratives enforce community compliance with conservation practices, ensuring sustainable use of natural resources. Another notable example is the **Haida Nation of Canada**, which incorporates spiritual beliefs into environmental stewardship [41]. Haida oral traditions emphasize respect for cedar trees, which are considered sacred. This belief system has led to sustainable forestry practices that have preserved old-growth forests in British Columbia for centuries.

Addressing Modern Environmental Challenges with Traditional Practices

Modern environmental challenges, such as climate change and deforestation, are increasingly addressed through Indigenous practices. In **India**, the **Dongria Kondh tribe** of Odisha safeguards the Niyamgiri Hills, which they consider sacred. By opposing mining projects, the tribe not only protects their cultural heritage but also preserves the region's biodiversity. Their resistance has inspired global environmental movements, highlighting how Indigenous wisdom can counteract ecological exploitation [42]. In another case, the **Indigenous peoples of the Amazon**

basin employ rotational farming and agroforestry techniques to combat deforestation. These methods reduce soil erosion, enhance carbon sequestration and sustain livelihoods, providing a viable model for climate-resilient agriculture [43].

Outcome: Integration of Indigenous Wisdom into Mainstream Policies

The Cultural Ecology Model offers a framework for integrating these traditional practices into mainstream legal and policymaking processes. For instance, in **New Zealand**, the Whanganui River was granted legal personhood in 2017, reflecting the Māori worldview of nature as a living entity. This recognition ensures the river's rights are upheld, blending Indigenous and state legal systems. Similarly, in **Ecuador**, the 2008 constitution enshrined the "Rights of Nature," inspired by Indigenous philosophies like Pachamama (Mother Earth). These cases underline the need to bridge Indigenous ecological wisdom with global environmental governance, promoting sustainability and equity. By adopting the Cultural Ecology Model, policymakers can honor Indigenous contributions and address modern ecological challenges more effectively.

1.12.2 Conflict Theory Model

- **Core Idea**: Investigates power dynamics, focusing on the marginalization of Indigenous legal systems in favor of dominant legal structures.
- **Approach**:
  - Study historical and contemporary conflicts over resource rights and land use.
  - Explore the imposition of state laws that undermine Indigenous environmental practices.
  - Advocate for participatory governance models that respect Indigenous sovereignty.
- **Outcome**: Policy recommendations to harmonize state laws with Indigenous environmental paradigms.

Conflict Theory Model and the Marginalization of Indigenous Legal Systems

Core Idea

The Conflict Theory model examines the power imbalances that arise when dominant legal systems marginalize Indigenous legal systems, often exacerbated by state interventions. This model emphasizes the role of historical and contemporary conflicts over resource rights and land use, where state laws and policies frequently undermine Indigenous traditions, particularly in environmental stewardship. By investigating these dynamics, the model advocates for participatory governance that respects Indigenous sovereignty and aligns with their environmental paradigms [44].

Approach

The model takes a structured approach:

- **Historical and Contemporary Conflicts**: It delves into cases where Indigenous communities faced dispossession and exploitation due to state-sponsored policies or resource extraction activities. For instance, in Canada, the Wet'suwet'en Nation has opposed pipeline constructions on their traditional lands, citing violations of their inherent rights and environmental practices [45].
- **Imposition of State Laws**: The imposition of Western-centric legal frameworks often disregards Indigenous ecological knowledge. An example can be found in Brazil, where the Indigenous Yanomami people face encroachments from illegal gold mining, backed indirectly by policies favoring industrial interests [46]. Their environmental practices, grounded in harmonious coexistence with nature, clash with exploitative state-driven economic policies.
- **Advocacy for Participatory Governance**: The model pushes for frameworks where Indigenous voices shape legal and policy decisions. In New Zealand, the Māori iwi (tribes) successfully negotiated the Treaty of Waitangi settlements, which respect Māori environmental guardianship through mechanisms like co-management of natural reserves, such as the Whanganui River being granted legal personhood [47].

Case Examples

- **Wet'suwet'en Nation, Canada**: In British Columbia, the Coastal GasLink pipeline project sparked significant conflict. The Wet'suwet'en hereditary chiefs argued that the project violated their ancestral rights, highlighting the tension between economic development and Indigenous sovereignty.
- **Yanomami People, Brazil**: The Yanomami people face systemic challenges from deforestation and illegal mining. State policies inadequately protect their lands, prioritizing extractive industries and disregarding traditional practices that sustain biodiversity.
- **Māori, New Zealand**: The legal recognition of the Whanganui River as a living entity underscores the potential for harmonizing state laws with Indigenous perspectives. This approach exemplifies participatory governance by embedding Māori concepts like *kaitiakitanga* (guardianship) into national law.

Outcome

The Conflict Theory model offers policy recommendations that harmonize state laws with Indigenous environmental paradigms. This involves:

- Enacting legal frameworks that recognize and integrate Indigenous knowledge.
- Facilitating co-management of resources and legal personhood for ecosystems, as demonstrated in New Zealand.
- Establishing dispute resolution mechanisms that respect Indigenous sovereignty.

By learning from real-world examples, policymakers can create governance models that bridge the gap between state priorities and Indigenous rights, fostering sustainable and equitable resource management.

1.12.3 Symbolic Interactionism Model

- **Core Idea**: Analyzes the meanings and symbols Indigenous communities attach to nature and how these influence environmental laws.
- **Approach**:
  - Document cultural narratives, rituals and symbols that reflect environmental stewardship.
  - Examine community interactions with sacred natural sites and their legal significance.
  - Develop interpretative tools to bridge Indigenous and modern legal terminologies.
- **Outcome**: Enhanced cross-cultural understanding of environmental ethics, fostering collaborative legal frameworks.

Symbolic Interactionism Model and Indigenous Environmental Stewardship

Core Idea

The Symbolic Interactionism model focuses on the meanings, symbols and cultural narratives that Indigenous communities associate with nature. These symbolic interactions shape their environmental ethics and influence their approach to stewardship. By understanding these cultural dimensions, this model aims to bridge Indigenous traditions and modern legal systems, fostering a collaborative approach to environmental governance [48].

Approach

This model uses a multi-faceted approach to uncover the deep-seated connections between Indigenous cultures and the natural world:

Documenting Cultural Narratives and Rituals: Indigenous communities often convey their relationship with nature through myths, rituals and oral traditions. For example, in Australia, the Aboriginal concept of *Dreamtime* embodies creation stories that tie specific landscapes to ancestral spirits. These narratives are crucial for understanding the spiritual and environmental value attributed to land [49].

Examining Sacred Natural Sites: Sacred sites are vital in Indigenous environmental frameworks. In India, the Bishnoi community's reverence for the *khejri* tree and local wildlife demonstrates their commitment to conservation, rooted in religious and ethical principles [50]. Legal disputes over the exploitation of such sites often highlight the need to consider these cultural dimensions in modern legal contexts.

Developing Interpretative Tools: Bridging Indigenous and modern legal terminologies is essential for creating mutually intelligible frameworks. For example, in Ecuador, the Kichwa people's belief in *Pachamama* (Mother Earth) has influenced the country's recognition of the Rights of Nature in its constitution, allowing the legal system to integrate Indigenous values into environmental protection policies [51].

Case Examples

Aboriginal Australians: The Uluru-Kata Tjuta National Park is a UNESCO World Heritage Site that is sacred to the Anangu people. Efforts to prohibit climbing Uluru reflect respect for Anangu cultural values and their symbolic interaction with the site. This case highlights the intersection of cultural significance and legal enforcement.

Cultural Significance of Uluru to the Anangu People

Uluru (formerly known as Ayers Rock) is a massive sandstone monolith in the heart of the Australian outback, central to the cultural and spiritual identity of the Anangu people, the traditional custodians of the land [52]. The site holds profound significance in Anangu cosmology, representing creation stories and the spiritual connection between the land, ancestors and the community. For thousands of years, Uluru has been a place of ritual, teaching and connection to the Dreamtime, the Anangu people's sacred mythology. The rock and the surrounding areas, including Kata Tjuta (the Olgas), are seen as living entities and are deeply embedded in Anangu laws and traditions. This belief system influences how the Anangu manage the land and their relationship with nature, emphasizing stewardship, respect and the sanctity of the environment.

The Colonial History and Impact on Uluru

The first non-Indigenous encounter with Uluru occurred in 1873 when European explorer William Gosse named it Ayers Rock, after the Chief Secretary of South Australia at the time. In the years that followed, Uluru became a popular tourist destination and its cultural significance to the Anangu people was largely ignored by Australian authorities [53]. In 1958, the Australian government took control of the land and in 1985, Uluru was officially handed back to the Anangu people under the condition that they would jointly manage the site with the government through a partnership known as the Uluru-Kata Tjuta National Park Board of Management. This marked a pivotal moment in recognizing the Anangu's traditional ownership, but the cultural impact of colonial policies on the site had already taken a toll.

The Controversy Over Climbing Uluru

One of the most contentious issues surrounding Uluru has been the practice of tourists climbing the rock. Despite the Anangu people's strong opposition to climbing, viewing it as a violation of cultural and spiritual beliefs, the practice continued for decades. The Anangu's requests to ban climbing were ignored by the tourism industry and government, with the climb seen as a key attraction to draw visitors. However, in 2017, after decades of advocacy by the Anangu community and growing awareness of the cultural sensitivity surrounding the issue, the Australian government and the Uluru-Kata Tjuta Board announced a decision to permanently close the climb. The closure, which took effect in October 2019, was seen as a major victory for the Anangu people and a step toward respecting Indigenous cultural values and sovereignty [54].

Intersection of Cultural Significance and Legal Enforcement

The decision to prohibit climbing Uluru is a landmark example of the intersection between cultural significance and legal enforcement. This action represents a recognition that legal frameworks must evolve to accommodate the values, rights and customs of Indigenous communities. The prohibition of climbing not only honors the Anangu people's wishes but also acknowledges their legal authority over the land as traditional owners. The decision was a result of years of advocacy, public education and dialogue between the Anangu people, the Australian government and the tourism sector [55]. It exemplifies a broader shift toward Indigenous rights and cultural preservation, as Australia confronts its colonial past and works toward reconciliation with its Indigenous peoples.

Global and Local Impact

The closure of Uluru to climbing has garnered widespread international attention, symbolizing the importance of respecting Indigenous cultural rights and land stewardship. It has also sparked discussions on the broader implications for tourism, Indigenous rights and land management. While some tourists initially resisted the closure, the overall response has been positive, with many visitors choosing to respect the cultural significance of the site. This decision aligns with global movements for the protection of Indigenous heritage and supports Australia's obligations under international conventions like the United Nations Declaration on the Rights of Indigenous Peoples (UNDRIP), which affirms the rights of Indigenous peoples to maintain and protect their cultural traditions and sacred sites [56].

The case of Uluru thus illustrates the growing recognition of Indigenous legal systems, the need for culturally sensitive legal frameworks and the importance of integrating Indigenous knowledge into modern environmental and tourism management.

Bishnoi Community, India: The Bishnoi people's protection of local wildlife and trees is rooted in spiritual practices dating back to the fifteenth century. Their environmental ethics have influenced legal policies in Rajasthan, where certain trees and animal species are now legally protected.

Origins of Bishnoi Environmental Ethics

The Bishnoi community, predominantly found in the western Indian state of Rajasthan is a group of eco-conscious people whose religious and cultural practices are deeply intertwined with the conservation of nature. Founded in the fifteenth century by Guru Jambheshwar (Jambhoji), the Bishnoi sect emphasizes a philosophy of environmental stewardship, emphasizing the protection of wildlife, trees and natural resources. Jambhoji's teachings promoted the sanctity of life and the need to protect nature, particularly the Khejri tree (Prosopis cineraria), which holds immense significance for the Bishnoi community. According to their beliefs, trees, animals and all living beings are sacred and should be respected and preserved.

One of the core principles of the Bishnoi community is the concept of "Ahimsa," or non-violence, which extends to all forms of life, including plants and animals. The community's commitment to environmental protection is evident in the religious practices that forbid the cutting of certain trees and the hunting of specific animals. The Bishnoi Code of Conduct includes the protection of wildlife, especially animals like the blackbuck, chinkara and peacock, as well as the preservation of forests and water sources. This philosophy has been practiced for over 500 years and continues to guide the Bishnoi people's actions today [57].

The Khejri Tree and Sacred Wildlife Protection

One of the most prominent aspects of Bishnoi environmental ethics is their protection of the Khejri tree, which has been central to their culture and survival. The Khejri tree is revered as sacred because it is seen as a provider of both ecological and economic benefits. Its deep roots prevent soil erosion and it provides shade and food to livestock and wildlife. Additionally, the tree's wood is used for fuel and its leaves are a valuable fodder for livestock in arid regions. The Bishnoi community's veneration of the Khejri tree and other local flora is based on the belief that nature provides for humanity and thus humans must reciprocate by protecting and conserving it. In the eighteenth century, the Bishnoi community's devotion to wildlife and trees was tragically put to the test during the famous Chipko Movement-like event in 1730, when a group of Bishnoi women, led by Amrita Devi, protested against the cutting of Khejri trees. As the Maharaja of Jodhpur ordered the cutting of trees for a new palace construction, Amrita Devi and over 360 Bishnois sacrificed their lives to protect the trees. This event, known as the Khejri Massacre, became an iconic moment in Indian environmental history and showcased the Bishnoi people's unwavering commitment to nature conservation.

Legal Impact and Environmental Policies in Rajasthan

The Bishnoi community's conservation efforts have had a profound impact on local and state-level environmental policies in Rajasthan. The community's long history of protecting sacred trees and animals has influenced the legal recognition and protection of specific species in the region. The Rajasthan government, recognizing the Bishnoi community's traditional ecological knowledge, has legally protected the Khejri tree, as well as other flora and fauna sacred to the Bishnois. Species such as the blackbuck (Antilope cervicapra), the chinkara (Indian gazelle) and the peacock (India's national bird) are now legally protected under Indian wildlife conservation laws, largely due to the Bishnoi community's long-standing efforts in protecting these species. In 1999, the Rajasthan High Court issued an order that the Khejri tree, along with other trees protected by Bishnoi religious customs, should be preserved. This legal protection was a direct outcome of the Bishnoi community's influence on conservation policies and the cultural significance they attach to the environment.

The Bishnois' environmental activism led to further formal recognition of sacred groves and biodiversity protection in Rajasthan.

Contemporary Influence and Continued Advocacy

Today, the Bishnoi community continues to play a key role in environmental conservation not only in Rajasthan but across India. The community's principles of ecological balance and sustainability are reflected in modern environmental movements, especially in the context of biodiversity conservation and sustainable land management. Their deep-rooted environmental ethics have inspired many conservationists and policymakers and their traditional practices are increasingly being integrated into contemporary conservation strategies. The Bishnoi model of conservation also aligns with global initiatives such as the United Nations Sustainable Development Goals (SDGs), particularly SDG 15, which focuses on protecting life on land and halting biodiversity loss. The community's efforts to conserve species and ecosystems, while integrating local knowledge into legal frameworks, provide a powerful example of how traditional ecological practices can be harmonized with modern environmental governance. The Bishnois' continued dedication to protecting nature serves as an invaluable resource for shaping sustainable, community-driven conservation policies in India and beyond.

Kichwa People, Ecuador: The enshrinement of the Rights of Nature in Ecuador's constitution was inspired by the Kichwa people's worldview. This legal innovation enables communities to defend ecosystems in court, ensuring that nature is protected as a living entity.

Origins of the Kichwa People's Worldview and Ecological Stewardship

The Kichwa people, an Indigenous group primarily located in the Amazon Basin of Ecuador, have long practiced a holistic approach to nature that integrates environmental stewardship with cultural and spiritual beliefs. For the Kichwa, nature is not a resource to be exploited, but a living entity that must be respected and maintained. This worldview is deeply rooted in their language, traditions and daily life. Central to their beliefs is the notion that humans are part of a larger ecological system where all beings, human, animal, plant and mineral, are interconnected. This philosophy emphasizes reciprocity between humans and the Earth, recognizing that the health of the environment is directly tied to the well-being of the community. The Kichwa have lived sustainably for centuries in the Amazon rainforest, using traditional knowledge to manage biodiversity, protect water sources and prevent deforestation. Their practices have always focused on balance and respect for the land, ensuring that ecosystems are preserved for future generations. These traditional ecological practices have shaped the Kichwa's relationship with nature, leading them to advocate for legal recognition of nature's intrinsic rights as a part of their ongoing fight for environmental justice [58].

The Emergence of the Rights of Nature Movement

The Rights of Nature movement, which gained global attention in the early twenty-first century, was directly influenced by the Kichwa people's deep understanding of the interdependence between humans and the environment. In Ecuador, this movement emerged as a response to the widespread degradation of ecosystems caused by oil extraction, deforestation and industrialization, practices that have severely impacted Indigenous territories and their way of life. The Kichwa, who have been on the front lines of these environmental battles, saw the need for a legal framework that would go beyond the protection of human rights and extend to the rights of ecosystems themselves. In the early 2000s, the Kichwa, alongside other Indigenous groups in Ecuador, began advocating for the legal recognition of nature's rights. They sought a legal mechanism that would allow them to defend not just the land but the ecosystems, rivers and forests that sustain life. Their advocacy was based on the belief that nature itself has rights to exist, regenerate and thrive, principles that align with the Kichwa worldview. This advocacy, rooted in both legal theory and traditional ecological knowledge, set the stage for a significant shift in Ecuador's environmental governance.

The Enshrinement of the Rights of Nature in Ecuador's Constitution

In 2008, Ecuador became the first country in the world to enshrine the Rights of Nature in its constitution, a legal innovation directly inspired by the Kichwa people's worldview. Article 71 of the Ecuadorian Constitution recognizes that nature has the right to exist, persist, maintain and regenerate its vital cycles. This groundbreaking provision allows ecosystems to be treated as legal entities with rights, meaning that communities, including Indigenous groups like the Kichwa, can now take legal action to protect the environment [59]. The incorporation of the Rights of Nature into Ecuador's Constitution was a direct result of decades of activism by the Kichwa and other Indigenous communities, who argued that traditional legal frameworks failed to adequately protect the environment. Their efforts culminated in the constitutional reform, which grants nature legal standing, enabling communities to represent ecosystems in court and seek reparations for environmental harm. This provision has been hailed as a revolutionary step in environmental law, offering a new paradigm for protecting ecosystems by recognizing their inherent rights.

The Kichwa and Their Role in Defending Nature

Since the enshrinement of the Rights of Nature, the Kichwa people have played a central role in the application of this legal framework. In the years following the constitutional reform, the Kichwa, particularly from the Amazonian region, have used the legal provisions to challenge practices that threaten their lands and ecosystems, such as oil extraction, mining and large-scale agriculture. One notable example is the Kichwa community of Sarayaku, which successfully used the Rights of Nature to halt oil exploration on their ancestral lands. The community argued that the exploration would violate the rights of the river and forest, which are central to their way of life. In 2012, the Sarayaku people won a landmark case when the Ecuadorian Constitutional Court ruled in their favor, affirming that the government and private companies must respect the rights of nature and consult Indigenous communities before carrying out activities that could harm the environment [60]. This victory demonstrated the potential of the Rights of Nature as a tool for Indigenous peoples to defend their territories and way of life and it reinforced the Kichwa's position as leaders in the global movement for environmental justice.

The Global Implications and Future of the Rights of Nature

The Kichwa people's influence on the Rights of Nature movement has extended beyond Ecuador's borders, inspiring similar legal reforms in other countries. Their work has sparked international debates on how legal systems can adapt to incorporate the rights of ecosystems and how Indigenous worldviews can contribute to shaping global environmental governance. As the climate crisis continues to intensify, the Kichwa and other Indigenous peoples are increasingly seen as key actors in the fight for environmental protection, offering valuable perspectives on sustainable living and ecological stewardship. The trajectory of the Rights of Nature in Ecuador, largely driven by the Kichwa's advocacy, serves as a model for other countries considering similar legal innovations. The movement challenges traditional legal paradigms and offers a more holistic approach to environmental protection, one that recognizes the intrinsic value of nature and the interconnectedness of all life. As more communities and governments embrace the principles of the Rights of Nature, the Kichwa's vision for a legal system that respects the rights of ecosystems may shape the future of environmental law on a global scale.

Outcome

The Symbolic Interactionism model promotes:

- Cross-cultural understanding of environmental ethics through the documentation of Indigenous narratives.
- Collaborative legal frameworks that respect and incorporate Indigenous symbols and values.
- A shift from anthropocentric to ecocentric legal paradigms, aligning with Indigenous worldviews.

By integrating Indigenous perspectives into modern legal systems, this model fosters more inclusive and sustainable environmental governance, ensuring that the symbolic and practical aspects of Indigenous environmental stewardship are preserved and respected.

1.12.4 Systems Theory Model

- **Core Idea:** Views Indigenous environmental laws as part of a larger socio-ecological system, emphasizing interdependence and feedback loops.
- **Approach:**
  - Model the interaction between Indigenous governance, biodiversity and community well-being.

  - Assess how external pressures (e.g., climate change, globalization) impact these systems.
  - Develop adaptive legal mechanisms that sustain the system's resilience.
- **Outcome:** Integrated governance models that respect Indigenous systems while addressing global environmental challenges.

Systems Theory Model and Indigenous Environmental Laws

Core Idea

The Systems Theory model frames Indigenous environmental laws as integral components of larger socio-ecological systems. It emphasizes the interdependence of governance, biodiversity and community well-being, along with feedback loops that maintain ecological and cultural balance. Recognizing the impact of external pressures like climate change and globalization, this model advocates for adaptive legal mechanisms that bolster system resilience while respecting Indigenous governance frameworks [61].

Approach

Modeling Socio-Ecological Interactions: Indigenous governance systems are often deeply intertwined with ecological processes. For instance, the Inuit in Canada rely on traditional knowledge systems to manage Arctic ecosystems, balancing their cultural practices with sustainable resource use. This interconnectedness ensures biodiversity conservation and supports community resilience [62].

Assessing External Pressures: Climate change and globalization pose significant challenges to Indigenous systems. In the Amazon, the Yanomami and Kayapo peoples face deforestation, mining and habitat loss due to commercial activities [63]. These pressures disrupt traditional ecological knowledge and governance, demanding legal responses that protect Indigenous territories and mitigate external impacts.

Developing Adaptive Legal Mechanisms: Adaptive governance systems must be flexible enough to integrate Indigenous laws while addressing broader environmental challenges. For example, in Kenya, the Ogiek community's traditional forest management practices were recognized by a landmark African Court of Human and Peoples' Rights decision, which upheld their land rights and emphasized the need for sustainable governance frameworks [64].

Case Examples

Inuit, Canada: The Inuit Tapiriit Kanatami organization represents Inuit communities in negotiations with the Canadian government. Their co-management of resources, such as polar bears and marine ecosystems, reflects an adaptive approach that integrates Inuit knowledge with modern legal frameworks to combat climate impacts.

Yanomami and Kayapo Peoples, Brazil: These communities actively resist deforestation and mining on their ancestral lands. Legal victories, like the demarcation of Yanomami territory, demonstrate the importance of integrating Indigenous governance with national laws to preserve biodiversity and community well-being.
Ogiek, Kenya: The Ogiek people have historically managed the *Mau* Forest sustainably, emphasizing the interdependence between their governance systems and forest biodiversity. The 2017 African Court ruling recognized these practices, reinforcing their importance in combating deforestation and climate change [65].

Outcome

The Systems Theory model promotes:

- **Integrated Governance Models**: By harmonizing Indigenous and state systems, it ensures that socio-ecological interdependencies are respected.
- **Resilience Against External Pressures**: Adaptive legal frameworks can mitigate the impacts of globalization and climate change.
- **Global Environmental Collaboration**: Recognizing Indigenous systems contributes to tackling global challenges like biodiversity loss and climate adaptation.

This model illustrates that Indigenous governance is not just about cultural preservation but is also crucial for sustaining resilient socio-ecological systems. By aligning modern legal structures with Indigenous laws, policymakers can enhance both local and global environmental outcomes.

1.12.5 Critical Theory Model

- **Core Idea**: Deconstructs colonial narratives that delegitimize Indigenous legal systems, advocating for their revival and adaptation.
- **Approach**:
  - Critique the erasure of Indigenous laws in environmental governance.
  - Promote the decolonization of legal frameworks through education and activism.
  - Collaborate with Indigenous communities to document and codify their environmental laws.
- **Outcome**: A shift toward legal pluralism that values Indigenous contributions as equal to state-centric laws.

Critical Theory Model and Reviving Indigenous Legal Systems

Core Idea

The Critical Theory model challenges colonial narratives that have historically undermined and erased Indigenous legal systems. It seeks to critique this erasure, advocate for decolonization and support the revival and adaptation of Indigenous environmental laws. This approach promotes a paradigm shift toward legal pluralism, where Indigenous contributions are valued equally alongside state-centric legal systems [66].

Approach

Critiquing the Erasure of Indigenous Laws: Colonization often marginalized Indigenous environmental governance, labeling it as primitive or irrelevant. For instance, in the United States, the Dawes Act of 1887 disrupted Native American land stewardship, imposing Western property laws that disregarded communal governance. Critiquing such policies is essential for understanding their long-term impact on Indigenous sovereignty and environmental degradation.

Promoting Decolonization Through Education and Activism: Education and activism are powerful tools for decolonization. In Australia, movements like the Uluru Statement from the Heart advocate for constitutional recognition and truth-telling about the history of dispossession. These efforts highlight the need for integrating Indigenous laws into national governance as a step toward reconciliation.

Documenting and Codifying Indigenous Environmental Laws: Collaboration with Indigenous communities is crucial to reviving and codifying their legal systems. For example, in Bolivia, the Quechua and Aymara peoples have worked with the government to document traditional laws governing land and water use. Bolivia's *Ley de Derechos de la Madre Tierra* (Law of the Rights of Mother Earth) incorporates Indigenous principles, emphasizing the interconnectedness of all living beings.

Case Examples

- **Maasai, Kenya and Tanzania**: The Maasai have long practiced sustainable grazing, guided by customary laws that balance land use with environmental conservation. Recent legal efforts aim to protect these practices against land grabs and state-imposed conservation models that often exclude Indigenous governance. The Maasai people of Kenya and Tanzania are renowned for their pastoralist lifestyle, which has been sustainably practiced for centuries. Guided by customary laws, the Maasai utilize rotational grazing techniques that balance land use with environmental conservation. This approach ensures that grasslands recover naturally while minimizing overgrazing and soil degradation. Their deep understanding of seasonal cycles and ecological dynamics enables the Maasai to manage resources efficiently, fostering biodiversity and maintaining the health of savannah ecosystems. Livestock, particularly cattle, are central to Maasai culture and livelihood and their grazing practices reflect a harmonious relationship with the environment [67].

Challenges to Indigenous Governance

These traditional practices face increasing threats from land grabs, privatization and state-imposed conservation models. Governments and private entities often appropriate Maasai lands for agricultural expansion, mining, or tourism without adequate consultation or compensation. State-led conservation strategies, such as the establishment of national parks and wildlife reserves, frequently exclude Indigenous governance, displacing communities and disrupting their livelihoods. These actions undermine the Maasai's sustainable practices and exacerbate land use conflicts.

Legal Protections for Maasai Practices

In response, legal efforts in both Kenya and Tanzania aim to protect Maasai land rights and traditional grazing practices. Policies recognizing communal land ownership and advocating for participatory conservation models are gaining traction. These measures align with global commitments like the United Nations Declaration on the Rights of Indigenous Peoples (UNDRIP), ensuring that the Maasai continue to contribute to ecological resilience while preserving their cultural heritage [68].

- **Standing Rock Sioux Tribe, USA**: The Dakota Access Pipeline protests highlighted the tribe's fight to protect their sacred lands and water sources. Their resistance brought global attention to the importance of Indigenous laws and sovereignty in environmental decision-making, challenging colonial-style resource extraction policies [69].

The Fight for Sacred Lands and Water

The Standing Rock Sioux Tribe's resistance to the Dakota Access Pipeline (DAPL) became a global symbol of Indigenous sovereignty and environmental justice. The pipeline, intended to transport crude oil across multiple U.S. states, was planned to pass under Lake Oahe, a crucial water source for the tribe and a site of profound spiritual significance. The Standing Rock Sioux argued that the project violated their treaty rights under the 1851 Treaty of Fort Laramie and posed significant risks to water quality, public health and sacred sites. Their fight underscored the ongoing marginalization of Indigenous voices in environmental decision-making and the dangers of colonial-style resource extraction policies [70].

Global Attention to Indigenous Sovereignty: The 2016 protests drew thousands of supporters, including other Indigenous nations, environmental activists and human rights organizations. The movement brought international attention to the role of Indigenous laws in safeguarding the environment. It also emphasized the importance of recognizing Indigenous sovereignty in decisions that affect their lands and resources. Despite intense opposition, the protests temporarily halted construction, setting a precedent for future legal and environmental advocacy.

Challenging Resource Extraction Policies: The Standing Rock protests highlighted systemic issues in environmental governance, challenging policies prioritizing economic development over ecological and cultural preservation. They align with global goals like the United Nations Declaration on the Rights of Indigenous

Peoples (UNDRIP) and Sustainable Development Goals (SDGs) 6 and 15, advocating for clean water and sustainable ecosystem management. The movement remains a testament to Indigenous resilience and the need for inclusive, equitable resource governance.

- **Quechua and Aymara Peoples, Bolivia:** Bolivia's recognition of Pachamama (Mother Earth) as a legal entity reflects the influence of Indigenous laws. These communities actively contribute to the country's environmental governance, emphasizing reciprocity and balance in human-nature interactions.

Recognition of Pachamama as a Legal Entity

Bolivia's groundbreaking decision to recognize *Pachamama* (Mother Earth) as a legal entity reflects the profound influence of Indigenous laws and worldviews, particularly those of the Quechua and Aymara peoples. Rooted in their spiritual and cultural beliefs, Pachamama symbolizes the interconnectedness of all living beings and the environment. By granting legal rights to nature through the *Ley de Derechos de la Madre Tierra* (Law of the Rights of Mother Earth) in 2010, Bolivia has created a framework that acknowledges nature's intrinsic value beyond its utility to humans. This legislation draws heavily from Indigenous traditions, emphasizing reciprocity, balance and respect in human-nature interactions.

Indigenous Contributions to Environmental Governance

The Quechua and Aymara peoples play an active role in Bolivia's environmental governance by incorporating traditional ecological knowledge into policies and practices. Their sustainable land use practices, such as terraced farming and rotational grazing, ensure soil fertility and water conservation. Additionally, their customs promote community-led conservation, protecting biodiversity in the Andean region. This integration of Indigenous wisdom strengthens Bolivia's ability to address pressing challenges like deforestation and climate change.

Global Implications of Indigenous Models

Bolivia's approach has inspired international discussions on ecological ethics and legal pluralism, aligning with global conventions like the United Nations Declaration on the Rights of Indigenous Peoples (UNDRIP) and SDG 15, which promotes the sustainable use of terrestrial ecosystems. By embracing Indigenous paradigms, Bolivia sets a precedent for balancing development and environmental preservation.

Outcome

The Critical Theory model advocates for:

- **Legal Pluralism**: Acknowledging Indigenous laws as equal contributors to environmental governance.
- **Cultural Revival**: Reviving Indigenous practices that offer sustainable solutions to modern environmental challenges.

- **Decolonization**: Reconfiguring national legal frameworks to respect and incorporate Indigenous worldviews.

By deconstructing colonial narratives and fostering collaboration with Indigenous communities, this model promotes a more equitable and inclusive legal landscape that values diverse approaches to environmental stewardship. These models provide a sociological foundation for exploring how Indigenous environmental laws, rooted in ethnoecological paradigms, can inform and transform global approaches to environmental governance.

1.13 Ecological Resilience and Human Adaptation

Exploring the intricate relationship between human societies and their own environmental laws, this chapter delves into how various cultures have adapted to environmental changes. This chapter includes different legal and traditional ecological knowledge, sustainable resource management and community-based conservation efforts. It share insights into how different societies navigate challenges such as climate change, deforestation and biodiversity loss, showcasing examples of laws, resilience and innovative adaptation strategies. Indigenous communities across the globe share a profound connection with their natural environment, a relationship that is deeply interwoven with their cultural, spiritual and social identities. This intricate bond has given rise to ethnoecological paradigms, a form of traditional ecological knowledge that serves as the foundation for many customary laws. However, religious beliefs, often manifesting as cultural norms, can sometimes create barriers to the development and evolution of these laws. This analysis explores the dynamics of ethnoecological paradigms within indigenous environmental law narratives, focusing on their symbiotic wisdom and the challenges posed by conflicting cultural norms.

1.14 Ethnoecological Paradigms

Ethnoecology refers to the way indigenous people perceive and manage their ecosystems through culturally rooted knowledge systems. These paradigms emphasize the interdependence between humans and nature, advocating sustainable practices long before the advent of modern environmental movements [71]. For instance, rotational farming, sacred groves and seasonal hunting restrictions are not mere practices but codified forms of customary laws that reflect deep ecological insights.

1.15 The Role of Religious Beliefs in Customary Laws

Religious beliefs often serve as the moral compass of a community, influencing its legal frameworks and societal norms. Among indigenous communities, spiritual connections to nature frequently underpin customary laws. For example, the belief in sacred landscapes or totemic species reinforces the conservation of biodiversity. However, when religious beliefs become rigid or are interpreted in ways that conflict with adaptive environmental needs, they can hinder the evolution of these laws. For instance:

- **Rigid Ritual Practices**: Certain rituals may mandate the use of rare natural resources, leading to unsustainable exploitation.
- **Gender-Based Restrictions**: Cultural taboos often exclude women from participating in environmental decision-making, despite their pivotal roles in resource management.
- **Resistance to Modernization**: Religious conservatism can resist the integration of scientific insights into traditional practices, creating gaps in addressing contemporary ecological challenges.

1.16 Symbiosis in Indigenous Environmental Law

Despite these challenges, indigenous environmental laws exhibit a remarkable ability to harmonize spiritual beliefs with ecological imperatives. This symbiosis can be seen in:

- **Sacred Landscapes**: Many communities designate forests, rivers, or mountains as sacred, thereby protecting these ecosystems from exploitation.
- **Seasonal Calendars**: The alignment of agricultural and fishing activities with lunar or solar cycles ensures resource regeneration.
- **Community-Centric Governance**: Decision-making processes often involve collective wisdom, reducing the risk of over exploitation and fostering accountability.

Case Studies

- **The Khasi Tribe of Northeast India**: Their belief in sacred groves has preserved biodiversity hotspots for centuries. However, pressures from modernization and shifting religious practices challenge these traditional norms [72].
- **The San People of Southern Africa**: The San's tracking and hunting laws, rooted in spiritual respect for prey, exemplify sustainable resource use. Yet, colonial and modern religious influences have disrupted their traditional governance [73].

1.17 Navigating the Barriers

Addressing the barriers posed by cultural norms requires a nuanced approach that respects indigenous sovereignty while promoting adaptability. Key strategies include:

- **Inclusive Dialogues**: Engaging diverse community members, including women and youth, ensures a more holistic understanding of environmental challenges.
- **Integrating Scientific Knowledge**: Bridging traditional wisdom with scientific insights can enhance the resilience of customary laws.
- **Legal Recognition**: Strengthening the legal status of indigenous environmental laws at national and international levels can provide protective frameworks against external pressures.

The symbiotic wisdom inherent in ethnoecological paradigms offers invaluable lessons for global environmental governance. While religious beliefs and cultural norms may pose challenges, they also enrich the narrative by embedding ethical dimensions into environmental law. By fostering a dialogue between tradition and modernity, we can ensure the preservation and evolution of these paradigms, honoring the wisdom of indigenous communities and safeguarding our planet's future.

References:

1. Wright, B. R., Laffineur, B., & Royé, D. (2021). Rainfall-linked megafires as innate fire regime elements in arid Australian Spinifex (*Triodia spp.*) grasslands. *Frontiers in Ecology and Evolution, 9*. https://doi.org/10.3389/fevo.2021.666241
2. Bang, H. (2024). Sustainable development goals, disaster risk management and indigenous knowledge: A critical assessment of the interlinkages. *Sustainable Earth Reviews, 7,* 29. https://doi.org/10.1186/s42055-024-00101-x
3. Kim, Y., Tanaka, K., & Perrings, C. (2023). The impact of international conservation agreements on protected areas: Empirical findings from the Convention on Biological Diversity using causal inference. *Environmental Management, 72,* 203–218. https://doi.org/10.1007/s00267-023-01818-9
4. Kim, J., & Kim, Y. (2024). Tweeting climate change: Analyzing actor diversity and influence in climate-change discourse post-Paris agreement. *Discover Sustainability, 5,* 258. https://doi.org/10.1007/s43621-024-00449-2
5. Frogner, R. O. (2022). The train from Dunvegan: Implementing the United Nations Declaration on the Rights of Indigenous Peoples (UNDRIP) in public archives in Canada. *Archival Science, 22,* 209–238. https://doi.org/10.1007/s10502-021-09373-0
6. Qi, Y., Shi, X., Chen, Y., et al. (2024). Country-level evenness measure in assessing progress towards Sustainable Development Goals (SDGs). *Humanities and Social Sciences Communications, 11,* 1117. https://doi.org/10.1057/s41599-024-03572-7
7. Garcia, B., Morgan, E. A., & Aruch, M. (2024). Large-scale forest protection: The successful case of the Kayapo people in the Brazilian Amazon. *Regional Environmental Change, 24*(4). https://doi.org/10.1007/s10113-024-02304-6
8. Ali, M. A., & Kamraju, M. (2023). Historical perspectives on resource use. In *Natural resources and society: Understanding the complex relationship between humans and the environment* (pp. 35–50). Springer. https://doi.org/10.1007/978-3-031-46720-2_2

9. Divya, C., Paul, M., Lata, C., et al. (2024). Ethnomedicinal survey of the Paliyar tribe: A case study of Kadamalaikundu, Theni District. *International Journal of Anthropology and Ethnology, 8*(15). https://doi.org/10.1186/s41257-024-00116-4
10. Frogner, R. O. (2022). The train from Dunvegan: Implementing the United Nations Declaration on the Rights of Indigenous Peoples (UNDRIP) in public archives in Canada. *Archival Science, 22*(3), 209–238. https://doi.org/10.1007/s10502-021-09373-0
11. Sanghera, G. S., Bhatia, D., & Thind, K. (2015). Access and benefit sharing on the use of Indigenous traditional knowledge. In R. K. Salgotra & B. B. Gupta (Eds.), *Plant genetic resources and traditional knowledge for food security* (pp. 175–190). Springer Singapore. https://doi.org/10.1007/978-981-10-0060-7_9
12. March, A., Woolley, M., & Failler, P. (2024). Integration of climate change mitigation and adaptation in Blue Economy planning in Africa. *Mitigation and Adaptation Strategies for Global Change, 29*, 38. https://doi.org/10.1007/s11027-024-10133-5
13. Lezak, S., & Rock, G. (2024). On micropolitics: Climate adaptation and Indigenous governance in Western Alaska. *Climatic Change, 177*, 135. https://doi.org/10.1007/s10584-024-03769-4
14. Sarmiento, F. O., & Bernbaum, E. (2024). Named and gendered mountains. In F. O. Sarmiento & A. Gunya (Eds.), *Mountain lexicon* (Vol. 2, pp. 199–212). Springer. https://doi.org/10.1007/978-3-031-64884-7_11
15. Reuter, K., & Sewall, B. (2016). *Taboos and sustainability of tenrec hunting in Madagascar*. Presented at the International Symposium on Managed Aquifer Recharge (ISMAR 10), Madrid, Spain, May 20–24, 2019.
16. Tshewang, U., Tobias, M. C., & Morrison, J. G. (2021). Animal rights and protection. In Bhutan: Conservation and environmental protection in the Himalayas (pp. 93–108). Springer. https://doi.org/10.1007/978-3-030-57824-4_4
17. Nulkar, G. (2024). Biodiversity. In G. Nulkar (Ed.), *The intersection of economics and ecology* (pp. 53–68). Springer. https://doi.org/10.1007/978-981-99-6893-0_3
18. Berning, H., North, C., & Stevens, S. (2024). Deconstructing the anthropocentrism versus ecocentrism binary through Māori oral fire traditions. *Journal of Outdoor and Environmental Education, 27*(3), 291–308. https://doi.org/10.1007/s42322-023-00128-2
19. Woyames Dreher, C. (2024). Assessing the application of consultation and Indigenous peoples' protocols. In *A legal assessment of the efficacy of consultation with Indigenous peoples* (pp. 151–172). Springer. https://doi.org/10.1007/978-3-031-50539-3_5
20. Kuliš, Z., & Šimundić, B. (2025). Heritage and territory: Tangible and intangible cultural resources as drivers of regional development in Croatia. In B. Neuts, J. Martins, & M. Ioannides (Eds.), *Advances in cultural tourism research* (pp. 103–116). Springer. https://doi.org/10.1007/978-3-031-65537-1_7
21. Johansson, P., Schaffer, J. K., & Johansson Lopez, S. (2023). Cultural expertise in Sami land rights litigation: Epistemic strategies in the Girjas and Fosen cases. *Jindal Global Law Review, 14*, 217–240. https://doi.org/10.1007/s41020-023-00211-1
22. Daily, J. W., & Park, S. (2024). Fermented marine foods of the Indigenous Arctic people (Inuit) and comparisons with Asian fermented fish. *Journal of Ethnic Foods, 11*, 38. https://doi.org/10.1186/s42779-024-00255-1
23. Smouts, M. C. (2003). The construction of a global issue. In *Tropical forests international jungle* (pp. 13–32). Palgrave Macmillan. https://doi.org/10.1057/9781403981851_2
24. Fernández Escalante, E., García Asensio, J. M., Ayuga, F., & San Sebastián Sauto, J. (2019). *Ancient techniques of managed aquifer recharge: Spanish Careos and Peruvian Amunas as an adaptive complex system.* Presented at the International Symposium on Managed Aquifer Recharge (ISMAR 10), Madrid, Spain, May 20–24, 2019.
25. Librán-Embid, F., Olagoke, A., & Martin, E. A. (2023). Combining Milpa and push-pull technology for sustainable food production in smallholder agriculture: A review. *Agronomy for Sustainable Development, 43*, 45. https://doi.org/10.1007/s13593-023-00896-7
26. Cenerini, R. (2023). The United Nations Declaration on the Rights of Indigenous People: A prototype for reconciliation? In L. E. Reimer & K. Standish (Eds.), *Perspectives on justice, indigeneity, gender and security in human rights research* (pp. 45–60). Palgrave Macmillan. https://doi.org/10.1007/978-981-99-1930-7_6

27. Chakrabarty, S. P., & Penteado, A. (2024). Towards a better access and benefit sharing mechanism to protect traditional knowledge in India: A platter in the offering. In A. Penteado, S. P. Chakrabarty, & O. H. Shaikh (Eds.), *Traditional knowledge and climate change* (pp. 199–214). Springer. https://doi.org/10.1007/978-981-99-8830-3_14
28. Majumdar, K. (2024). Comparative perspective on social welfare policies for the Indigenous peoples in Taiwan and India: Exploring best practices and lessons. *Discover Global Society, 2*(1), 2. https://doi.org/10.1007/s44282-023-00021-9
29. Chirkin, S. (2024). Bolivia's MERCOSUR membership. *Eurasian Integration Studies, 7*(3), 37–49. https://doi.org/10.24412/2072-8042-2024-7-37-49
30. Nguyen, T. M. P., Davidson, K., & Farrelly, M. (2025). Embedding transformative innovation into mission-oriented policy and innovation districts: The case of Melbourne. In N. Frantzeskaki, M. Moglia, P. Newton, D. Prasad, & M. Pineda Pinto (Eds.), *Future cities making: Theory and practice of urban sustainability transitions* (pp. 313–336). Springer. https://doi.org/10.1007/978-981-97-7671-9_11
31. Thakur, A. (2024). Why nature deserves a seat at the table: A case study on nature's personhood. *Jindal Global Law Review, 15*(2), 147–162. https://doi.org/10.1007/s41020-024-00247-x
32. Gould, J., Smyth, D., & Rassip, W. (2021). Recognizing the contribution of Indigenous protected areas to marine protected area management in Australia. *Maritime Studies, 20*(1), 5–26. https://doi.org/10.1007/s40152-020-00212-z
33. Bruce, K., & Mulrennan, M. E. (2024). A typology of national park co-management agreements in the era of reconciliation in Canada. *Environmental Management, 74*(3), 564–589. https://doi.org/10.1007/s00267-024-01997-z
34. Cenerini, R. (2023). The United Nations Declaration on the Rights of Indigenous People: A prototype for reconciliation? In L. E. Reimer & K. Standish (Eds.), *Perspectives on justice, indigeneity, gender and security in human rights research* (pp. xx–xx). Palgrave Macmillan. https://doi.org/10.1007/978-981-99-1930-7_6
35. Akpoviri, F. I., Baharum, S. N., & Zainol, Z. A. (2023). Digital sequence information and the access and benefit-sharing obligation of the Convention on Biological Diversity. *Nanoethics, 17*(1). https://doi.org/10.1007/s11569-023-00436-3
36. Sun, Y., Wang, Y., Liu, L., et al. (2024). Large-scale cultural heritage conservation and utilization based on cultural ecology corridors: A case study of the Dongjiang-Hanjiang River Basin in Guangdong, China. *Heritage Science, 12*, 44. https://doi.org/10.1186/s40494-024-01162-z
37. Mtey, A. R. (2024). Community involvement in education provision for indigenous pastoral community girls in Tanzania. *Interchange, 55*(1), 27–49. https://doi.org/10.1007/s10780-024-09511-4
38. Dudgeon, P., Bray, A., Walker, R., Wright, M., & Sutherland, S. (2024). Caring for country: Indigenous well-being, law and environmental justice. In R. J. Moore (Ed.), *Climate change and mental health equity* (pp. xx–xx). Springer. https://doi.org/10.1007/978-3-031-56736-0_15
39. Susemihl, G. (2023). Collaboration and cooperation: SGang Gwaay and Gwaii Haanas. In *Claiming back their heritage* (pp. xx–xx). Springer. https://doi.org/10.1007/978-3-031-40063-6_5
40. Jackson, H. (2024). Variation in population assemblage of Acanthuridae and Scaridae across human concentration levels during a bleaching event affecting the coral reefs of Guna Yala, Panama. *University of Colorado Honors Journal.* https://doi.org/10.33011/cuhj20242861
41. Susemihl, G. (2023). Collaboration and Cooperation: SGang Gwaay and Gwaii Haanas. In *Claiming Back Their Heritage. Heritage Studies.* Springer. https://doi.org/10.1007/978-3-031-40063-6_5
42. Syali, M. (2025). Nature-based solutions for riparian decision-making in South Asia: A legal perspective. In P. Singh, P. Srivastava, & A. Sorokin (Eds.), *Nature-based solutions in achieving sustainable development goals* (pp. xx–xx). Springer. https://doi.org/10.1007/978-3-031-76128-7_1
43. Marcías, C. (2024). *Resilience of indigenous food systems: A study of cacao production in agroforestry systems in the Northern Ecuadorian Amazon.* (Master's thesis).

44. Tsuchiya, R. (2024). Balance of power in a conflict model. *Economics of Governance, 25*(4), 379–399. https://doi.org/10.1007/s10101-024-00318-8
45. Ballard, A. (2024). "Are they getting it?": Texting with water in Leanne Betasamosake Simpson's "Big Water." In F. Mussi (Ed.), *Indigenous storytelling and connections to the land* (pp. xx–xx). Palgrave Macmillan. https://doi.org/10.1007/978-3-031-65591-3_7
46. Siqueira, A. L., Santos Amorim, T., Vasconcelos, M. M., & others. (2024). Implications and geotechnological propositions for the Yanomami Indigenous peoples due to illegal exploration of gold minings. *Revista Contemporânea, 4*(10), e6174. https://doi.org/10.56083/RCV4N10-105
47. Burns, C., Hetaraka, M., & Jones, A. (2024). Te Tiriti o Waitangi: The Treaty of Waitangi, principles and other representations. *New Zealand Journal of Education Studies, 59*(1), 15–29. https://doi.org/10.1007/s40841-024-00312-y
48. Orsini, A. (2024). Symbolic interactionism. In *Sociological theory* (pp. xx–xx). Palgrave Macmillan. https://doi.org/10.1007/978-3-031-52539-1_11
49. Poelina, A., & others. (2024). Personal stories. In *Declaration of peace for Indigenous Australians and nature* (pp. xx–xx). Springer. https://doi.org/10.1007/978-981-99-9327-7_3
50. Kaushal, N. (2023). The role of Indian culture in enlightening the notions of environmental stewardship and sustainable living mechanism. In S. Dhiman (Ed.), *Sustainable development and environmental stewardship* (pp. xx–xx). Springer. https://doi.org/10.1007/978-3-031-28885-2_5
51. Bautista-Valarezo, E., Duque, V., Verdugo Sánchez, A. E., et al. (2020). Towards an indigenous definition of health: An explorative study to understand the indigenous Ecuadorian people's health and illness concepts. *International Journal for Equity in Health, 19*, 101. https://doi.org/10.1186/s12939-020-1142-8
52. Retallack, G. J. (2022). Lichens and till. In *Soil grown tall* (pp. xx–xx). Springer. https://doi.org/10.1007/978-3-030-88739-1_12
53. Spennemann, D. H. R., & Hurford, S. (2024). Badges of (dis-)honour: Manifesting the 'conquest' of Uluṟu via wearable material culture. *Heritage, 8*(1), 8. https://doi.org/10.3390/heritage8010008
54. Tombleson, B., & Wolf, K. (2022). Sustainable tourism and public opinion: Examining the language surrounding the closure of Uluru to climbers. In M. Sigala, A. Yeark, R. Presbury, M. Fang, & K. A. Smith (Eds.), *Case-based research in tourism, travel, hospitality and events* (pp. 349–366). Springer. https://doi.org/10.1007/978-981-16-4671-3_22
55. Kearney, A., & Others. (2023). Conceptualising indigenous law. In *Indigenous law and the politics of kincentricity and orality* (pp. 1–19). Palgrave Macmillan. https://doi.org/10.1007/978-3-031-19239-5_1
56. Harris, B. (2024). Terminology, values and identity. In *Indigenous peoples and constitutional reform in Australia* (pp. 23–41). Springer. https://doi.org/10.1007/978-981-99-7121-3_1
57. Rathoure, A. K. (2024). Cultural practices to protect biodiversity through cultural heritage: Preserving nature, preserving culture. *Biodiversity International Journal, 7*(2), 71–75. https://doi.org/10.15406/bij.2024.07.00213
58. Díaz, S. C., Quezada, L. C., Álvarez, L. J., & Others. (2023). Indigenous use of fire in the paramo ecosystem of southern Ecuador: A case study using remote sensing methods and ancestral knowledge of the Kichwa Saraguro people. *Fire Ecology, 19*(5). https://doi.org/10.1186/s42408-022-00164-1
59. Mührel, J. (2024). Rights of nature in liberal legal systems. In *Rights of nature in liberal legal systems and international law* (pp. 143–158). Springer. https://doi.org/10.1007/978-3-031-69059-4_8
60. Suzina, A. C. (2023). Towards a circular theory of communication: The case of the Wayusa ritual of the traditional Kichwa people of Sarayaku. *Journal of Alternative & Community Media, 8*(2), 145–167. https://doi.org/10.1386/jacm_00124_1
61. Zhang, J., Zhang, R., Zhou, Y., & Others. (2024). A novel model predictive observer for switched systems using dissipativity theory. *Multiscale and Multidisciplinary Modeling, Experiments and Design, 7*, 3977–3991. https://doi.org/10.1007/s41939-024-00450-2

62. Healey Akearok, G. K. (2024). Arctic security: A reflection on security of community health, wellbeing and resilience. In G. Adlakha-Hutcheon & C. Kelshall (Eds.), *Identifying the invisible disruptors of security*. Springer. https://doi.org/10.1007/978-3-031-67608-6_8
63. Smouts, M. C. (2003). The construction of a global issue. In *Tropical forests international jungle* (pp. 21–36). Palgrave Macmillan. https://doi.org/10.1057/9781403981851_2
64. Zocchi, D. M., Volpato, G., Chalo, D., & Others. (2020). Expanding the reach: Ethnobotanical knowledge and technological intensification in beekeeping among the Ogiek of the Mau Forest, Kenya. *Journal of Ethnobiology and Ethnomedicine, 16*, 57. https://doi.org/10.1186/s13002-020-00409-w
65. Voda, M., Kithiia, S., Jackiewicz, E., & Others. (2019). Geosystems' pathways to the future of sustainability. *Scientific Reports, 9*, 14446. https://doi.org/10.1038/s41598-019-50937-z
66. McNaughton, N., & Martimianakis, M. A. (2023). Critical theory. In D. Nestel, G. Reedy, L. McKenna, & S. Gough (Eds.), *Clinical education for the health professions* (pp. 233–247). Springer. https://doi.org/10.1007/978-981-15-3344-0_35
67. Tamarozzi, F., Kibona, T., de Glanville, W. A., & Others. (2022). Cystic echinococcosis in northern Tanzania: A pilot study in Maasai livestock-keeping communities. *Parasites & Vectors, 15*, 396. https://doi.org/10.1186/s13071-022-05518-x
68. Timmins, H. L., Mupeta-Muyamwa, P., Marubu, J., Schouten, C., Lekaita, E., & Peterson, D. (2022). Securing communal tenure complemented by collaborative platforms for improved participatory landscape management and sustainable development: Lessons from northern Tanzania and the Maasai Mara in Kenya. In M. B. Holland, Y. J. Masuda, & B. E. Robinson (Eds.), *Land tenure security and sustainable development* (pp. 123–142). Palgrave Macmillan. https://doi.org/10.1007/978-3-030-81881-4_12
69. Kinefuchi, E. (2023). Environmental racism and environmental justice in North America. In R. Brinkmann (Ed.), *The Palgrave handbook of global sustainability* (pp. 601–621). Palgrave Macmillan. https://doi.org/10.1007/978-3-031-01949-4_74
70. Beisaw, A. M., & Olin, G. E. (2020). From Alcatraz to Standing Rock: Archaeology and contemporary Native American protests (1969–today). *Historical Archaeology, 54*, 537–555. https://doi.org/10.1007/s41636-020-00252-6
71. WinklerPrins, A. M. G. A., & Barrera-Bassols, N. (2005). Introduction: Ethnoecology. *Journal of Latin American Geography, 4*(1), 7–8. https://doi.org/10.1353/lag.2005.0032
72. Kharshiing, K. D. (2024). How matrilineal are the Khasis in Northeast India? A critical discourse analysis of gender and identity. *Human Arenas*. https://doi.org/10.1007/s42087-024-00422-5
73. Scott, B. K. (2024). Conflicting colonial, racial and tribal claims to southern Africa. In *Taking place: Geocriticism and spatial literary studies* (pp. 33–52). Palgrave Macmillan. https://doi.org/10.1007/978-3-031-48355-4_3

Chapter 2
Environmental Justice and Indigenous Perspectives

Abstract The complex link between environmental justice and indigenous viewpoints is examined in this chapter, with a focus on the critical role that indigenous communities play in protecting ecosystems while battling environmental and socioeconomic injustices. The chapter illustrates how indigenous knowledge systems, cosmologies and traditional practices support environmental stewardship by looking at instances from throughout the world. It also shows how these people often suffer the most from environmental degradation brought on by industrialization and policy marginalization. Indigenous beliefs on environmental justice are firmly anchored in holistic worldviews, which see nature as a living being that merits respect and preservation rather than simply as a resource. This chapter examines important cases, including Native American tribes' fights in the US for control over natural resources and the preservation of sacred sites under laws like the National Historic Preservation Act of 1966 and the Indian Self-Determination and Education Assistance Act of 1975. The Te Awa Tupua Act, 2017, which gave the Whanganui River legal personality and acknowledged Māori cosmology in New Zealand, is another example of how indigenous worldviews are influencing creative approaches to environmental justice.

Keywords Environmental racism · Indigenous perspectives · Sustainable development · Health equity

2.1 Overview

An essential framework called environmental justice (EJ) aims to address how marginalized communities, especially communities of color, low-income groups and Indigenous peoples are disproportionately affected by environmental degradation [1]. The detrimental impacts of environmental policies and practices on resources, land and human health have been the main emphasis of the conventional environmental justice narrative. Indigenous perspectives on environmental justice, however, make it clear that the problem goes beyond simply enforcing equitable policies; it also entails

T. Pradhan et al., *Symbiotic Wisdom: Exploring Ethnoecological Paradigms within Indigenous Environmental Law Narratives*,
https://doi.org/10.1007/978-981-95-1042-9_2

acknowledging the close, interdependent link that exists between Indigenous peoples and the land they live on. The relationship between indigenous peoples and the environment is based on cultural and spiritual practices that regard the planet as sacred, rather than just resource extraction or land rights. The Western, capitalist-driven patterns of resource exploitation that frequently serve as the foundation for environmental injustices are contested by this viewpoint. Therefore, in order to develop truly equitable solutions to environmental issues, the Environmental Justice movement must take Indigenous worldviews into consideration. The historical causes of injustice, the function of Indigenous knowledge systems and the contributions of Indigenous-led movements to a more equitable and sustainable future are all examined in this essay, which examines the relationship between environmental justice and Indigenous perspectives.

Addressing the unequal distribution of environmental benefits and burdens among various communities, particularly underprivileged and vulnerable groups, is the focus of the critical and multidisciplinary area of environmental justice. With a focus on addressing the disproportionate effects of environmental degradation on low-income, minority and Indigenous communities, it explores the connections between environmental policy, human rights, social justice and equity. In order to ensure that no group suffers an undue share of environmental harm while others benefit from environmental goods, this idea has grown into a potent social and political movement that promotes fairness in environmental decision-making. The main ideas, background and importance of environmental justice are summarized in this introduction, which also looks at how it developed in reaction to environmental injustices, the difficulties it encounters and the solutions it suggests for building a more sustainable and just society.

2.2 Origins and Historical Contexts

The origins of environmental justice can be found in the 1960s and 1970s, when American communities and activists realized that marginalized groups, especially low-income communities and ethnic minorities, were disproportionately affected by environmental risks. These communities frequently found themselves in close proximity to hazardous waste sites, polluting industries and other environmental risks that endangered their general well-being, livelihood and health [2]. The 1982 demonstration against the location of a hazardous waste landfill in a community with a large African American population in Warren County, North Carolina, was one of the most important early incidents that sparked the environmental justice movement. A broader national awareness of environmental racism—the notion that communities of color are disproportionately exposed to environmental hazards—began with this demonstration. Widespread action and a call for legislative measures to address these injustices were energized by the protests.

Communities of color were more likely than white communities to be situated close to toxic waste sites, according to a landmark 1987 report titled Toxic Wastes and Race in the United States by the United Church of Christ's Commission for Racial Justice. This report, which emphasized the necessity of addressing the social and racial aspects of environmental policy, became a basic text for the environmental justice movement. The movement's political objectives and philosophical underpinnings were further cemented in 1991 at the First National People of Color Environmental Leadership Summit in Washington, D.C. Leaders from community organizations, environmental organizations and grassroots activists came together for the summit to create a framework for environmental justice, which resulted in the endorsement of the "17 Principles of Environmental Justice." These tenets demanded that environmental racism be eradicated, that everyone's right to a healthy environment be acknowledged and that sustainable development that does not take advantage of marginalized communities be encouraged.

2.3 Key Concepts of Environmental Justice

At its core, environmental justice is concerned with the fair distribution of environmental risks and benefits. Several key concepts define the movement:

The term "environmental racism" describes how communities of color are disproportionately exposed to environmental risks such as air pollution, contaminated water and hazardous waste. Redlining, zoning regulations and industrial siting decisions that disproportionately affect low-income, Black, Indigenous and people of color (BIPOC) communities are only a few examples of the historical discriminatory practices that form the basis of environmental racism.

Disproportionate Effects, Environmental justice draws attention to the fact that societal distribution of environmental deterioration is frequently uneven. The burden of environmental devastation is borne more heavily by vulnerable groups, who may already be dealing with health, social and economic issues. This covers the consequences of climate change, limited access to green spaces and pollution exposure. **Sustainable Development,** Environmental justice promotes growth that satisfies current demands without jeopardizing the capacity of future generations to satisfy their own. This entails taking into account the long-term effects of development on the environment, society and economy and making sure that advantages are distributed fairly among groups. **Health Equity,** Environmental justice highlights the connection between public health and environmental quality. It is well recognized that exposure to dangerous chemicals, contaminated water and poor air quality can all have a negative impact on one's health, especially in areas where resources are scarce. Therefore, a key component of the environmental justice movement is health equity. **Empowerment and Participation,** The right of communities to have a say in choices that impact their environment and well-being is a fundamental component of environmental justice. This entails promoting inclusive policymaking procedures that enable historically underrepresented groups to hold polluters accountable and take part in decision-making. **Intersectionality,** Environmental justice acknowledges that environmental damages are entwined with wider societal injustices rather than occurring in a vacuum. Individuals' susceptibility to environmental hazards and their capacity to defend themselves are influenced by social characteristics such as gender, race and class. Therefore, efforts to promote environmental justice must tackle the underlying causes of social inequality in addition to environmental concerns.

2.4 Environmental Justice and Climate Change

The growing threat posed by climate change has been incorporated into the concept of environmental justice in recent years. groups that are already at risk from environmental risks, such as low-lying coastal areas, impoverished urban districts and rural Indigenous groups, are disproportionately impacted by climate change. Extreme weather events like hurricanes, floods, heat waves and wildfires, as well as the social and economic repercussions of relocation brought on by climate change, are more likely to affect these communities. Workers and communities that have historically relied on fossil fuels should not be left behind in the change to renewable energy, according to the environmental justice movement, which promotes a "just transition" to a green economy. The foundation of this shift should be equality, which includes giving frontline communities access to clean energy, good jobs and resilience to the effects of climate change [4]. Thus, proponents of environmental justice demand that climate policy acknowledge and compensate for the past and present exploitation of Indigenous lands and resources, as well as the disproportionate emissions from developed countries that fuel climate change. Given that the nations in the Global South, which have made the least contribution to climate change, are frequently the ones most impacted by its effects, this is especially pertinent in international discussions (Fig. 2.1).

2.5 Key Issues in Environmental Justice

Environmental justice and social justice connect with a number of urgent challenges. Among these problems are; **(a) Air and Water Pollution,** high levels of air and water pollution are caused by the proximity of industrial facilities, landfills and transportation infrastructure to underserved populations. For instance, urban African American communities are more likely to be situated close to highways, which increases the prevalence of respiratory conditions like asthma. (b) **Waste Disposal and Toxic Sites,** low-income and communities of color neighborhoods are disproportionately situated next to landfills, hazardous waste sites and other health-risky establishments. These locations have the potential to pollute the air, water and soil, which could result in long-term health issues like cancer, birth deformities and developmental disorders. **(c) Food Deserts and Green Space Access,** in many urban and rural regions, there is a shortage of access to nutritious food and green spaces, which is another issue that environmental justice addresses. "Food deserts," or places with limited access

Fig. 2.1 Key issues in environmental justice

to fresh, healthful food, are frequently found in communities without parks or other recreational spaces. Poor health outcomes, such as obesity, heart disease and mental health problems, are exacerbated by the lack of these services. (d) **Environmental Displacement,** communities are being compelled to relocate as a result of extreme weather, rising sea levels and environmental degradation brought on by the acceleration of climate change. While displaced communities frequently deal with issues including poverty, loss of livelihood and insufficient housing availability, indigenous peoples in particular are losing their ancestral territories and traditional ways of life.

The right of impacted communities to pursue legal action and hold polluters responsible is one of the fundamental tenets of environmental justice [5]. However, historically underrepresented groups frequently encounter obstacles when trying to access the courts and legal counsel, which restricts their capacity to remedy environmental harms.

2.6 Strategies and Remedies for Environmental Justice

To address these problems and advance more equity in environmental policy and practice, the environmental justice movement supports a number of tactics, including; (a) **Community-Based Lobbying**, the movement's main goal is to enable local communities to take the lead in addressing environmental injustices. At the municipal, state and federal levels, grassroots organizations, neighborhood activists and community groups are essential in recognizing problems, planning demonstrations and promoting legislative changes. (b) **Policy Reform,** Proponents of environmental justice work to amend laws to take into account the racial and social aspects of environmental problems. To guarantee that vulnerable populations are not disproportionately burdened by environmental concerns, this involves changes to land use planning, pollution controls and zoning laws. **(c) Environmental Monitoring and Data Collection,** finding and correcting environmental injustices requires accurate data on health effects and environmental threats. Affected communities can gather information on pollution levels, health consequences and environmental conditions through community-based environmental monitoring projects, providing them with the proof they need to push for change. **(d) Just and Sustainable Development,** The movement advocates for a change to sustainable development that puts economic fairness, community well-being and environmental health first. This entails funding conservation and environmental restoration initiatives that help underserved populations, encouraging green infrastructure and supporting renewable energy projects. **(e) Education and Public Awareness,** Creating widespread support for change requires increasing public knowledge of environmental justice issues. Campaigns for education can motivate grassroots action by relating environmental suffering to larger social injustices [6].

2.7 History and Evolution of Environmental Justice

Due in large part to the concentration of polluting businesses in underprivileged and minority neighborhoods, the modern Environmental Justice movement began to take shape in the United States in the latter half of the twentieth century. The 1982 demonstrations in Warren County, North Carolina, where a landfill with toxic waste was to be constructed in a neighborhood that was predominately African American, were a pivotal point in the movement's history. The demonstrations led to a nationwide campaign that broadened the definition of environmental harm to encompass racial and socioeconomic injustices [7]. According to professionals like Dr Robert Bullard, environmental justice acknowledges that historically underprivileged groups are frequently disproportionately affected by environmental deterioration [8]. Around the world, environmental justice has expanded to include concerns about human rights, biodiversity and climate change in addition to racial and economic challenges.

(a) Fair Treatment, according to environmental justice, no group should be disproportionately affected by environmental damage, regardless of their color, ethnicity or financial status [9]. (b) **Inclusive Decision-Making,** the environmental decision-making process should incorporate all communities, particularly those that are marginalized. **(c) Fair Distribution of Environmental Benefits and Burdens,** the advantages of protecting the environment and the costs of pollution and degradation have to be divided equally. (d) **Relation to Sustainability,** because it promotes a comprehensive approach to the environment that puts the health and well-being of all communities above short-term financial gain at the expense of vulnerable populations, environmental justice is closely related to sustainability.

2.8 Traditional Ecological Knowledge (TEK)

Based on years of observation and lived experience, indigenous peoples all over the world have created complex systems of knowledge about the environment. Indigenous communities' perspectives on ecosystems, biodiversity and environmental management are referred to as Traditional Ecological Knowledge (TEK). Understanding the land's cycles, the relationships between species and sustainable harvesting methods are all part of this knowledge. TEK is frequently transmitted orally through customs, rituals and stories that demonstrate a strong bond with the natural world [10].

2.9 Sacredness of the Environment

Many Indigenous cultures view the environment as a sacred thing that has to be revered and protected, rather than just a resource to be used. Numerous origin myths and religious doctrines that establish a mutually beneficial interaction between people and the land, plants, animals and elements are clear examples of this worldview. These ideas are frequently reflected in conservation strategies that prioritize sustainability and balance, including switching up hunting areas or letting ecosystems recover before using them once more [11].

2.10 Stewardship and Conservation Practices

A long-term perspective of ecological health is frequently the foundation of indigenous conservation methods. These methods include managing water resources, agroforestry, sustainable hunting and fishing and controlled fires to preserve the health of forests. These are comprehensive techniques that encompass the community's social and cultural fiber in addition to the land [12].

2.11 Colonialism, Land Dispossession and Environmental Racism

Indigenous groups have seen significant disruptions in their relationship with the land as a result of colonization. Indigenous peoples have endured policies aimed at erasing their cultures and ways of life throughout history, as well as being violently forcibly relocated from their ancestral territories [2]. Additionally, resource extraction was linked to this land expropriation, which had a direct impact on environmental deterioration. In many respects, colonial practices are still being carried out in the environmental injustices that Indigenous populations still experience. For example, resource exploitation (oil drilling, mining, etc.) frequently occurs on Indigenous lands and Indigenous peoples continue to oppose environmental racism that results in the loss of their lands.

The histories of numerous oppressed populations worldwide have been influenced by the intertwined problems of colonialism, land dispossession and environmental racism. These problems are not just remnants of the past; they still show up in the current battles over resources, land and environmental justice. A historical perspective that takes into consideration the lingering effects of colonial practices and an understanding of the ways in which race, class and environment are entwined in contemporary systems of exploitation and inequality are necessary to comprehend the junction of these three elements.

2.12 Colonialism and Land Dispossession

The concepts of economic exploitation and territory domination served as the foundation for colonialism as an expansionist endeavor. In an attempt to control large swaths of the globe, colonial powers like Britain, Spain, France and Portugal uprooted native populations in order to obtain resources. Since the land was frequently the main source of income and power, the act of land dispossession was essential to colonial goals. From the Americas to Africa, Australia and the Pacific, indigenous peoples were either forced from their native lands or relocated to smaller, less productive regions. For instance, in order to create agricultural and urban communities in the Americas, European colonizers committed enormous land theft and killings. While their ancestral grounds were taken and turned into lucrative lands for settlers, Native American tribes in the United States were evicted and placed onto reservations, frequently in hostile areas. Despite the fact that Aboriginal peoples had lived in Australia for thousands of years, the British designated the country "terra nullius" (nobody's land), which resulted in the violent eviction of landowners and the devastation of ecosystems [13]. Colonial powers ignored the land rights and cultural links of indigenous peoples to the land when they split Africa in accordance with European objectives. Local inhabitants were systematically cut off from their natural resources as a result of the construction of exploitative institutions such as forced labor in agriculture and mining, as well as the imposition of artificial borders. In both situations, colonization aimed to establish a new socioeconomic structure based on the exploitation of native resources and labor in addition to displacing land.

2.13 Environmental Racism

The term "environmental racism" describes how marginalized racial and ethnic groups are disproportionately exposed to environmental risks, frequently as a result of discriminatory laws and practices. This type of racism has its origins in the colonial worldview, which saw indigenous peoples and their lands as inferior and disposable.

Many of the lands stolen from indigenous people were turned into resource-rich areas during and after the colonial era and they were extensively used for mining, agriculture and extraction. The same populations that had been evicted were frequently severely hit by the environmental damage these enterprises generated. Due to industrial pollution, particularly in the vicinity of chemical companies, refineries and waste dumps, African American communities in the South of the United States many of whom were descended from enslaved people were exposed to hazardous chemicals and endured substandard living circumstances [14]. The environmental practices that still have an impact on indigenous communities around the world are another clear example of colonialism's legacy. For instance, while businesses work to extract natural resources, Indigenous peoples in Canada and the United States who live in or close to pipelines, mining operations and oil extraction sites frequently have their lands destroyed, their water supplies contaminated and their soil contaminated. Because of this environmental racism, these communities which have already been damaged by centuries of colonial displacement are more susceptible to long-term health problems including cancer and respiratory disorders.

Similar to this, many postcolonial regimes in Africa have carried on with resource extraction under new leadership, a priority of colonial powers. Indigenous and rural communities are disproportionately affected by environmental degradation brought on by the oil and mineral extraction industries in nations like South Africa, Nigeria and the Democratic Republic of the Congo [15]. These communities suffer from poor health outcomes and the loss of livelihoods based on agriculture and land.

2.14 The Intersection of Colonialism, Land Dispossession and Environmental Racism

Understanding the connections between environmental racism, land dispossession and colonialism is essential to comprehending the larger oppressive structures that have persisted after formal colonialism. During the colonial era, land dispossession was linked to the eradication of indigenous cultures, customs and ways of life in addition to being an economic and territorial issue. Land was a living thing that was entwined with social institutions, spiritual beliefs and cultural identity; it was more than just a resource. These cultural linkages were broken by the loss of land, which paved the path for ongoing marginalization, particularly as colonized countries found it difficult to adjust to a new global order that placed a higher value on European lifestyles. In a number of respects, this dispossession process set the groundwork for environmental racism. First, ecosystems were frequently harmed as a result of colonial powers' exploitation of natural resources. The land and local residents suffered as a result of mining, over farming and deforestation. Indigenous people were nonetheless impacted by these practices after colonial rule ended, frequently being sidelined by industrialization or postcolonial economic objectives centered on resource exploitation. Second, colonial powers' social and political legacies, including racial hierarchies, resource allocation schemes and land ownership laws, perpetuated environmental injustice trends. Indigenous peoples and other oppressed groups were frequently denied their legal land rights or forced to live in places unsuitable for sustainable cultivation or habitation [16]. These populations were allowed to suffer the most from environmental degradation because they were frequently viewed as "expendable" by colonial and postcolonial regimes.

2.15 Contemporary Struggles and Resistance

The fight against environmental racism and land dispossession is far from done for vulnerable people. Indigenous peoples around the world are still fighting for their ancestral territories and to keep the environment from being exploited. These communities have been at the vanguard of environmental activism, drawing attention to the connections between racial, environmental and land-based injustices, from the Standing Rock Sioux's opposition to the Dakota Access Pipeline in the United States to the ongoing land disputes in Brazil's Amazon. Thus, colonialism's legacy still influences contemporary environmental problems like climate change. The current environmental crises are largely a result of colonial powers' exploitation of natural resources and the imposition of exploitative industrial and agricultural systems. Formerly colonized nations and communities often those least accountable for the emissions causing global warming are disproportionately affected by climate change.

Due to colonial pasts, resource exploitation and the global push for economic growth at the expense of Indigenous rights and ecosystems, Indigenous communities worldwide deal with a variety of environmental challenges. These problems are especially critical since they jeopardize these communities' cultural customs and spiritual links to the land in addition to endangering their physical well-being [17].

2.15.1 Resource Extraction (Mining, Oil Drilling, Logging, Etc.)

One of the biggest environmental risks that Indigenous peoples are currently confronting is resource extraction. Multinational firms frequently want to take advantage of the abundant natural resources found in many Indigenous territory, such as lumber, minerals and oil. Nevertheless, the environmental and cultural rights of the local Indigenous communities are rarely respected by these companies [18]. Large-scale forestry projects, oil drilling and mining operations harm ecosystems irreversibly by contaminating streams, destroying habitats and reducing biodiversity.

For example, Canada's Oil Sands, protests against the oil sands' expansion, which has resulted in extensive deforestation, air and water pollution and the devastation of traditional grounds, have been led by Indigenous communities in Alberta. **Mining in the Amazon,** indigenous groups in Brazil's Amazon rainforest are battling against illicit gold mining, which pollutes the environment with mercury, destroys forests and targets Indigenous leaders who oppose the projects.

The livelihoods of Indigenous peoples, whose survival frequently depends on the condition of their natural surrounds, are disrupted by these activities in addition to harming the environment.

2.15.2 Pollution and Toxic Waste Sites

Landfills, toxic waste sites and other contaminated regions are close to many Indigenous villages. Systemic racism and discriminatory environmental policies that have traditionally singled out Indigenous peoples for the installation of dangerous enterprises are directly responsible for this. Uranium mining in the US has contaminated Native American villages by leaving behind radioactive waste that contaminates water supplies and damages nearby ecosystems. For example, uranium mining has caused major health problems for the Navajo Nation, including high incidence of cancer and other ailments. Numerous First Nations communities in Canada are coping with tainted water supplies [19]. In many isolated Indigenous communities, which have been overlooked by government infrastructure projects, the lack of access to safe drinking water is a persistent crisis. In addition to posing health hazards, pollution and toxic waste are destroying the environment, endangering cultural activities like fishing, hunting and harvesting medicinal herbs that depend on a healthy environment.

2.15.3 Deforestation and Habitat Destruction

Deforestation, particularly in tropical and boreal rainforests, is another significant threat to Indigenous lands. The removal of trees for logging, agriculture or urban development not only destroys vital habitats but also contributes significantly to climate change by releasing carbon into the atmosphere [20]. The livelihood and cultural customs of Indigenous peoples in Borneo and Sumatra are under jeopardy due to the extensive deforestation caused by the growth of palm oil plantations in Indonesia. Strong corporate interests are a major obstacle to indigenous people' efforts to prevent the loss of their forests. Both legal and illicit logging have significantly decreased the Amazon's rainforest acreage, which has resulted in the extinction of species and a decline in biodiversity. Indigenous civilizations who depend on the forest for everything from food to housing to medicine are also impacted by this destruction.

2.15.4 Climate Change Impacts on Indigenous Lands and Cultures

Indigenous communities are disproportionately impacted by climate change, especially those that reside in high-altitude, coastal and Arctic locations that are susceptible ecosystems. The physical environment and the cultural traditions associated with it are under threat from rising temperatures, more frequent and severe weather events, altered animal migration patterns and biodiversity loss. Melting glaciers and thawing permafrost are threatening traditional hunting methods and coastal villages for Indigenous peoples in Alaska, including the Yupik and Iñupiat. Additionally, coastal villages are being eroded by rising sea levels, forcing residents to migrate. Rising sea levels are posing a threat to the homes and ancestral lands of indigenous tribes in the Pacific Islands, such as the Marshall Islands [21]. Since these groups have lived in these areas for millennia, their relocation signifies a loss of identity, culture and language.

2.15.5 Water Rights and Contamination

Although many Indigenous people are deprived of this essential resource because of contamination, privatization and disregard by state and corporate players, access to clean water is a fundamental human right. Key water supplies are located on Indigenous lands in many parts of the world and the fight for access to water frequently crosses over into larger conflicts for environmental justice and land sovereignty. Due to government incompetence, African American and Indigenous populations in Flint, Michigan, were disproportionately impacted by the water crisis and exposed to drinking water tainted with lead. Concerns about water contamination from pipeline breaches were brought to light at the Sacred Stone Camp at Standing Rock in North Dakota, when Indigenous peoples and allies demonstrated against the Dakota Access Pipeline (DAPL) [22]. In addition to protecting the environment, many Indigenous peoples view water as having cultural and spiritual value, which is why the fight for clean water is so important.

2.16 Movements for Environmental Justice: Indigenous Activism and Leadership

Using both traditional knowledge and contemporary action, Indigenous peoples have been in the front of environmental justice movements, fighting to preserve their lands, rivers and cultures [23]. Achieving long-lasting, systemic change requires the inclusion of Indigenous leadership in the larger environmental justice movement.

- **The Standing Rock Sioux and the Dakota Access Pipeline Protest**

  One of the most high-profile environmental justice movements in recent years was the resistance to the Dakota Access Pipeline (DAPL) led by the Standing Rock Sioux Tribe in North Dakota [24]. The pipeline, which was to carry oil across the Missouri River, threatened to contaminate the water supply of the Standing Rock Sioux and other nearby communities. The protest, which began in 2016, garnered international attention and led to widespread solidarity actions across the globe. This demonstration was about protecting Indigenous rights, water and sovereignty, not just about a pipeline. The Standing Rock Sioux demanded a reassessment of how environmental regulations frequently ignore Indigenous people and underlined the significance of upholding treaty rights. As a rallying cry for more environmental and social justice, the movement brought allies and Indigenous peoples together to oppose government indifference and corporate greed.

- **The Fight Against the Pebble Mine**

  One of the biggest sockeye salmon fisheries in the world is found in the Bristol Bay watershed, whose pristine waters are in danger due to the contentious Pebble Mine project in Alaska. The Yup'ik, Dena'ina and Alutiiq peoples are among the indigenous groups in the area who have been outspoken in their opposition to the project, claiming that it will destroy their way of life and disturb vital fish habitats [25]. The struggle over Pebble Mine brings to light the larger problem of resource extraction on Indigenous territory, where the requirements of Indigenous peoples on a cultural, ecological and spiritual level frequently clash with the financial objectives of big corporations.

- **Global Indigenous-Led Resistance**

  Resistance movements conducted by Indigenous peoples are not just found in North America. Indigenous peoples have been in the vanguard of environmental movements all across the world. Indigenous leaders in Brazil, such as Raoni Metuktire and Sônia Guajajara, have spearheaded initiatives to stop illicit logging and destruction in the Amazon jungle [26]. The practices of the Brazilian government that have enabled land grabs and the devastation of Indigenous areas are criticized by these leaders. Similar efforts have been made by Indigenous activists in Australia, such as Lydia Bevege, to defend sacred sites and oppose the mining of natural fuels

[27]. In nations like New Zealand, where Māori tribes have resisted resource extraction and industrialization that endangers the environment and their cultural legacy, the struggle to prevent mining on holy areas is also visible.

2.17 Legislative and Policy Frameworks for Indigenous Environmental Rights

Indigenous peoples' environmental rights are recognized and protected by a number of international legal systems. For Indigenous communities to have a voice in choices that affect their land and ecology, these frameworks are crucial.

- **Indigenous Peoples' Rights Declaration of the United Nations (UNDRIP)**

  The UNDRIP, which was adopted in 2007, upholds the rights of Indigenous peoples around the world, including the right to self-determination, the right to preserve and enhance their traditional customs and the right to free, prior and informed consent (FPIC) for projects that impact their territories [28]. Although the political will of particular states will determine how this declaration is implemented, it offers Indigenous communities a potent instrument for promoting environmental justice.

- **Environmental Laws and Treaties**

  Due to national and international treaties, Indigenous communities in many nations are entitled to certain legal safeguards. Indigenous peoples frequently find themselves in legal disputes with strong governments and businesses and the implementation of these safeguards can be uneven. Although Indigenous rights, such as the right to land and resources are recognized by the Constitution Act of 1982 in Canada, many Indigenous communities still encounter legal obstacles when attempting to exercise these rights, especially when they clash with commercial interests [29]. Indigenous lands in the United States are partially protected by federal laws like the National Environmental Policy Act (NEPA) and the Indian Environmental General Assistance Program, but corporate interests and government policies that put economic development ahead of environmental protection have frequently undermined these laws [30].

2.18 Indigenous Solutions to Environmental Justice: A Path Forward

Although Indigenous people suffer disproportionately from environmental devastation, they also provide priceless answers because of their centuries-long expertise in resilient communities and sustainable land management. Integrating social, ecological and spiritual well-being, these solutions are based on holistic, culturally sensitive methods.

2.18.1 Reviving Ecological Knowledge and Indigenous Governance

Reviving Indigenous governance institutions is a key element of an environmental justice movement headed by Indigenous peoples (Fig. 2.2). Indigenous cultures have historically used institutions that guaranteed sustainability and reverence for the natural environment to manage their territories. These governing bodies, which are frequently ingrained in cultural customs and beliefs, provide a template for dealing with today's environmental emergencies. The seven-generation concept, which is emphasized by the Great Law of Peace in the Haudenosaunee (Iroquois) Confederacy, emphasizes the necessity of making decisions that will have a lasting impact on future generations. By emphasizing long-term sustainability, this type of government can serve as a model for tackling environmental problems like climate change [31].

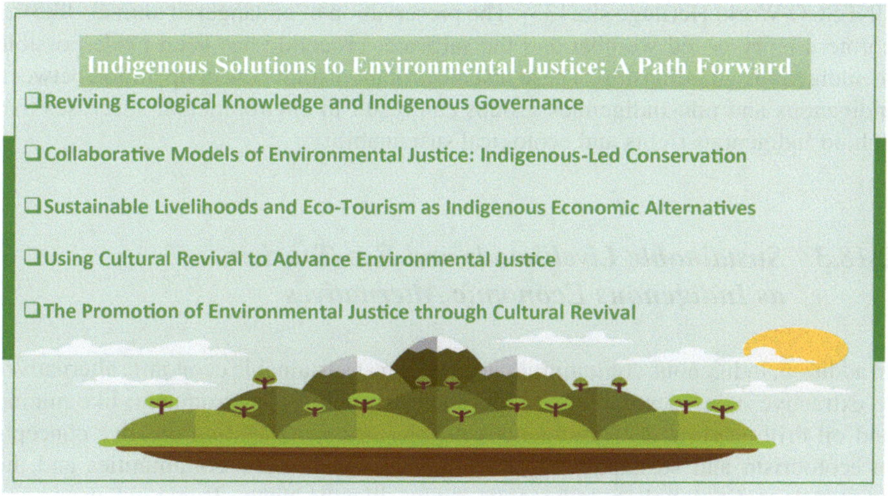

Fig. 2.2 Indigenous solutions to environmental justice: A path forward

Traditional Ecological Knowledge (TEK), also known as indigenous knowledge systems, is an essential tool for managing natural resources, comprehending biodiversity and keeping an eye on ecosystems. TEK places a strong emphasis on links with animals and the land, demonstrating the functioning of natural cycles and providing coping mechanisms for periods of environmental change. By incorporating TEK into contemporary environmental management, traditional practices like animal monitoring, community-based fisheries management and the restoration of ecosystems vulnerable to fire can be balanced with conservation.

2.18.2 *Collaborative Models of Environmental Justice: Indigenous-Led Conservation*

The effectiveness of collaborative models, in which Indigenous communities collaborate with governments, scientists and non-governmental organizations to preserve ecosystems while preserving their cultural and economic customs, is demonstrated by an increasing number of successful conservation initiatives (Fig. 2.2). An effective illustration of conservation led by Indigenous peoples is the Great Bear Rainforest in British Columbia, Canada. The Coast Salish, Nuu-chah-nulth and other Indigenous people played a key role in the fight against industrial development and logging in one of the world's greatest temperate rainforests [32]. This cooperative model has protected ecosystems and upheld Indigenous rights by establishing land use agreements that strike a balance between conservation and the needs of Indigenous people. Similar to this, the Bininj/Mungguy people and the Australian government work together to administer the Indigenous Kakadu National Park, which is a UNESCO World Heritage site [33]. The preservation of endangered animals like the northern hairy-nosed wombat and the saltwater crocodile has been made possible by indigenous guardianship. These instances demonstrate how cooperation between Indigenous and non-Indigenous groups can result in environmental successes that uphold Indigenous rights and ecological sustainability.

2.18.3 *Sustainable Livelihoods and Eco-Tourism as Indigenous Economic Alternatives*

In addition, indigenous communities are looking at sustainable economic alternatives to extractive industries that have historically harmed the environment, like mining and oil drilling (Fig. 2.2). Indigenous peoples are spearheading creative concepts in ecotourism and sustainable agriculture that benefit their communities and the environment. **Ecotourism,** indigenous groups, like the Ngäbe-Buglé in Panama and the Maasai in East Africa, are using their special environmental knowledge to create ecotourism businesses that highlight their culture and the natural beauty of their regions. These businesses offer a substitute for exploitative sectors and produce revenue that can be used to support conservation and community development efforts. **Sustainable forestry and agriculture,** Native American agricultural methods like permaculture and agroforestry place a strong emphasis on growing crops in balance with the environment. In addition to preserving biodiversity, these strategies give communities robust food systems that can withstand the effects of climate change [34].

Alternatives that support Indigenous principles of sustainability and stewardship provide a route to environmental justice without sacrificing financial security.

2.18.4 Using Cultural Revival to Advance Environmental Justice

Maintaining the cultural and spiritual customs that are intrinsically linked to the land is just as important to environmental justice as safeguarding the natural environment (Fig. 2.2). Cultural customs that respect the soil and bring the ecology back into balance are being revived by numerous Indigenous tribes. A crucial component of their opposition to the exploitation of their lands is cultural revival [35].

2.18.5 The Promotion of Environmental Justice Through Cultural Revival

As crucial to environmental justice as protecting the natural environment is preserving the spiritual and cultural traditions that are inextricably linked to the land (Fig. 2.2). Many Indigenous groups are reviving cultural practices that honor the earth and restore ecological equilibrium [36]. Cultural rebirth is an important part of their resistance to the exploitation of their lands. In the end, achieving environmental justice for Indigenous peoples entails acknowledging the interdependence of community, culture and land as well as creating environments that support simultaneous cultural and environmental healing.

2.19 Case Studies in Indigenous Environmental Justice

2.19.1 The Dakota Access Pipeline and the Standing Rock Sioux (DAPL)

The Standing Rock Sioux Tribe's opposition to the Dakota Access Pipeline (DAPL) is one of the most well-known campaigns for Indigenous environmental justice in the world. By passing beneath the Missouri River, which serves as the main supply of water for the Standing Rock Sioux and other tribal communities downstream, the pipeline was intended to move crude oil from North Dakota to Illinois [37].

- **Environmental Injustice:** The main worry was that a pipeline rupture may contaminate the Missouri River, which is vital for fishing, farming and drinking water. In addition, the pipeline was being constructed on Indigenous land that was considered sacred and protected by the 1851 Treaty of Fort Laramie [38]. The tribe claimed that because they had not been adequately consulted in accordance with the United Nations Declaration on the Rights of Indigenous Peoples (UNDRIP)'s free, prior and informed consent (FPIC) principle, the construction infringed upon their sovereignty and legal rights.
- **Activism and Resistance:** Standing Rock's resistance turned into a global emblem for environmental justice and Indigenous rights. The Standing Rock Sioux protest camp, also known as Sacred Stone Camp, was formed when thousands of activists and allies joined the tribe in protest. Protesters brought attention to more general problems such environmental racism, water contamination and the history of environmental harm to Indigenous communities.
- **Result and Impact:** The Trump administration approved the pipeline's construction in 2017, but the court struggle went on despite the protests raising awareness of the problems. However, the Standing Rock movement contributed to a wider discussion about environmental justice and Indigenous sovereignty. A number of groups devoted to Indigenous rights, water conservation and environmental justice were also founded as a result of the movement, such as the Water Protectors network [39].

2.19.2 The Battle Against Deforestation and the Amazon

Often referred to as the "lungs of the Earth," the Amazon rainforest is vital to the Indigenous peoples that inhabit there as well as to biodiversity and climate management worldwide [40]. For many years, indigenous groups including the Kayapo, Xingu and Yanomami have been battling against land expansion and deforestation [41].

- **Environmental Injustice:** Illegal logging, agricultural growth (particularly for soy and livestock ranching) and mining activities are major causes of the Amazon's extreme deforestation. The rights of the Indigenous peoples who have inhabited the jungle for thousands of years are being violated by these actions, which also endanger the biodiversity of the area. Specifically, the growth of illicit gold mining has resulted in land grabs, violence and mercury poisoning, while the spread of soy crops and cattle ranching has caused extensive deforestation.

- **Indigenous Leadership and Resistance:** Sônia Guajajara, a Guajajara leader and Raoni Metuktire, a Kayapo leader are two examples of indigenous leaders who have drawn international prominence for their support of Amazon conservation [42]. By highlighting the fact that deforestation rates are significantly lower on Indigenous lands that are actively managed and preserved, they have brought attention to the role that Indigenous peoples play as stewards of the land. These leaders have urged governments and international organizations to respect Indigenous communities' land rights and make companies responsible for environmental damage.
- **Achievements and Difficulties:** Indigenous-led initiatives have been successful in ensuring the protection of significant areas of the Amazon, despite the difficulties. For example, the Kayapo was able to expand their protected territories, which now total more than 9 million hectares, in 2016 through successful negotiations with the Brazilian government [43]. But under President Jair Bolsonaro's current administration, environmental safeguards have been undermined, which has resulted in an increase in illicit mining and deforestation. Indigenous groups, however, are still fighting back and they are receiving support from all across the world.

2.19.3 The Fight Against the Pebble Mine in Alaska

One of the most controversial environmental challenges that Indigenous people in Alaska have had to deal with is the proposed Pebble Mine project. Located close to the headwaters of the Bristol Bay watershed, which supports one of the world's largest salmon fisheries, the Pebble Mine is a proposed open-pit mine that would extract copper, gold and molybdenum [44].

- **Environmental Injustice:** The main issue facing the Bristol Bay region's Indigenous communities is the possible devastation of the salmon fishery, which is not only a vital source of food and revenue but also has cultural and spiritual significance for the Dena'ina, Yup'ik and Alutiiq peoples, among others [45]. In order to build the mine, mountains would have to be removed and hazardous waste would be dumped into neighboring streams, endangering the ecosystem's health and the quality of the water.
- **Opposition and Indigenous Leadership:** The Tribal Council of Bristol Bay has been spearheading the opposition to the project, working with environmental organizations, local activists and Indigenous leaders. They contend that the mine's risks greatly exceed any potential financial gains, highlighting the irreversible destruction of their traditional way of life, which is based on fishing and subsistence

hunting [46]. In addition to mobilizing efforts to put pressure on the U.S. government and project-related firms, indigenous resistance has been instrumental in stopping the project from proceeding.

- **Result and Impact:** Due to environmental concerns, the U.S. Army Corps of Engineers denied the mine's permission application in 2020[44]. The hard efforts of Indigenous groups, who partnered with environmental organizations to gather scientific evidence, public testimony and international pressure, were significantly responsible for this win. The battle is still continuing on, though, as political figures and business interests are still trying to have the mine approved, underscoring the continuous fight for environmental preservation and Indigenous sovereignty.

2.19.4 The Battle Against Wind Turbine Projects and the Sámi

Industrial development and the growth of renewable energy projects have resulted in environmental degradation for the Sámi people, who are indigenous to northern Norway, Sweden, Finland and Russia. The establishment of massive wind farms on indigenous Sámi land has been one of the most contentious topics in recent years. **Environmental Injustice,** although wind turbines help produce renewable energy, they are being constructed in locations that are essential to the Sámi's methods of herding reindeer. Traditional activities, grazing places and migration patterns that are essential to Sámi culture and the economy are disrupted by wind farm construction. Reindeer, a major resource for the Sámi, have also been displaced, habitats have been destroyed and noise pollution has resulted from the fast urbanization of these areas. **Indigenous Resistance:** Protests against the growth of wind farms have been spearheaded by Sámi organizations, such as the Sámi Council and Indigenous youth activists. They contend that the development is occurring without adequate consultation and endangers their people's cultural legacy. The Sámi Reindeer Herders' Association has defended their right to keep their ancestral territories safe from damaging industrialization by fighting legal fights to halt these projects. **Legal and Political Battles:** The Sámi have battled for their rights under International Labour Organization (ILO) Convention 169, which protects Indigenous peoples' right to be involved in decisions that impact their lands and resources, both in court and through demonstrations. Even though these conflicts have received some attention, there are still conflicts between the state's demand for renewable energy projects and the Sámi people's right to preserve their ecosystem [47].

2.19.5 The Maasai and Conservation in East Africa

The Maasai people have a long tradition of living in harmony with the environment and wildlife in East Africa. However, Maasai tribes now face many difficulties, especially in places like Kenya and Tanzania, as a result of conservation legislation and the expansion of commercial agriculture and tourism [45].

Environmental Injustice, the Serengeti and Maasai Mara environments, which are also important wildlife conservation sites, are home to many Maasai communities. Indigenous people have been forcibly removed from their land in the name of conservation, causing them to lose their means of subsistence, be uprooted and have their culture disrupted. Furthermore, the commodification of Maasai traditional territory is facilitated by tourism ventures such as safari excursions and opulent hotels, which frequently disregard their land rights. **Indigenous Leadership and Resistance,** the Maasai have long opposed these practices and fought for their land rights and involvement in conservation decision-making. Maasai livelihoods and conservation objectives are integrated by groups like the Maasai Wilderness Conservation Trust (MWCT), which enables the Maasai to manage animals and natural resources responsibly while maintaining their culture.

The creation of community-based conservation programs that enable Maasai people to oversee protected areas while reaping financial rewards from ecotourism and sustainable livestock grazing has proven to be one of the most effective methods. According to this concept, Maasai land is valued as an essential part of the wider ecosystem and the community actively participates in decision-making, wildlife protection and the advantages of sustainable land use and tourism.

A route to a fair and sustainable future; Indigenous groups are claiming their rights to land, water and natural resources in a wide range of ways, as illustrated by the case studies that are being presented. The fact that Indigenous peoples frequently take the lead in defending the environment and their way of life further demonstrates the close ties between environmental justice and cultural identity preservation. These case studies' examples of leadership and resistance make a strong case for acknowledging Indigenous sovereignty, integrating traditional knowledge into contemporary environmental management and working with Indigenous communities to develop sustainable solutions. Governments, businesses and international organizations must recognize the rights of Indigenous peoples and their special contribution to preserving the planet's future going ahead. In order to ensure that Indigenous peoples have the authority, respect and power to continue being stewards of their lands, cultures and communities for future generations, environmental justice goes beyond simply protecting ecosystems.

Just like ecology is a concern from the global indigenous perspective, similarly Indian subcontinent has a lot to offer in terms of environmental narrative. Indigenous peoples, also known as Adivasi (meaning "original inhabitants"), have a long history in India and have lived in close proximity to the soil for thousands of years [48]. They frequently experience marginalization, exploitation and displacement as a result of mining, deforestation, industrialization and other large-scale development initiatives, making their fight for environmental justice crucial. Here are some in-depth case studies from India that highlight the difficulties faced by Indigenous-led environmental justice campaigns.

2.20 The Save the Narmada Movement, also Known as the Narmada Bachao Andolan

One of the most well-known environmental justice campaigns in India is the Narmada Bachao Andolan (NBA), which began in the 1980s and is spearheaded by rural and Indigenous people. One of India's biggest and most ambitious irrigation and hydroelectric projects, the Sardar Sarovar Dam on the Narmada River, sparked the movement [49]. The dam, which was situated on the border between Madhya Pradesh, Gujarat and Maharashtra, was intended to supply the areas with energy and water, but it had significant negative effects on the environment and society.

Environmental Injustice, approximately 40,000 families, mostly from Adivasi communities residing along the Narmada Valley's riverbanks, were under danger of being displaced due to the dam's development [50]. Large areas of forest land would be submerged by the dam, which would have an impact on the local biodiversity, farming methods and means of subsistence for these communities, who relied on the river for farming, fishing and resource collection. It was also anticipated that the dam will ruin sacred sites and force numerous Indigenous towns to relocate. **Depletion of Forests and Resources,** the Narmada River's communities depended on the forests for food, fuelwood and medicinal herbs (Fig. 2.3). These forests would be submerged by the dam, depriving Indigenous peoples of essential resources that they have been managing responsibly for many generations. **Cultural and Social Impact,** with temples, burial grounds and holy groves located in the areas designated for submersion, many of the communities were also deeply ingrained in their local cultures and beliefs. Being displaced meant losing one's cultural identity in addition to one's means of subsistence. **Activism and Resistance,** the Narmada Bachao Andolan (NBA), led by social activist Medha Patkar, attracted a lot of notice for opposing the dam and fighting for the rights of displaced people, particularly Indigenous communities. The campaign formed partnerships with academics, political leaders and environmentalists while organizing the local populace.

Key Aspects of the Movement Included:

The NBA used non-violent protest strategies like blockades, sit-ins and hunger strikes to raise awareness of the problem. **Legal and Political Advocacy,** the campaign brought the dam's construction under legal attack, pointing out that displaced Indigenous villages had not received proper rehabilitation or compensation. A restoration plan that guaranteed the relocation of displaced families with stable means of subsistence was what they requested. **Outcome,** the Narmada Bachao Andolan raised awareness of the social and environmental problems associated with major infrastructure projects in India on a national and worldwide level. The effort was successful in slowing down the dam's construction, which compelled officials to reevaluate how the project would affect communities that were already at risk. Although a large portion of the promised compensation was never paid, the Supreme Court of India eventually ordered that appropriate rehabilitation measures be implemented. The movement continues to be a significant representation of Indigenous peoples'

A depiction of the Narmada Bachao Andolan (NBA), illustrating the resilience and determination of rural and Indigenous communities protesting against the Sardar Sarovar Dam.

Fig. 2.3 A depiction of the Narmada Bachao Andolan (NBA), illustrating the resilience and determination of rural and indigenous communities protesting against the Sardar Sarovar Dam

opposition to development initiatives that endanger their environment and way of life.

2.21 The Chipko Movement

One of India's oldest and most recognizable environmental groups, the Chipko Movement (1973), has Indigenous origins in Uttarakhand (then a part of Uttar Pradesh). The campaign was mostly led by rural, forest-dwelling people, especially Adivasi and Gurkha women, who used non-violent protest by embracing the trees to try to stop logging in their woods. Sunderlal Bahuguna, Chandi Prasad Bhatt, Gaura Devi and other grassroots activists played a major role in leading the movement [51]. **Environmental Injustice,** to boost the timber sector, the Indian government allowed widespread commercial logging in the Himalayan forests in the 1970s. Significant soil erosion, biodiversity loss and the drying up of natural springs essential water sources for the nearby communities were all results of this deforestation. **Degradation of woods,** local populations, especially those who rely on the woods for supplies like fuelwood, fodder and lumber for home construction, discovered that their access to these resources had decreased. Additionally, the forests held spiritual and cultural significance. **Impact on Livelihoods,** Because Adivasi and rural populations relied on trees for their livelihoods, their destruction forced them into economic marginalization.

2.21.1 Activism and Resistance

In reaction to the extensive deforestation in the area, the Chipko Movement was born as a direct action movement. The logging operation was stopped when a local woman named Gaura Devi famously organized a group of women to "hug" the trees to stop contractors from felling them. In India, this peaceful protest method came to represent Indigenous environmental justice.

Women's Involvement and Local Leadership, one of the first environmental movements in India to emphasize the importance of women in environmental preservation was the Chipko movement. Adivasi communities' values, which held that the land, forests and their own well-being are all intertwined, were also firmly ingrained in it.

Political and Public Support, as a result of individuals like Sunderlal Bahuguna spreading the word on national and worldwide stages about the importance of preserving the forest for the sake of the ecology and the welfare of nearby populations, the movement grew in strength. Result, the Chipko Movement brought about important policy reforms, such as the creation of protected forest reserves and the prohibition of tree-cutting in the Uttarakhand region. Additionally, it served as a catalyst for the Forest Conservation Act of 1980 and other forest conservation regulations passed by the Indian government. The movement is still a potent illustration of Indigenous opposition to resource exploitation and community-based environmental advocacy (Fig. 2.4).

Fig. 2.4 An Artistic representation of the Chipko, movement, illustrating the peaceful and determined protest led by Gaura Devi and other women to protect the forest from deforestation

Fig. 2.5 An artwork illustrating the Dongria Kondh struggle in the Niyagmiri Hills against bauxite mining. It captures the emotional depth of their resistance and the environment and cultural significance of their fight

2.22 The Struggle Against Mining in the Niyamgiri Hills (Dongria Kondh Tribe)

An indigenous tribe known as the Dongria Kondh lives in the eastern Indian state of Odisha, in the Niyamgiri Hills [52]. The projected bauxite mining project by the multinational company Vedanta Resources, which aimed to mine bauxite from the hills to supply its aluminum smelting plant, is at the center of their fight for environmental justice (Fig. 2.5).

2.23 Environmental Injustice

The Dongria Kondh people hold the Niyamgiri Hills in high regard in addition to their biodiversity. Their identity and spiritual existence revolve around the Niyam Raja, the hill deity. The tribe relies on the hills' fauna, rivers and thick forests for cultural practices, food and medicine.

Deforestation and Sacred Land Loss: The mining project posed a threat to the forests and sacred hilltops, resulting in irreparable environmental harm. The Dongria Kondh contended that mining would destroy their sacred territory, contaminate their water supplies and upset the ecosystem. **Cultural Impact,** because the project would force the tribe to leave their ancestral territory and jeopardize their cultural legacy, it was perceived as a direct assault on their way of life in addition to the environmental damage. **Activism and Resistance,** with the help of environmental groups like Survival International and the Odisha State Tribal Forum, the Dongria Kondh themselves spearheaded the opposition to the mining proposal. According to the United Nations Declaration on the Rights of Indigenous Peoples (UNDRIP), the tribe possessed the right to free, prior and informed consent (FPIC), which served as the foundation for their objection. **Direct Action and Legal Battles,** to halt the mining proposal, the Dongria Kondh and its allies planned demonstrations, rallies and court cases. Following years of opposition, the mining project was put on hold in 2013 after the Supreme Court of India decided in favor of the Dongria Kondh and other nearby tribal people. **International Solidarity,** the movement also attracted international attention, with groups and individuals from all over the world supporting the Dongria Kondh's rights and the preservation of the Niyamgiri Hills. **Result,** Vedanta was unable to move on because the Supreme Court of India ordered a community referendum in which the majority of the 12 villages involved voted against the mining proposal. This was a major gain for Indigenous rights, demonstrating that strong corporate interests can be successfully resisted by local communities when they are cohesive and well-organized.

2.24 Fishermen's and Indigenous Peoples' Opposition to the Koodankulam Nuclear Power Plant Protest

Background, from the beginning, the Koodankulam Nuclear Power Plant (KKNPP) in Tamil Nadu has been the subject of criticism [53]. Local people have long opposed the project, especially fishing communities and Adivasi tribes, despite the Indian government's assertion that it is necessary for the country's energy security. **Environmental Injustice,** the Koodankulam Nuclear Power Plant was built in a coastal region with abundant marine species that is ecologically sensitive. These waters are vital to the local fishing community, many of which are Adivasi. There was a serious risk to the fishery and the environment from the plant's waste disposal and possible radioactive contamination. **Threat to Livelihoods,** because radioactive contamination might cause the fisheries to collapse, the fishing community feared that their main source of food and money would be destroyed. **Lack of Consultation and Displacement,** Many Adivasi and fishing communities in the area felt excluded or displaced throughout the decision-making process since they were not sufficiently consulted before to the project's start. Another major worry was the possibility of radioactive leaks in a heavily populated coastal area (Fig. 2.6). **Activism and Resistance,** the main voice of opposition was the People's Movement Against Nuclear Energy (PMANE), which was headed by local leaders like S.P. Udayakumar. Hunger strikes, demonstrations and legal challenges were among the strategies used by the movement to stop the plant's construction and guarantee adequate consultation with the impacted communities. **International Solidarity,** by drawing attention to the

Fig. 2.6 Representational image depicting fishermen indigenous people protesting against the Koondankulam nuclear power plant in Tamilnadu

risks associated with nuclear energy in densely populated regions, environmental organizations and activists from all over the world supported the demonstration. **Outcome,** the Indian government was under a lot of pressure following years of protests, especially from the impacted populations. Although the facility eventually started operating in 2013, the demonstrations were successful in delaying its completion and bringing attention to the necessity of safety precautions and public consultation. In India, the Koodankulam battle became a pivotal issue that brought attention to the relationship between Indigenous rights and environmental justice.

The various and intricate challenges that Indigenous people encounter in their pursuit of environmental justice are reflected in these case studies from India. Indigenous peoples in India have continuously demonstrated tenacity, leadership and a strong bond with their land, whether it is by rejecting massive dams, defending holy forests, opposing extractive industries like mining, or defending traditional livelihoods from industrial developments. The vital role that the Adivasi communities play in the larger environmental justice movement is highlighted by their capacity to use their traditional knowledge systems, cultural customs and spiritual beliefs in their resistance. These case studies serve as a reminder that Indigenous peoples need to be viewed as both active change agents and victims of environmental degradation in order to create just and sustainable futures.

2.25 Environmental Justice and Indigenous Perspective as Reflected in Film and Literature

Both literature and film have effectively portrayed environmental justice and Indigenous viewpoints, providing a diverse range of stories that emphasize the rights, tenacity and hardships of Indigenous communities in the face of exploitation, displacement and environmental degradation. These platforms are essential for elevating Indigenous perspectives, drawing attention to international concerns and subverting popular conceptions of growth and advancement [54]. The emotional and physical hardships of Indigenous communities as they strive for their land, rights and environment are vividly depicted in movies thanks to the visual narrative power. Indigenous authors have frequently employed storytelling in their works to critique the devastation caused by colonization and modernization, maintain indigenous customs and increase public awareness of environmental issues. With examples that emphasize important concerns and themes, we examine below how environmental justice and Indigenous views are represented in literature and film.

2.25.1 Documentary Works that Show Indigenous Environmental Justice

(a) 1992's "the Last of the Mohicans"

"The Last of the Mohicans" tells a moving story of the Mohican people's forced removal from their ancient homeland, albeit taking place during the American colonial era. The impact of European colonialism and the British-French conflict on Indigenous tribes is the main topic of the Michael Mann-directed movie [55]. The film emphasizes the close relationship between Indigenous people and their environment through the Mohicans' fight to preserve their territory and way of life. **Environmental Themes,** current battles for Indigenous sovereignty and environmental justice are reminiscent of the Mohicans' struggle to defend their country against colonial powers. Their relationship with environment, hunting methods and spiritual respect for the land are depicted in a way that mirrors the larger Indigenous perspective, which views nature as a sacred, interwoven aspect of life rather than a resource to be used for profit.

(b) "Avatar" (2009)

One of the most recognizable and well-liked movies that combines science fiction and Indigenous themes is probably James Cameron's "Avatar." The Na'vi, a humanoid Indigenous species, live in harmony with their environment, which is abundant in natural resources, on the fictitious moon of Pandora. A human named Jake Sully fights alongside the Na'vi's against human forces that want to take advantage of Pandora's resources, especially the lucrative material unobtanium [56]. The movie depicts many of the actual issues faced by Indigenous communities, especially those involving resource exploitation, land grabbing and the environmental destruction brought on by multinational corporations. Modern Indigenous conflicts are directly paralleled by the Na'vi's relationship to nature, their spiritual practices and the devastation of their sacred sites by human colonists, especially in locations like Standing Rock and the Amazon. Indigenous groups battling to maintain their sovereignty and save their environment against extractive industries like mining, oil drilling and deforestation can be compared to the Na'vi's opposition to the exploitation of their territory.

(c) "the Eagle Huntress" **(2016)**

Aisholpan, a 13-year-old girl from the Kazakh Indigenous community in Mongolia, is the first woman in her family to become an eagle hunter. Her tale is told in this documentary, which was directed by Otto Bell. The movie emphasizes the age-old technique of eagle hunting, which has been practiced by the Kazakh people for many years. Environmental Themes: In light of contemporary issues, the movie emphasizes the value of conserving traditional knowledge about the environment and hunting techniques [57]. Aisholpan's story also highlights the conflict between traditional ways of life and modernity, as well as the significance of gender equality in Indigenous communities. **Preservation of Culture and the Environment,** The movie subtly criticizes how contemporary development and globalization jeopardize local ecosystems and sustainable methods. It draws attention to the ways that traditional Indigenous practices might support biodiversity preservation and ecological balance if they are respected.

(d) "Even the Rain" (2010)

The focus of this Spanish film, which was directed by Icíar Bollaín, is a Spanish film crew working on a film about Christopher Columbus and the colonization of the Americas. Unknowingly, the filmmakers get entangled in Bolivia's current water crisis, as indigenous people demonstrate against the privatization of their water source [58]. **Environmental Justice,** the movie connects current battles for resources like water to the historical colonial exploitation of Indigenous peoples. It is a potent critique of the ways in which Indigenous communities, both historical and contemporary, have been exploited for their resources, first through colonization and later through contemporary capitalist businesses that monopolize resources that are critical to their life, such as water. **Resistance and Solidarity,** the historical abuse of Indigenous peoples by colonizers is comparable to the fight of Indigenous peoples to defend their water rights. Aymara and Quechua villages are impacted by the Bolivian government's decision to privatize water and the film illustrates how contemporary Indigenous resistance to resource extraction is an extension of the fight for environmental justice.

2.25.2 Indigenous Environmental Justice in Literature

In order to address the disproportionate environmental burdens experienced by vulnerable communities, environmental justice emphasizes the equitable treatment and participation of all individuals in environmental policymaking. It does this by tying together social, economic and environmental concerns. Since authors have long tackled ecological degradation, social inequity and the human cost of environmental exploitation, there are many methods to examine environmental justice in international literature.

These are some significant examples of how environmental justice is portrayed in international literature;

2.25.2.1 Illustration of Environmental Degradation and How It Affects Vulnerable Groups

Numerous literary works highlight the connection between environmental harm and its disproportionate impact on underprivileged groups, especially people of color, poor communities and Indigenous peoples. Authors frequently examine how environmental deterioration, such as pollution, deforestation and climate change, directly affects these populations and exacerbates socioeconomic injustices.

2.25.2.2 John Steinbeck's "The Grapes of Wrath" (1939)

The Joad family is at the heart of this book as they abandon the Dust Bowl in Oklahoma and travel westward during the Great Depression. Due to the eviction of impoverished migrant workers and their exploitation by affluent landowners, the Dust Bowl environmental disaster is portrayed as both an ecological calamity and a type of social injustice [59].

2.25.2.3 Wangari Maathai's "The Battle for the Forests"

This book, written by Nobel laureate and Kenyan environmental campaigner Wangari Maathai, emphasizes the link between social justice, human rights and environmental degradation [60]. By reclaiming the environment to empower oppressed groups, Maathai's Green Belt Movement, which enabled women in Kenya to plant trees and combat deforestation, exemplifies environmental justice.

Indigenous worldviews are typically reflected in literature that emphasizes environmental justice issues and Indigenous cultures have a strong, spiritual bond with the land. These pieces emphasize the importance of sustainable practices, land management and the moral obligation to safeguard the planet from exploitation.

2.25.2.4 Leslie Marmon Silko's 1977 work "Ceremony"

One of the best examples of Native American literature that tackles environmental justice is Silko's book. It centers on Tayo, a young man who battles the psychological effects of war after returning from World War II [61]. The degradation of the land

and the traditional Native American worldview which views humans as stewards of nature rather than conquerors are also explored in the book. Silko's work makes the case that mending the earth is entwined with healing communities and individuals.

2.25.2.5 Cherie Dimaline's "The Marrow Thieves" (2017)

The story of Indigenous people who are persecuted for their bone marrow, which contains the key to preventing the extinction of the human race, is told in this dystopian novel set in a future where climate change has devastated much of the earth [62]. Because Indigenous people experience both ecological and cultural erasure, the novel connects colonialism and environmental catastrophe. As climate change has gained international attention, authors have looked more closely at how the poorer, less developed parts of the world, known as the Global South, are disproportionately affected by the effects of environmental degradation. Despite making the least contribution to the issue, these areas frequently suffer the most from climate-related calamities.

2.25.2.6 Paolo Bacigalupi's "The Water Knife" (2015)

Set in a near-future America devastated by environmental collapse, water scarcity and climate change, Bacigalupi's book explores the disparities brought about by resource scarcity [63]. The story focuses on the struggle for water rights in the American Southwest and examines how the consequences of climate change further isolate vulnerable groups, such as the poor and migrants.

2.25.2.7 Octavia Butler's 1993 work "Parable of the Sower"

A bleak future influenced by social unrest, economic inequality and climate breakdown is depicted in Butler's science fiction book. In a society devastated by social and environmental breakdown, the main character, Lauren, a young Black woman, aims to establish a new religious movement that places an emphasis on adaptability and survival. Butler's work critiques environmental injustice by examining issues of racism, class and environmental devastation [64]. The study of the connection between literature and the environment is known as ecocriticism. This covers how authors handle the human involvement in environmental deterioration as well as how environmental justice topics are portrayed in literature. Many writers have been reflecting on humanity's evolving relationship with nature in world literature, either within or in tandem with this tradition.

2.25.2.8 Richard Powers' 2018 Book "The Overstory"

Powers' book explores the value of forests to human groups and natural systems by fusing the lives of trees with that of different humans. Powers reflects on the pressing need for increased ecological awareness and action while presenting a vision of the environmental problem through a convoluted narrative [65]. The novel challenges environmental justice concerns associated with the destruction of natural habitats as well as human exploitation of nature.

2.25.2.9 Rachel Carson's "Silent Spring" (1962)

Despite being non-fiction, Carson's seminal book addressed the effects of pesticide use, especially DDT and ignited the environmental movement. By showing how dangerous chemicals disproportionately impact underprivileged communities, such as farmworkers and Indigenous peoples, it increased awareness of environmental justice. "Silent Spring" was crucial in influencing environmental discourse and promoting stronger environmental regulations [66]. Critiques of colonialism and its lingering effects on indigenous cultures and the environment frequently touch on environmental justice in postcolonial literature. Numerous postcolonial authors draw attention to the ways in which colonial powers exploited the land, resulting in social and ecological inequities.

2.25.2.10 Chinua Achebe's 1958 Book "Things Fall Apart"

Although Achebe's book does not specifically address environmental justice in the contemporary sense, it does examine how colonialism disrupted traditional Igbo life and how European settlers forced changes on the land [67]. The larger story of cultural and social upheaval that Achebe criticizes in his writing includes the colonial abuse of the environment.

2.25.2.11 Tayeb Salih's 1966 Book "Season of Migration to the North"

The aftermath of colonialism and its effects on the land and its inhabitants are the subject of this Sudanese novel. Salih examines the interwoven history of ecological devastation and social inequality in former colonies as she criticizes the environmental damage brought on by both colonial practices and postcolonial exploitation [68]. In World Literature, authors use environmental justice as a lens to examine the power disparity in the exploitation of both people and the environment. Literature is essential in bringing attention to and promoting a more equitable and sustainable future because it addresses climate change and its worldwide injustices, looks at how environmental degradation affects underprivileged communities and incorporates Indigenous viewpoints and postcolonial critiques. In addition to being a kind of social critique, this literature also serves as a call to action, imploring readers to understand how social, environmental and economic issues are intertwined and the necessity of an equitable, group response to the global environmental catastrophe.

2.25.2.12 Thomas King's book "The Inconvenient Indian"

A Curious Account of This highly regarded book by Cherokee author Thomas King combines Indigenous storytelling, introspection and history. It criticizes the way Indigenous peoples have been marginalized and displaced throughout North America [69]. Themes related to environmental justice, king discusses the past and present battles of Indigenous people to preserve their relationships to the land, which have been continuously taken away and exploited by colonization, treaties and governmental policies. He emphasizes that Indigenous peoples have long been the land's caretakers and incorporates their thoughts on environmental stewardship. King criticizes the contemporary idea of progress, which frequently leads to environmental damage and the infringement of Indigenous rights. The book investigates the connections between colonialism and capitalist exploitation and the eviction of people from their land and resources.

2.25.2.13 Cherie Dimaline's "the Marrow Thieves"

The dystopian novel "The Marrow Thieves," written by Métis author Cherie Dimaline, tackles the environmental and social breakdown in a future in which the land has turned poisonous and Indigenous people are targeted for their bone marrow, which is thought to hold the secret to treating a worldwide illness [70]. The story draws a clear comparison between the forced extraction of resources from Indigenous peoples and the environmental deterioration of the planet by symbolizing the exploitation of Indigenous bodies and territories for their resources. The book offers a compelling analysis of how colonialism, resource exploitation and environmental degradation continue to affect Indigenous peoples. The book highlights how resilient Indigenous cultures are when they are subjected to discrimination. The struggle for survival of the Indigenous characters symbolizes their struggle to maintain their cultural identity and their ties to the land, both literally and figuratively.

2.25.2.14 "Ceremony" by Leslie Marmon Silko

The spiritual and natural landscapes of the Southwest United States are powerfully explored in this landmark work by Laguna Pueblo author Leslie Marmon Silko. The story revolves around Tayo, a young Native American man who is attempting to recover from post-traumatic stress disorder (PTSD) through a customary Laguna ceremony after returning home from World War II [71]. **Native American Cosmology and Environmental Protection,** in Indigenous societies, where the spiritual and the natural are intricately linked, the novel emphasizes the holistic approach to existence. The collective healing of Indigenous lands devastated by colonialism and exploitation is reflected in Tayo's recovery path. **Land and Healing,** Tayo's awareness of the land and its rhythms is entwined with his spiritual path, reaffirming that land is not only a commodity but is vital to Indigenous peoples' individual and collective well-being. Silko criticizes the destructive nature of contemporary capitalism and its disrespect for cultural heritage and ecological balance.

2.25.2.15 "The Round House" by Louise Erdrich

The setting of Louise Erdrich's book "The Round House" is a Native American reservation in North Dakota. After his mother is attacked on the reservation, the story follows young Joe Coutts as he pursues justice [72]. The book interweaves the narrative of personal pain with more general issues of Indigenous sovereignty, the rule of law and the fight to preserve sacred areas. **Environmental Justice,** the conflict between the traditional communal life of the reservation and the intrusion of outside forces, including as resource extraction, mining and land exploitation, is discussed in the book. One of the main themes is the community's bond with the land and their obligation to preserve it. **Cultural Sovereignty,** Erdrich examines the relationship between environmental justice, gender violence and justice, demonstrating how external factors consistently jeopardize Indigenous peoples' rights to self-determination and land management. World music and indigenous environmental narratives are two diverse, intertwined fields that provide deep insights into how people relate to the natural world, spirituality and the universe. Indigenous civilizations all around the world have created stories that provide advice on how to coexist peacefully with nature in addition to explaining it. These tales, which reveal a strong bond with the land, frequently focus on land, animals, ancestors and the cycles of life.

2.26 Native American Environmental Stories

2.26.1 Ecological Knowledge and Stewardship

Indigenous environmental stories frequently rest on a perspective that regards people as a part of nature, not as something distinct from or superior to it. These tales highlight stewardship, reciprocity and balance. Many Indigenous cultures, for instance, believe that the earth is a living entity that deserves respect [73]. Creation myths, which describe the origins of the world and the place of humans in it, reflect this. For example, the Earth is revered in many Native American traditions and people and the land have a mutually responsible connection.

2.26.2 Sacred Landscapes and Place-Based Knowledge

Passed down through the years, many Indigenous peoples possess in-depth knowledge of the land. Their stories frequently relate specific flora, fauna, weather patterns and landscapes to historical occurrences, spiritual beliefs and survival techniques. The locations themselves hold cultural value and are considered sacred. The Australian Aboriginal "Dreamtime" traditions, for instance, combine mythology with ecological knowledge to explain how ancestor beings created the earth and its features [74]. Similar to this, the Māori people of New Zealand view the land (whenua) and the ocean (moana) as ancestral entities and they believe that every aspect of nature has spiritual and cultural importance.

2.26.3 Sustainability and Life Cycles

The significance of sustainability is emphasized in many Indigenous cultures. Seasonal cycles and the processes by which nature regenerates are frequently depicted in their legends. The interdependence of the earth's resources is exemplified by Indigenous agriculture traditions such as the Three Sisters (corn, beans and squash) in North America. Lessons regarding the harmony between consumption and renewal, how to hunt, fish, produce, or collect in a way that preserves resources for future generations are frequently found in narratives.

2.26.4 Spiritual Bond with Nature

The land is regarded as a living thing that provides both material and spiritual sustenance and the environment is revered by many Indigenous peoples. For example, the "spirit" of the forest is believed among Amazonian tribes, where animals, rivers and trees are all considered to have spiritual meaning [75]. One of these stories' key themes is the interdependence of all life.

2.27 The Relationship Between World Music and Indigenous Environmental Stories

These environmental themes can be richly represented acoustically by world music, which includes the traditional music of many different nations around the world. The way that music reflects a people's spiritual, cultural and ecological worldviews is how world music and Indigenous environmental narratives are related. Stories may be told, information can be passed down and preserved and the natural world can be celebrated via music.

2.28 The Relationship Between World Music and Indigenous Environmental Soundscapes and Nature

Bird calls, running water, wind rustling and animal noises are just a few examples of the environmental sounds that are included into the music of many Indigenous musical traditions. The idea that the environment is alive with spirit is reflected in these sounds, which evoke the presence of nature. For example, the traditional songs of the San people of southern Africa frequently make references to animals and the land, while Inuit throat singing imitates the sounds of nature, such as wind and water [77]. This depicts a vision where music becomes a medium for communication with the land and humans are in a continuous dialogue with the environment.

2.28.1 Rhythm and Cycles

The cycles of nature are reflected in the melodies and rhythms of many Indigenous musical traditions. African drumming patterns, for instance, can reflect the day-night cycles or the earth's heartbeat. Drums are utilized by certain Native American cultures in the Americas to signal seasonal shifts and customs related to the cycles of planting, hunting and harvest [78]. Invoking blessings from the spirits of nature and pursuing harmony with the environment, music also serves as a kind of prayer.

2.28.2 Ceremonial Music and Rituals

Indigenous ceremonies, many of which center on healing, environmental sustainability and fostering a connection with nature, are intricately interwoven with music. Among Native American tribes, for example, the peyote ceremony entails singing holy songs while consuming peyote, a psychotropic cactus used for environmental and spiritual vision [79]. The songs frequently have a direct connection to nature and the idea that the Earth is a living, breathing thing.

2.28.3 *Transmission of Ecological Knowledge*

Songs are a common way for Indigenous societies to transmit vital ecological knowledge. Songs can explain the moon's phases, animal migration patterns, or when it's best to plant and harvest [80]. Native American or Inuit musical traditions, for example, can narrate tales about particular plants, animals or landscapes, storing environmental knowledge in a form that is simple to recall and transmit between generations.

2.28.4 *Healing and Environmental Restoration*

Music has a function in healing people and the environment in various cultures. People who are out of balance with nature may benefit from the use of music by traditional healers. For example Andean traditional music is frequently utilized in ceremonies to bring the ecosystem back into balance and to call upon spirits to safeguard the land [81]. The premise is that illness or imbalance can result from environmental damage and that music can heal and bring about equilibrium.

2.28.5 *Examples of Indigenous Music from Around the World:*

2.28.5.1 Native American Music

The usage of flutes, drums and chanting are characteristics of Native American music. The land, environment and the sacred are frequently its main topics. Rituals like the harvest, the sweat lodge ceremony or the sun dance may have music to go with them [82].

2.28.5.2 Aboriginal Australian Music

The didgeridoo, a traditional wind instrument that is said to replicate the sounds of the ground, is frequently used in Aboriginal music [83]. Music is an essential component of the Dreamtime, a complex system of beliefs about the world's origins and nature and Aboriginal songs are closely linked to the land and its creation stories.

2.28.5.3 African Drumming

Drumming is a common way for people in many African cultures to interact with nature. Natural cycles, including those of the seasons, animal life stages and agricultural cycles are frequently reflected in the rhythms and patterns [84]. In rituals, drums are frequently used to worship natural spirits or to request bountiful harvests.

2.28.5.4 Andean Music

The Quechua and Aymara communities in the Andes region of South America have a strong connection to the land and the universe through their music [85]. Songs that celebrate the earth and the spirits of the mountains are accompanied by traditional instruments like the charango, a tiny stringed instrument and the pan flute (zampoña).

Native to the northern parts of Norway, Sweden, Finland and Russia, the Sami people have a rich musical heritage that includes joik, a type of song that is used to symbolize a person, animal, or location. The Sami people have a strong bond with the land, reindeer and the natural world, which is reflected in these songs' strong environmental connections. Literature and film as well as music are effective mediums for illustrating Indigenous peoples' fight for environmental justice and the conservation of their natural and cultural heritage. Both Indigenous and non-Indigenous audiences are drawn into a larger discussion about the significance of preserving the environment, honoring Indigenous knowledge and defending the rights of Indigenous peoples by these works' striking depictions of resistance to resource exploitation, land dispossession and cultural erasure. The idea that Indigenous peoples are active change agents who fight environmental injustice and defend their rights to their lands, cultures and identities is a recurrent topic in both literature and film. As long as these tales are repeated, they will motivate action, increase consciousness and foster unity in the struggle for social and environmental justice. Indigenous environmental narratives and world music are powerful ways to understand the relationship between humans and the natural world. Through stories and songs, Indigenous cultures teach us about respect, sustainability and spiritual connection with the land. Music, with its ability to transcend language and convey deep emotion, becomes a tool for expressing these profound environmental philosophies. Together, these traditions offer wisdom for navigating contemporary environmental challenges, reminding us of the importance of listening to the earth and living in harmony with it.

2.29 Indigenous Women and Environmental Justice: A Crucial Intersection

A framework known as environmental justice (EJ) aims to guarantee that everyone, irrespective of gender, race, ethnicity or class, has equal access to a healthy environment and that the communities that are most impacted by environmental degradation often marginalized communities are given the tools they need to address the harms they experience [86]. As vulnerable groups dealing with the combined weight of environmental deterioration and gendered discrimination, Indigenous women are vital in this regard. They are also important advocates for environmental stewardship. This essay examines how environmental justice and Indigenous women's experiences interact, illuminating their leadership, challenges and the significance of acknowledging gendered aspects in environmental movements.

2.30 The Confluence of Indigenous Rights and Environmental Justice

The 1980s saw the emergence of environmental justice in the US, mostly in response to the disproportionate environmental costs that poor communities of color had to bear [87]. It highlighted how vulnerable groups, particularly Black, Indigenous and People of Color (BIPOC), frequently suffer the most from habitat degradation, environmental pollution and climate change. Protecting their ancestral lands, cultures and ways of life is just as important to Indigenous populations as having access to clean air and water.

Because they have a strong connection to and understanding of the earth, indigenous peoples around the world have long practiced sustainable environmental management. The interdependence of all living things, equilibrium and reverence for the natural world are all emphasized by these traditional ecological knowledge systems (TEK). Particularly important to these activities have been Indigenous women, who frequently serve as the main stewards of the environment and keepers of information passed down through generations. They have particular difficulties that are entwined with their social duties, obligations and the patriarchal structures that are prevalent in many Indigenous countries and they are also disproportionately impacted by environmental degradation.

2.31 Gender and the Environment: The Role of Indigenous Women

Indigenous women hold a special place in the social and environmental spheres. They have traditionally been considered stewards of the land, the water, the flora and the fauna. They have a very intimate and spiritual contact with the environment because of their roles as mothers, daughters and sisters, which connect them to the continuous transmission of information and culture. The sanctity of nature is frequently emphasized in indigenous cosmologies, where women are viewed as the life-givers tasked with preserving and caring for the planet.

However, outside forces like colonization, industrialization and globalization are progressively undermining these old positions. Lands that Indigenous peoples rely on for their sustenance, cultural customs and spiritual well-being have been destroyed as a result of the growth of extractive industries like mining, oil extraction and logging. These environmental changes disproportionately affect Indigenous women. In addition to being in charge of ensuring food security and access to water, they are frequently the first to suffer from the negative health effects of environmental contamination, including exposure to hazardous chemicals, air pollution and water-borne illnesses. Gender and environmental inequities frequently interact for Indigenous women. Indigenous communities' patriarchal norms, which were made worse by colonialism, might hinder women from playing a major role in choices about land control. Women are increasingly marginalized in their communities and in larger environmental movements as a result of their voices being silenced in environmental discussions.

2.32 The Effects of Environmental Injustice on Indigenous Women

When some groups, especially those with less political clout, are disproportionately exposed to environmental risks, the idea of environmental injustice emerges. The social, cultural and economic roles that Indigenous women play in their communities exacerbate the effects of environmental injustice. Indigenous women encounter the nexus of gender and environmental inequality in a number of important areas, such as:

Loss of Traditional Livelihoods and Food Security, many Indigenous societies depend on subsistence farming, fishing and hunting and Indigenous women are frequently the main producers of food. These women's capacity to provide for their families and preserve their customs is directly threatened by environmental degradation brought on by deforestation, water pollution and soil erosion. For example, fish populations, which are a major source of food for many Indigenous communities, can be severely damaged when rivers are contaminated with harmful chemicals. In addition to having an impact on community members' physical health, this also jeopardizes the customs associated with hunting and fishing. **Health Effects,** Indigenous women are more susceptible to the negative health effects of environmental degradation, including exposure to toxic air, contaminated water and dangerous chemicals. Women are disproportionately harmed by environmental injustices, as evidenced by the higher rates of cancer, respiratory ailments and reproductive health issues in areas impacted by industrial pollution. The effects of environmental degradation on the health of Indigenous women are further compounded by the fact that many of them lack access to quality treatment. **Land Loss and Displacement,** There is a gendered influence on the forced relocation of Indigenous people brought on by the growth of mining, oil extraction and major development projects. Although both men and women experience displacement, women frequently lose more than simply their houses; they also lose their livelihood, their traditional role and their connection to the land. Migration away from ancestral lands can often result in the disintegration of cultural customs and communal institutions, which impacts women's capacity to transmit information to future generations.

2.32.1 Climate Change

The climate catastrophe also directly affects Indigenous women. Indigenous women, particularly those residing in rural or isolated locations, are disproportionately impacted by natural disasters such floods and droughts, changing weather patterns and rising temperatures. Food hunger, water scarcity and health concerns are made worse by climate change and women are disproportionately affected because they are the primary caregivers and community leaders [88]. Furthermore, women are frequently pushed into hazardous situations, such as migration and relocation, as a result of the effects of climate change on agriculture and food production, which can cause social instability.

2.32.2 The Leadership of Indigenous Women in Environmental Justice

Indigenous women have led global environmental justice initiatives in spite of the obstacles they confront. Their activism aims to ensure the planet's survival in addition to protecting their neighborhoods. Indigenous women's spiritual ties to the land and traditional ecological knowledge serve as the foundation for their environmental leadership. They support the acknowledgment of Indigenous land rights, the conservation of holy sites and the preservation of biodiversity.

Standing Rock and the Dakota Access Pipeline, the 2016–2017 demonstrations against the Dakota Access Pipeline (DAPL) in the United States are among the most notable recent instances of Indigenous women's environmental activism [89]. Along with other Indigenous nations, the Standing Rock Sioux Tribe tried to stop the pipeline from being constructed beneath the Missouri River, a vital source of water. As leaders and caregivers, indigenous women were essential to the demonstrations. Through community mobilization and organization, they used social media to raise awareness of the problem on a global scale. Standing Rock's indigenous women battled for the acknowledgement of their sovereign rights over the land in addition to their communities' right to clean water. Latin American Environmental Advocacy, Indigenous women have spearheaded campaigns throughout Latin America to stop the exploitation of the region's natural resources. Indigenous women, for example, have played a key role in anti-extraction campaigns in Ecuador and Bolivia that contest the negative social and environmental effects of mining, oil drilling and hydropower dams [90]. These women have pushed for legislation that acknowledges the rights of Indigenous peoples to environmental preservation and self-determination, as well as increased political engagement. Global Indigenous Women's Network, Indigenous women have united to create coalitions and networks centered on human rights and environmental justice all around the world. For instance, the International Indigenous Women's Forum (FIMI) has played a significant role in promoting the rights of Indigenous women on global stages like the UN [91]. Indigenous women can support one another, share expertise and organize for group action through these networks.

2.32.3 Gender's Significance in Environmental Justice Campaigns

The need to incorporate gender into environmental discourse is one of the most important lessons to be drawn from the experiences of Indigenous women in environmental justice movements. Due to the diverse roles and duties that each gender has in society, environmental challenges do not effect men and women equally. Understanding the unique ways that environmental degradation impacts Indigenous women and making sure that their opinions are heard during decision-making processes are crucial for a truly inclusive environmental justice movement. Supporting Indigenous women's leadership in environmental governance and policymaking is part of this. Climate change mitigation, natural resource conservation and sustainable land management have all benefited greatly from the leadership and expertise of indigenous women. Indigenous women should therefore be given more authority to make decisions at the local, national and international levels in addition to protecting the environment.

Indigenous women's struggles are intrinsically linked to environmental justice. Indigenous women, who are the most vulnerable and marginalized members of society, bear the dual burden of gendered oppression that limits their authority and involvement in decision-making, as well as environmental degradation that endangers their communities, customs and ways of life. Nevertheless, in spite of these obstacles, Indigenous women remain at the vanguard of the battle for environmental justice, fighting to safeguard their communities, lands and health. Environmental justice movements must recognize and respect the special needs and contributions of Indigenous women in order to create a more equitable and sustainable world. We can promote a more comprehensive, inclusive and successful approach to environmental justice that benefits not only Indigenous peoples but also all of humanity by elevating their voices and leadership.

In Australia, the Native Title Act, 1993, has empowered Aboriginal communities to reclaim ancestral lands and integrate traditional fire management techniques, demonstrating the efficacy of indigenous ecological practices in mitigating modern environmental challenges [92]. In Brazil, the 1988 Constitution acknowledges indigenous rights to Amazonian lands, yet challenges persist in enforcing these protections amidst rising deforestation [93]. Africa's community-based conservation initiatives, guided by laws like Kenya's Wildlife Conservation and Management Act, 2013, underscore the importance of integrating cultural practices with modern conservation policies [94]. Furthermore, international treaties such as the Convention on Biological Diversity (CBD) and the UN Declaration on the Rights of Indigenous Peoples (UNDRIP) advocate for the inclusion of indigenous perspectives in global environmental governance. This analysis underscores the need for an equitable approach to environmental justice, where the voices of indigenous populations are not only heard but actively shape policies. By integrating indigenous worldviews and practices into legal frameworks, nations can address historical injustices and foster sustainable, inclusive environmental solutions.

2.33 Environmental Justice and Indigenous Perspectives

Focusing on the intersection of environmental issues and social justice, this chapter theme examines how different communities, particularly indigenous populations, experience and respond to environmental challenges. Presentations may cover topics such as land rights, environmental racism and the impact of industrial development on marginalized groups. The session aims to amplify voices that are often underrepresented, fostering a dialogue on equitable and inclusive approaches to environmental conservation and management. The intersection of environmental challenges and social justice reveals profound impacts on marginalized communities, particularly indigenous populations. Indigenous peoples, often stewards of biodiversity, face unique challenges due to their deep cultural, spiritual and physical ties to ancestral lands. Exploring this intersection across various countries highlights shared struggles and innovative responses to environmental injustices.

2.33.1 United States: Environmental Racism and Sacred Land Protection

In the United States, environmental racism disproportionately affects Native American tribes. For instance, the Dakota Access Pipeline (DAPL) controversy underscored the violation of indigenous land rights and environmental justice. The Standing Rock Sioux Tribe protested the pipeline's proximity to their water sources and sacred lands, sparking a global movement [95]. This case highlights the broader struggle of indigenous groups to protect their environment from industrial encroachments.

2.33.2 Brazil: Deforestation and Amazonian Tribes

In Brazil, deforestation and illegal mining threaten the livelihoods of Amazonian tribes. The Yanomami and Kayapo people face displacement and environmental degradation due to logging and industrial development [96]. Despite these challenges, indigenous groups have organized efforts to safeguard their territories, often collaborating with international environmental organizations to combat deforestation and advocate for sustainable policies.

2.33.3 Australia: Aboriginal Land Rights and Mining

Australia's Aboriginal communities have long fought for recognition of their land rights. Projects like the Juukan Gorge destruction, where sacred rock shelters were irreparably damaged by mining operations, illustrate the tension between industrial development and indigenous heritage. Indigenous groups are increasingly using legal mechanisms, such as native title claims, to reclaim their land and influence conservation policies [97].

2.33.4 India: Tribal Resistance to Industrial Projects

In India, tribal communities like the Dongria Kondh have opposed mining projects on sacred mountains such as the Niyamgiri Hills [98]. Their resistance, grounded in cultural and spiritual connections to the land, successfully halted a multinational corporation's plans. This highlights how indigenous activism can influence environmental governance.

2.33.5 Canada: Land and Water Defenders

In Canada, First Nations communities are at the forefront of battles against pipelines and industrial pollution. The Wet'suwet'en protests against the Coastal GasLink pipeline exemplify efforts to preserve land and water from harmful development. These movements often emphasize the need for indigenous-led conservation strategies, rooted in traditional ecological knowledge [99].

2.33.6 Global Perspectives: Amplifying Marginalized Voices

Across the globe, indigenous peoples have responded to environmental injustices with resilience and innovation. They often advocate for land rights, legal protections and sustainable practices. The inclusion of indigenous voices in environmental decision-making is crucial for equitable solutions to climate change and biodiversity loss. This dialogue calls for a shift from tokenistic inclusion to active empowerment of underrepresented communities. Collaborative approaches, respecting indigenous knowledge systems and prioritizing their rights, are vital to achieving global environmental justice.

A complicated but extremely significant relationship between land, people and justice is revealed by the intersection of environmental justice and indigenous perspectives. Indigenous communities around the world have long recognized that their ability to preserve and uphold their ancestral lands is essential to their survival as unique peoples and that environmental health is inextricably linked to community health. The environmental injustices that Indigenous peoples experience have their roots in colonization, dispossession and exploitation history and are not solely the product of bad policies or carelessness. Nonetheless, Indigenous peoples have led environmental justice movements by providing solutions based on sustainable, culturally sensitive land management strategies as well as opposition to destructive practices. Indigenous worldviews must be acknowledged and respected by the environmental justice movement and they must be included in decisions that have an impact on their lands. Although the United Nations Declaration on the Rights of Indigenous Peoples (UNDRIP) and other legal frameworks provide valuable advice, more work must be done to uphold these rights both locally and internationally. Furthermore, the larger environmental justice movement can be guided by the effective models provided by Indigenous-led conservation initiatives, cultural revival and sustainable economic options.

In the end, the fight for environmental justice is a fight for the survival of the cultures, languages and ways of life that have cultivated the land for thousands of years, as well as for cleaner air and water. We need to look to Indigenous knowledge systems, governance methods and leadership for direction as we face global issues like resource depletion, biodiversity loss and climate change. Respecting the rights, wisdom and leadership of Indigenous peoples is essential to the future of environmental justice and, in fact, the future of our world. This includes making sure that their voices are heard, their territories are safeguarded and their cultures are maintained for future generations. Traditional frameworks that only address ecosystem preservation or human rights must give way to environmental justice. When all components of an ecosystem, people, plants, animals and spiritual beings are acknowledged as interdependent and worthy of preservation, true justice will be served. Through the integration of Indigenous leadership, knowledge and legal rights into environmental policy and practice, we can build a more just, sustainable and equitable world for everybody.

References

1. Morrison, J. (2024). *Indigenous peoples.* Palgrave Macmillan. https://doi.org/10.1007/978-3-031-69848-4_5
2. Ergene, S., Banerjee, S. B., & Ergene, E. (2024). Environmental racism and climate (in)justice in the anthropocene: Addressing the silences and erasures in management and organization studies. *Journal of Business Ethics, 193,* 785–800. https://doi.org/10.1007/s10551-024-05723-x
3. Kaswan, A. (2023). Background on environmental justice and racism. In R. Brinkmann (Ed.), *The Palgrave handbook of global sustainability* (pp. 123–140). Palgrave Macmillan. https://doi.org/10.1007/978-3-031-01949-4_70
4. Márquez, G. (2025). The biosphere reserve concept, seaflower and climate change. In J. E. Mancera Pineda, A. F. Osorio, C. Toro, & C. S. Velásquez-Calderón (Eds.), *Climate change adaptation and mitigation in the Seaflower biosphere reserve.* Springer. https://doi.org/10.1007/978-981-97-6663-5_7
5. Malakar, K. D., Kumar, M., Anand, S., & Kuzur, G. (2023). *Climate change, justice and rights.* Springer. https://doi.org/10.1007/978-981-99-4390-6_8
6. Izah, S. C., Onwudiegwu, C. A., Sylva, L., & Etim, N. G. (2024). Health and environmental justice strategies for mitigating air pollution. In M. C. Ogwu & S. C. Izah (Eds.), *Sustainable strategies for air pollution mitigation.* Springer. https://doi.org/10.1007/698_2024_1121
7. Ali, M. A., & Kamraju, M. (2023). *Environmental justice and resource distribution.* In Natural resources and society. https://doi.org/10.1007/978-3-031-46720-2_11
8. Liebersohn, H. (2009). Entries. In A. Iriye & P. Y. Saunier (Eds.), *The Palgrave dictionary of transnational history.* Palgrave Macmillan. https://doi.org/10.1007/978-1-349-74030-7_1
9. White, T. M., Borrell, L. N., & El-Mohandes, A. (2024). A review of the public health literature examining the roles of socioeconomic status and race/ethnicity on health outcomes in the United States. *Journal of Racial and Ethnic Health Disparities.* https://doi.org/10.1007/s40615-024-02195-7
10. Moojen, F. G., Ryschawy, J., Wulfhorst, J. D., et al. (2024). Case study analysis of innovative producers toward sustainable integrated crop-livestock systems: Trajectory, achievements and thought process. *Agronomy for Sustainable Development, 44,* 26. https://doi.org/10.1007/s13593-024-00953-9
11. Enciso, S. W. (2024). The Indigenous tutorial assistance scheme from a tutor's point of view: Groundwork for a critical pedagogy. *Australian Educational Researcher.* https://doi.org/10.1007/s13384-024-00776-3
12. Mishra, H. (2024). The role of ethnoeconomics in promoting sustainable consumption and production patterns: A pathway to environmental protection and economic prosperity. In W. Leal Filho & V. Kuzmanović (Eds.), *Sustainable development seen through the lenses of*

ethnoeconomics and the circular economy. Springer. https://doi.org/10.1007/978-3-031-72676-7_6

13. Ratuva, S. (2022). The politics of imagery: Understanding the historical genesis of sinophobia in pacific geopolitics. *East Asia, 39*, 13–28. https://doi.org/10.1007/s12140-021-09376-9
14. Banks, A. S., & Muller, T. C. (1980). Governments. In A. S. Banks & T. C. Muller (Eds.), *Political handbook of the world: 1998*. Palgrave Macmillan. https://doi.org/10.1007/978-1-349-14951-3_1
15. Katusiime, E., & Igba, S. A. (2024). History repeats itself: A reflection of civil-military relations in post-colonial Uganda. In J. Mushomi & C. Wielenga (Eds.), *Mobility, identity and conflict resolution in Africa*. Palgrave Macmillan. https://doi.org/10.1007/978-3-031-61745-4_4
16. Halidu, O. B., Amidu, M., Asiedu, E., & Asare, N. (2024). Effective and sustainable management of natural resources in Africa: The roles of environmental tax and public participation. In M. Amidu, A. Ali-Nakyea, & J. Y. Abor (Eds.), *Taxation and management of natural resources in Africa*. Springer. https://doi.org/10.1007/978-3-031-58124-3_9
17. Madrigal, R. A. G. (2023). Critical relationalities: Centering Indigenous land, presence and sovereignty in immigrant/migrant rights discourses. *Latino Studies, 21*, 305–322. https://doi.org/10.1057/s41276-023-00434-2
18. Saidi, U. (2022). Against the grain: The tragedy of Zimbabwe in the context of 4IR. In E. Benyera (Ed.), *Africa and the Fourth Industrial Revolution*. Springer. https://doi.org/10.1007/978-3-030-87524-4_4
19. Engel-Di Mauro, S. (2024). *First peoples and ecosocialism*. Springer. https://doi.org/10.1007/978-3-031-74288-0_7
20. Geetha, B. V., Shreenidhi, K. S., Nethra, L., & Padhmalakshmi, S. (2024). Microbial communities: A promising tool for treatment of wastewater and solid waste. In M. P. Shah (Ed.), *Microbial remediation of hazardous chemicals from water & industrial wastewater treatment plant* (pp. 1–25). Springer. https://doi.org/10.1007/978-3-031-62898-6_9
21. Hoang, N. T., & Kanemoto, K. (2021). Mapping the deforestation footprint of nations reveals growing threat to tropical forests. *Nature Ecology & Evolution, 5*, 845–853. https://doi.org/10.1038/s41559-021-01417-z
22. Duarte Santos, F. (2021). Anthropocene, technosphere, biosphere and the contemporary utopias. In *Time, progress, growth and technology* (pp. 155–178). Springer. https://doi.org/10.1007/978-3-030-55334-0_7
23. Coleman, C. L. (2020). How Sioux-settler relations underscore the Dakota access pipeline. In *Environmental clashes on Native American land* (pp. 123–139). Palgrave Macmillan. https://doi.org/10.1007/978-3-030-34106-0_7
24. Mayes, E. (2024). Young people learning climate justice: Education beyond schooling through youth-led climate justice activism. In J. Wyn, H. Cahill, & H. Cuervo (Eds.), *Handbook of children and youth studies*. Springer. https://doi.org/10.1007/978-981-99-8606-4_99
25. Friedline, T. (2024). A conversation with Matt Remle: Settler colonialism, fossil fuel divestment and public banking advocacy. *Journal of Family and Economic Issues, 45*(2), 308–314. https://doi.org/10.1007/s10834-024-09946-y
26. Kugo, Y. (2022). Community voices, practices and memories in environmental communication: Iliamna lake yup'ik place names, Alaska. In A. Sjölander-Lindqvist, I. Murin, & M. E. Dove (Eds.), *Anthropological perspectives on environmental communication* (pp. 95–116). Palgrave Macmillan. https://doi.org/10.1007/978-3-030-78040-1_5
27. Linstroth, J. P. (2022). Cultural genocide, genocide and Amerindian genocide. In *Politics and racism beyond nations* (pp. 79–101). Palgrave Macmillan. https://doi.org/10.1007/978-3-030-91720-3_4
28. Thimm, T. (2024). Indigenous art and Indigenous tourism in Western Australia: A model of interrelations. *Journal of Sustainable Tourism, 28*(4), 1–22. https://doi.org/10.52230/MSSO3601
29. Frogner, R. O. (2022). The train from Dunvegan: Implementing the United Nations Declaration on the Rights of Indigenous Peoples (UNDRIP) in public archives in Canada. *Archival Science, 22*, 209–238. https://doi.org/10.1007/s10502-021-09373-0

30. Singh, S., & Trask, B. (2024). Faded by design: Manufacturing agnosis of settler-colonialism in an era of Indigenous truth and reconciliation in Canada. In J. Gacek & R. Jochelson (Eds.), *Justice in the age of agnosis* (pp. 143–162). Palgrave Macmillan. https://doi.org/10.1007/978-3-031-54354-8_6
31. Mostafavi, N., Fiocchi, J., & Dellacasa, M. G. (2022). Resilience of environmental policy amidst the rise of conservative populism. *Journal of Environmental Studies and Sciences, 12*, 311–326. https://doi.org/10.1007/s13412-021-00721-1
32. Pöhl, F. (2022). Das imaginierte und instrumentalisierte Imperium der Haudenosaunee. In M. Gehler & R. Rollinger (Eds.), *Empires to be remembered: Universal- und kulturhistorische Studien* (pp. 451–476). Springer VS. https://doi.org/10.1007/978-3-658-34003-2_20
33. Popken, L. R., Griffin, P. J., & Cote, C. (2023). Indigenous food sovereignty through resurgent self-governance: Centering Nuu-chah-nulth principles in sea otter management in Canada. Ecology and Society, *28*(2), Article 12. https://doi.org/10.5751/ES-13702-280212
34. Grant, E., & Greenop, K. (2018). Affirming and reaffirming Indigenous presence: Contemporary aboriginal and torres strait islander community, public and institutional architecture in Australia. In E. Grant, K. Greenop, A. Refiti, & D. Glenn (Eds.), *The handbook of contemporary Indigenous architecture* (pp. 45–72). Springer. https://doi.org/10.1007/978-981-10-6904-8_3
35. Gallegos, M. C., Buizer, M., Hobbis, S. K., et al. (2024). Knitting for conservation: A social practice perspective on a social and behavior change communication intervention. *Environment, Development and Sustainability, 26*, 8687–8707. https://doi.org/10.1007/s10668-023-03066-7
36. Wang, S., & Gu, K. (2023). From aspirational to operational: Towards an integrated approach to spatial justice. In *Spatial justice and planning* (pp. 89–113). Springer. https://doi.org/10.1007/978-3-031-38070-9_3
37. Cuéllar-Padilla, M., Haro Pérez, I., & Di Masso Tarditti, M. (2024). Socioeconomic and political-cultural criteria for agroecology: Learnings from participatory guarantee systems. *Agriculture and Human Values*. https://doi.org/10.1007/s10460-024-10656-2
38. Friedline, T. (2024). A conversation with Matt Remle: Settler colonialism, fossil fuel divestment and public banking advocacy. *Journal of Family and Economic Issues, 45*, 308–314. https://doi.org/10.1007/s10834-024-09946-y
39. Fukurai, H., & Krooth, R. (2021). The Lakota Nation's search for independence: The Nation of Lakota versus the state of the United States of America and the constitutional amendments for national liberation. In *Original nation approaches to inter-national law* (pp. 205–230). Palgrave Macmillan. https://doi.org/10.1007/978-3-030-59273-8_5
40. Munabari, F., & Hamdani, H. (2023). The implementation of the Jerusalem embassy act under president Donald Trump (2017–2019). *Budi Luhur Journal of Strategic & Global Studies*, 1(1), 49–66. https://doi.org/10.36080/jsgs.v1i1.9
41. Susemihl, G. (2023). Collaboration and cooperation: SGang Gwaay and Gwaii Haanas. In *Claiming back their heritage* (pp. 117–134). Springer, Cham. https://doi.org/10.1007/978-3-031-40063-6_5
42. Brazil's Indians and the onslaught of civilization. (2006). The Yanomami and the Kayapo. *Luso-Brazilian Review, 43*(1), 150–151. https://doi.org/10.1353/lbr.2006.0032
43. Linstroth, J. P. (2022). Cultural genocide, genocide and Amerindian genocide. In Politics and racism beyond nations (pp. 57–76). Palgrave Macmillan, Cham. https://doi.org/10.1007/978-3-030-91720-3_4
44. Garcia, B., Morgan, E. A., Aruch, M., & Hugh, S., et al. (2024). Large-scale forest protection: The successful case of the Kayapo people in the Brazilian Amazon. *Regional Environmental Change, 24*(4). https://doi.org/10.1007/s10113-024-02304-6
45. Johansen, B. E. (2023). Mining: Tearing at mother's breast. In *Resource devastation on Native American lands* (pp. 121–137). Springer, Cham. https://doi.org/10.1007/978-3-031-21896-5_8
46. Iliamna Lake Nanvarpak ethnogeography: Yup'ik and contemporary place names and stories of these places. (2021). *The Northern Review*. https://doi.org/10.22584/nr52.2021.001

47. Palgrave Macmillan. (2016). United Kingdom of Great Britain and Northern Ireland. In *The Statesman's yearbook*. Palgrave Macmillan, London. https://doi.org/10.1007/978-1-349-68398-7_351
48. Dunér, D. (2013). The wave. In The natural philosophy of Emanuel Swedenborg. *Studies in the History of Philosophy of Mind* (vol. 11, pp. 53–75). Springer, Dordrecht. https://doi.org/10.1007/978-94-007-4560-5_4
49. Tian, X. (2024). Pastoralism and pastoralist children in East Africa. In Maasai childhood. Palgrave Studies on the Anthropology of Childhood and Youth (pp. 21–39). Palgrave Macmillan, Cham. https://doi.org/10.1007/978-3-031-73780-0_2
50. Srivastava, V. K. (2022). Adivasi. In Long, J. D., Sherma, R. D., Jain, P., & Khanna, M. (Eds.), *Hinduism and tribal religions. Encyclopedia of Indian Religions*. Springer, Dordrecht. https://doi.org/10.1007/978-94-024-1188-1_1874
51. Vincent, S. (2024). Distribution, recognition and participation: The paradigm for the human right to a sustainable environment and eco-justice in Mahasweta Devi's eco-critical writing. *Journal of Human Rights and Social Work*. https://doi.org/10.1007/s41134-024-00321-3
52. Kolhe, N. P., Dhote, K. K., & Parihar, A. (2023). Mapping the access of internet facility to Scheduled Tribe population: An approach towards digital education. In Choudhury, A., Biswas, A., & Chakraborti, S. (Eds.), *Digital learning-based education. Advanced Technologies and Societal Change* (pp. 1–21). Springer, Singapore. https://doi.org/10.1007/978-981-19-8967-4_1
53. James, G. A., & Mallick, K. (2023). Environmental movements of India: Chipko, Narmada Bachao Andolan, Navdanya. *DHARM, 6*, 275–277. https://doi.org/10.1007/s42240-024-00158-z
54. Pandey, A. D. (2024). Partnering with the mountains for reclaiming their land: Conflict between indigenous and capitalist perspectives. In Pattnaik, B. K. (Ed.), *Environmental and ecological sustainability through indigenous traditions* (pp. 157–174). Springer, Singapore. https://doi.org/10.1007/978-981-19-7079-5_9
55 Declaration of the Young Asian Indigenous Peoples. (2024, May). Conference: Voices of Asian Indigenous Peoples. Kep Province, Cambodia.
56. Lash, S. (2023). Civic associations and polycentric approaches to environmental justice in Louisiana. *Constitutional Political Economy*. https://doi.org/10.1007/s10602-023-09409-w
57. Piegler, T. (2023). Kampf um Identität. In Schumacher, H. (Ed.), Michael Mann (pp. 91–109). Springer VS, Wiesbaden. https://doi.org/10.1007/978-3-658-41673-7_6
58. George, R., & V, S. (2024). Navigating the ecological self: A deep ecological analysis of self-realization in the film Avatar. Human Arenas. https://doi.org/10.1007/s42087-024-00446-x
59. Reddick, Y. (2024). Pascale Petit: Entanglement, animals and the 'Anthropocene extinction'. In *Anthropocene poetry. Literatures, cultures and the environment*. Palgrave Macmillan, Cham. https://doi.org/10.1007/978-3-031-39389-1_6
60. Stanly, S., Rasana, N., & Rajendrakumar, S. (2024). Eco-centric approaches: Integrating indigenous agricultural wisdom and practices in realizing the sustainable development agendas. *Water, Air, & Soil Pollution, 235*(742). https://doi.org/10.1007/s11270-024-07525-3
61. Mackenthun, G. (2023). In search of paradise: Providential plots and political myth in Upton Sinclair's Oil! and John Steinbeck's The grapes of wrath. In L. Lutz-Auras & D. B. Rudolf (Eds.), Menschen, Macht und Mythen. Springer VS, Wiesbaden. https://doi.org/10.1007/978-3-658-39221-5_2
62. Kinefuchi, E. (2023). Wangari Maathai. In R. Brinkmann (Ed.), *The Palgrave handbook of global sustainability*. Palgrave Macmillan, Cham. https://doi.org/10.1007/978-3-031-01949-4_185
63. Sarkowsky, K. (2021). Relationality, autobiographical voice and the posthumanist paradox: Decentering the human in Leslie Marmon Silko's life writing. In I. Batzke, L. Espinoza Garrido, & L. M. Hess (Eds.), *Life writing in the posthuman anthropocene. Palgrave studies in life writing*. Palgrave Macmillan, Cham. https://doi.org/10.1007/978-3-030-77973-3_2

64. Hintz, C. (2022). Young adult (YA) fiction. In P. Marks, J. A. Wagner-Lawlor, & F. Vieira (Eds.), *The Palgrave handbook of utopian and dystopian literatures*. Palgrave Macmillan, Cham. https://doi.org/10.1007/978-3-030-88654-7_15
65. Jacobson, K. J. (2022). Novel climates, national catharsis: Local vs. global environmentalism in Californian cli-fi. *Comparative American Studies, 19*(2), 1–19. https://doi.org/10.1080/14775700.2022.2095194
66. Messimer, M. (2023). Hyperobjects and hyperempathy in Octavia Butler's Parable of the sower. In *Apocalyptic California*. Palgrave Macmillan, Cham. https://doi.org/10.1007/978-3-031-29920-9_4
67. Otjen, N. (2022). The climate of extinction: Resistant multispecies communities in Barbara Kingsolver's Flight behavior and Richard Powers's The overstory. In S. Borkfelt & M. Stephan (Eds.), *Literary animal studies and the climate crisis. Palgrave studies in animals and literature*. Palgrave Macmillan, Cham. https://doi.org/10.1007/978-3-031-11020-7_9
68. Joseph, S. (2025). Silent spring: The rise of the environmental movement. In P. Calvi (Ed.), *The literary journalist as a naturalist. Palgrave studies in literary journalism*. Palgrave Macmillan, Cham. https://doi.org/10.1007/978-3-031-56634-9_7
69. Afejuku, T. E. (2023). The meaning of solitude/loneliness/isolation in Chinua Achebe's Things fall apart and Arrow of god. In C. A. Hornbuckle, J. S. Smith, & W. S. Smith (Eds.), *Posthumanism and phenomenology. Analecta Husserliana*, 125. Springer, Cham. https://doi.org/10.1007/978-3-031-10414-5_12
70. Brodsky, G. W. S. (2024). Conrad's influence in postmodern literature and abroad and in the performing arts. In *Intimations of Joseph Conrad*. Palgrave Macmillan, Cham. https://doi.org/10.1007/978-3-031-67918-6_5
71. Eh Htoo, S., & Waters, T. (2024). Why ne win's burmanization policies are still important sixty years later: The Burmese burden. In *General ne win's legacy of burmanization in Myanmar*. Palgrave Macmillan, Singapore. https://doi.org/10.1007/978-981-97-1270-0_2
72. King, A. L., McNeil, B., Phipps, H., & Ricketts, K. (2022). Exploring polyvocal stories of space, place, movement and migration. In T. Vine & S. Richards (Eds.), *Stories, storytellers and storytelling*. Palgrave Macmillan, Cham. https://doi.org/10.1007/978-3-031-07234-5_6
73. Däwes, B., & Georgi-Findlay, B. (2024). Indigen-amerikanische Literatur. In H. Zapf & T. Müller (Eds.), *Amerikanische Literaturgeschichte*. J.B. Metzler, Berlin, Heidelberg. https://doi.org/10.1007/978-3-662-68062-9_7
74. Roza, M. (2024). Revision, change and the Native American oral tradition in Louise Erdrich's Love Medicine(s). In M. Gieskes & M. Roza (Eds.), *Retrospection and revision in modern and contemporary art, literature and music*. Palgrave Macmillan, Cham. https://doi.org/10.1007/978-3-031-39598-7_6
75. Beehner, C. G. (2024). Introduction: The nexus of spirituality and sustainability. In Spirituality, sustainability and success. Palgrave Studies in Workplace Spirituality and Fulfillment. Palgrave Macmillan, Cham. https://doi.org/10.1007/978-3-031-47643-3_1
76. Zerafa-Payne, E., Kerby, M., & Tualaulelei, E. (2024). Not just in black and white: Aboriginal and Torres strait Islander peoples in Australian children's picture books. *Australian Journal of Language and Literacy, 47*, 1–16. https://doi.org/10.1007/s44020-023-00048-0
77. Chacon, R. J. (2023). Supernatural gamekeepers/animal masters among the Munduruku (Wuy Jugu), Tukano, Embera and Achuar (Shiwiar) of the Neotropics. In *The history and environmental impacts of hunting deities: Conflict, environment and social complexity*. Springer, Cham. https://doi.org/10.1007/978-3-031-37503-3_14
78. Scott, B. K. (2024). Conflicting colonial, racial and tribal claims to Southern Africa. In *Taking place: Geocriticism and spatial literary studies*. Palgrave Macmillan, Cham. https://doi.org/10.1007/978-3-031-48355-4_3
79. Scott, B. K. (2024). Conflicting colonial, racial and tribal claims to Southern Africa. In Taking place. Geocriticism and spatial literary studies (pp. 39–55). Palgrave Macmillan, Cham. https://doi.org/10.1007/978-3-031-48355-4_3
80. Prichard, R. (2022). Masculinities and performativities in Native American dance. In D. Risner & B. Watson (Eds.), *Masculinity, intersectionality and identity* (pp. 145–161). Palgrave Macmillan, Cham. https://doi.org/10.1007/978-3-030-90000-7_7

81. Engel, L., Barratt, M., Ferris, J., & Winstock, A. R. (2023). Mescaline, peyote and San Pedro: Is sustainability important for cacti consumers? *Journal of Psychedelic Studies, 7*(2). https://doi.org/10.1556/2054.2023.00252
82. Dineen, M. (2023). Digital convergence and musical ethics. In D. C. Poff & A. C. Michalos (Eds.), *Encyclopedia of business and professional ethics.* Springer, Cham. https://doi.org/10.1007/978-3-030-22767-8_401
83. Zurita-Gallegos, R. M., Bastidas-Arauz, M. B., & Saeteros-Hernandez, A. M. (2024). The indigenous bioculture of the Pungalá parish of Ecuador: An approach to their culinary and medicinal heritage. *Journal of Ethnic Foods, 11*(6). https://doi.org/10.1186/s42779-023-00219-x
84. Prue-Owens, K. (2024). People of American Indian/Alaskan Native heritage. In E. A. Fenkl & L. D. Purnell (Eds.), *Handbook for culturally competent care* (pp. 65–84). Springer, Cham. https://doi.org/10.1007/978-3-031-70492-5_5
85. Martellotta, E., Brumm, A., & Langley, M. (2023). Tales of multifunctionality: A systematic quantitative literature review of boomerangs used as retouchers in Australian Aboriginal cultures. *Journal of Archaeological Method and Theory, 30*(3), 310–334. https://doi.org/10.1007/s10816-022-09561-x
86. Pombo, P. (2024). Afro-Indic archipelagos: Searching for African heritages in the materialities, visual cultures and art practices of the Western Indian Ocean Islands. In U. Fendler & Y. Chang (Eds.), *Asia-Africa - Multifaceted engagement in the contemporary world* (pp. 85–106). Palgrave Macmillan, Singapore. https://doi.org/10.1007/978-981-97-0696-9_5
87. Mendoza-Zapata, R. (2022). The dimension of the sacred in the Quechua youth of Southern Peru. *Journal of Anthropology and Youth Studies, 5*, 297–315. https://doi.org/10.1007/s43151-022-00086-4
88. Liddell, J. L., Kington, S. G., & Wright, D. C. (2024). Environmental reproductive justice, Indigenous health knowledge and Indigenous women on the climate frontlines. *Social Justice Research, 37*(4), 424–446. https://doi.org/10.1007/s11211-024-00439-9
89. Jeelani, A. H. (2024). Interplay of climate change and the emergence of sustainability. In P. Singh & N. Yadav (Eds.), The climate-health-sustainability nexus (pp. 1–16). Springer, Cham. https://doi.org/10.1007/978-3-031-56564-9_1
90. Biswas, D. (2024). Literary solastalgia: Indigenous communities and narratives of precarity in the Global South. Regional Environmental Change, 24(168). https://doi.org/10.1007/s10113-024-02335-z
91. Beisaw, A. M., & Olin, G. E. (2020). From Alcatraz to standing rock: Archaeology and contemporary Native American protests (1969–today). *Historical Archaeology, 54*(3), 537–555. https://doi.org/10.1007/s41636-020-00252-6
92. Franco, D., Cardozo, E., & Mahan, A. (2024). Social work and support for climate-related Indigenous migrants from South America. *Journal of Human Rights and Social Work.* https://doi.org/10.1007/s41134-024-00339-7
93. McIntyre-Mills, J. J., Makaulule, M., & Lethole, P. (2023). Ecocentric living: A way forward towards zero carbon: A conversation about Indigenous law and leadership based on custodianship and praxis. *Systemic Practice and Action Research, 36*(3), 275–319. https://doi.org/10.1007/s11213-022-09604-0
94. van Reekum, R. (2023). Re-membering the native public. In Out of character: Cultural sociology (pp. 77–98). Palgrave Macmillan, Cham. https://doi.org/10.1007/978-3-031-48898-6_4
95. Martins, L. O. M., dos Reis, M. F., & Chaoubah, A. (2024). Distributive justice and equity in resource allocation: A temporal analysis of hospitalization costs in Indigenous populations in Brazil. International Journal for Equity in Health, 23(21). https://doi.org/10.1186/s12939-024-02102-w
96. Didarali, Z., Kuiper, T., & Brink, C. W. (2022). Awareness of environmental legislation as a deterrent for wildlife crime: A case with Maasai pastoralists, poison use and the Kenya Wildlife Act. *Ambio, 51*(12), 1632–1642. https://doi.org/10.1007/s13280-021-01695-8

97. Coleman, C. L. (2020). How Sioux-settler relations underscore the Dakota Access Pipeline. In *Environmental clashes on Native American land* (pp. 89–103). Palgrave Pivot, Cham. https://doi.org/10.1007/978-3-030-34106-0_7
98. Pattnaik, B. K. (2024). Introduction: Re-modernizing the modern, a syncretic perspective. In B. K. Pattnaik (Ed.), Environmental and ecological sustainability through Indigenous traditions (pp. 1–20). Springer, Singapore. https://doi.org/10.1007/978-981-19-7079-5_1
99. Crocetti, A. C., Walker, T., & Mitchell, F. (2024). *Making big business everybody's business: Aboriginal leaders' perspectives on commercial activities influencing Aboriginal health in Victoria*, Australia. Global Health, 20(33). https://doi.org/10.1186/s12992-024-01038-8
100. Sekher, M., Awasthi, M., Nayak, S., & Kumar, R. (2022). Resource extraction and conflict in India. In H. E. Ali & L. E. Cederman (Eds.), *Natural resources, inequality and conflict* (pp. 167–192). Palgrave Macmillan, Cham. https://doi.org/10.1007/978-3-030-73558-6_6
101. Budd, B. (2024). "Reconciliation is dead": News coverage of the Wet'suwet'en land defense. In *News framing of indigenous politics in Canada* (pp. 119–137). Palgrave Macmillan, Cham. https://doi.org/10.1007/978-3-031-64758-1_6

Chapter 3
Legal Dimensions of Conservation Practices

Abstract This chapter delves into the legal frameworks that govern conservation practices, with a particular focus on how indigenous rights and cultural beliefs are integrated into environmental law narratives. By exploring both historical and contemporary legislative measures, the chapter examines how legal structures have evolved to recognize the critical role indigenous communities play in the stewardship of biodiversity and ecosystems worldwide. Environmental laws serve as critical tools for balancing development with conservation. They act as a mechanism for regulating human activities, ensuring that ecological resources are utilized responsibly while safeguarding the rights of future generations. This book examines the evolution of environmental laws and their role in addressing global challenges, from climate change mitigation to biodiversity conservation. Through a detailed analysis of case studies, this work highlights the transformative potential of laws informed by indigenous worldviews. For instance, the Rights of Nature framework in Ecuador and the joint management of Kakadu National Park by the Mirarr people and the Australian government showcase how legal systems can incorporate traditional ecological knowledge to enhance biodiversity protection. These examples illuminate how the fusion of legal principles and cultural values can lead to more inclusive and effective solutions to environmental challenges.

Keywords Indigenous knowledge · Conservation laws · Biodiversity protection · Legal integration

3.1 Historical Evolution of Conservation Laws with Indigenous Contributions

This chapter uniquely traces the historical trajectory of conservation laws, showcasing how Indigenous practices have influenced legal frameworks over time. It explores case studies where customary laws, such as the Bishnoi community's protection of wildlife in India or the Māori's kaitiakitanga (guardianship) in New Zealand, have shaped modern conservation policies. By bridging the gap between traditional

T. Pradhan et al., *Symbiotic Wisdom: Exploring Ethnoecological Paradigms within Indigenous Environmental Law Narratives*,
https://doi.org/10.1007/978-981-95-1042-9_3

and contemporary legal systems, the chapter emphasizes the enduring relevance of Indigenous knowledge in global environmental governance [1]. This historical perspective offers readers a comprehensive understanding of how conservation laws have evolved to incorporate Indigenous wisdom, making it a valuable resource for policymakers, legal scholars and conservationists.

3.2 Indigenous Roots of Conservation Laws

Indigenous communities have practiced sustainable living and environmental stewardship for centuries, predating modern legal systems. Their understanding of biodiversity and ecosystem balance has significantly influenced the development of conservation laws globally. This chapter examines how these traditional practices have transitioned into formal legal frameworks, becoming vital in today's efforts to combat biodiversity loss and climate change [2]. By drawing upon examples such as the Bishnoi community in India and the Māori in New Zealand, the chapter highlights the role of Indigenous wisdom in shaping conservation laws, providing a blueprint for addressing contemporary environmental challenges.

3.2.1 Bishnoi Community: A Model for Legal Wildlife Protection in India

The Bishnoi community of Rajasthan, India, has been a symbol of environmental conservation since the fifteenth century. Guided by spiritual principles established by Guru Jambheshwar, the Bishnois prioritize the protection of wildlife and trees, treating them as sacred. Their non-violent resistance to deforestation and poaching, epitomized in the 1730 Khejarli Massacre, where over 360 Bishnois sacrificed their lives to protect trees, directly influenced the legal recognition of wildlife and forest protection in India [3]. Today, the Wildlife Protection Act, 1972, and Forest Conservation Act, 1980, embody principles aligned with the Bishnoi ethos, emphasizing the role of local communities in preserving biodiversity. These legal provisions have reinforced India's commitment to international conventions like the Convention on Biological Diversity (CBD) and the UN's Sustainable Development Goals (SDG 15).

3.2.2 *The Māori's Kaitiakitanga and Its Legal Integration in New Zealand*

The Māori concept of *kaitiakitanga,* guardianship of nature has deeply influenced New Zealand's environmental laws. Historically, the Māori viewed their relationship with the environment as reciprocal, emphasizing balance and responsibility. This worldview gained legal prominence with the Treaty of Waitangi (1840), which recognized Māori rights, although inconsistently enforced. In contemporary times, legal frameworks like the Resource Management Act (1991) and the Te Awa Tupua (Whanganui River Claims Settlement Act, 2017) have solidified Māori values within New Zealand's legal system [4]. By granting the Whanganui River legal personhood, the law respects Māori traditions while offering a modern governance model for resource management (Fig. 3.1). This integration serves as a global precedent, illustrating how Indigenous perspectives can drive innovative legal mechanisms to address environmental degradation.

Fig. 3.1 An artistic depiction of the Whanganui River, reflecting the Māori concept of kaitiakitanga and its integration into modern legal frameworks. It captures the harmony between nature and culture, showcasing the river's significance as a living entity in Māori traditions

3.3 Bridging Customary Practices and Formal Legal Systems

One of the key challenges in modern conservation law is bridging the gap between customary Indigenous practices and formal legal structures. Historically, many Indigenous conservation methods were dismissed or marginalized by colonial powers, leading to conflicts over land rights and resource use. However, legal systems have increasingly recognized the need to integrate traditional knowledge into conservation strategies. For instance, Canada's establishment of Indigenous Protected and Conserved Areas (IPCAs) reflects a shift toward collaborative governance, blending traditional ecological knowledge with state-supported conservation efforts [5]. These co-management models not only empower Indigenous communities but also enhance biodiversity conservation by leveraging localized expertise. This trend aligns with international frameworks like the UN Declaration on the Rights of Indigenous Peoples (UNDRIP), which advocates for the inclusion of Indigenous governance in environmental decision-making.

3.4 Contemporary Legal Relevance and Challenges

In today's scenario, the integration of Indigenous knowledge into conservation laws is more relevant than ever. Climate change, habitat destruction and biodiversity loss demand innovative solutions rooted in sustainability. Legal frameworks inspired by Indigenous practices address these challenges by emphasizing coexistence rather than exploitation. However, implementation remains fraught with obstacles. Land-grabbing, industrialization and lack of political will often undermine Indigenous contributions. For example, while the Pachamama Law in Bolivia recognizes Mother Earth's rights, enforcement has been inconsistent due to competing economic interests [6]. Similarly, the Dakota Access Pipeline protests by the Standing Rock Sioux Tribe in the U.S. underscore the ongoing struggle for Indigenous sovereignty in environmental governance [7].

3.5 International Legal Instruments Supporting Indigenous Contributions

The increasing acknowledgment of Indigenous contributions to conservation is supported by international legal instruments. Agreements like the Paris Agreement and the Convention on Biological Diversity (CBD) emphasize the integration of traditional knowledge into climate adaptation and biodiversity strategies. The Aichi Biodiversity Targets specifically highlight the role of Indigenous and local communities in achieving conservation goals. Moreover, the Sustainable Development Goals

(SDG 13 on Climate Action and SDG 15 on Life on Land) stress the importance of involving Indigenous communities in legal and policy frameworks to ensure sustainable resource management [8]. These global commitments offer a pathway for nations to harmonize traditional practices with modern legal systems.

3.6 A Path Forward for Conservation Laws

The historical evolution of conservation laws demonstrates the indispensable role of Indigenous knowledge in shaping sustainable governance models. Case studies from the Bishnoi community, Māori guardianship and Indigenous Protected Areas in Canada illustrate how traditional practices have influenced and continue to inform legal frameworks. These examples highlight the need for a paradigm shift toward participatory governance that values Indigenous contributions equally [9]. In the face of escalating environmental crises, recognizing and integrating Indigenous perspectives is not just a legal necessity but a moral imperative. By drawing upon the wisdom of the past, conservation laws can evolve to address the challenges of the future, ensuring ecological balance and resilience for generations to come.

3.7 Indigenous Sovereignty in Conservation Law

The chapter delves into the legal recognition of Indigenous sovereignty and its role in conservation practices. It examines landmark cases, such as the granting of legal personhood to the Whanganui River in New Zealand, inspired by Māori cultural, beliefs and the establishment of Indigenous Protected and Conserved Areas (IPCAs) in Canada. These examples illustrate how recognizing Indigenous governance fosters effective conservation while preserving cultural heritage [10]. The chapter emphasizes the importance of participatory governance models that empower Indigenous communities to manage their lands, demonstrating how legal acknowledgment of Indigenous sovereignty benefits both conservation and Indigenous rights. Indigenous sovereignty, the inherent right of Indigenous communities to govern their own territories and resources, has gained increasing legal recognition in recent decades. This shift in legal frameworks is a response to the long-standing marginalization of Indigenous knowledge and governance systems in favor of state-centric approaches. Indigenous sovereignty is now recognized not only as a matter of cultural and human rights but also as a crucial element of effective environmental conservation. This chapter explores the legal acknowledgment of Indigenous sovereignty in conservation law, highlighting landmark cases and initiatives that demonstrate how empowering Indigenous communities in land management and environmental governance can yield sustainable outcomes. Examples like the granting of legal personhood to the Whanganui River in New Zealand and the establishment of Indigenous Protected and Conserved Areas (IPCAs) in Canada highlight the role of Indigenous governance in modern conservation practices.

3.8 Legal Personhood of the Whanganui River: A Case Study in Māori Sovereignty

One of the most significant legal recognitions of Indigenous sovereignty in conservation law is the granting of legal personhood to the Whanganui River in New Zealand. This landmark case is rooted in the Māori concept of *iwi* (tribal) governance and the belief that the river is a living entity, central to their cultural, spiritual and physical existence. In 2017, the New Zealand government passed the *Whanganui River Claims Settlement Act*, granting the Whanganui River legal personhood. This law recognizes the river as an entity with legal rights, including the right to be represented in court and protected by a governance structure that includes both Māori and state representatives. The legal personhood of the Whanganui River is a pioneering model for integrating Indigenous sovereignty into environmental law. The recognition of the river as a legal entity directly aligns with Māori values, where rivers and other natural elements are regarded as ancestors with whom people have reciprocal relationships. This legal innovation provides a framework for ensuring that the environmental governance of such resources is led by Indigenous knowledge and customs [11]. By empowering the Māori people to directly participate in the governance of the Whanganui River, the law preserves both the river's ecological integrity and Māori cultural heritage. This case sets a powerful precedent for recognizing the legal rights of other ecosystems, demonstrating how the acknowledgment of Indigenous sovereignty fosters more effective conservation efforts and protects traditional knowledge.

3.9 Indigenous Protected and Conserved Areas (IPCAs) in Canada: A Collaborative Governance Model

Another critical example of Indigenous sovereignty in conservation law is the creation of Indigenous Protected and Conserved Areas (IPCAs) in Canada. These areas are designated and managed by Indigenous communities, using their traditional knowledge of the land and ecosystems to ensure their protection. IPCAs are part of a broader movement toward reconciliation and recognition of Indigenous land rights. In Canada, Indigenous communities have been at the forefront of conservation efforts, advocating for the recognition of their governance systems in managing natural resources and protecting biodiversity. IPCAs are established through collaborative governance models that blend Indigenous traditional ecological knowledge with Western scientific approaches. This integration ensures that conservation efforts are culturally appropriate and environmentally effective. For example, the Dehcho First Nations in the Northwest Territories have established the Dehcho Land Use Plan, which integrates traditional knowledge and scientific research to guide conservation practices [12]. By recognizing Indigenous sovereignty in the management of protected areas, Canada is empowering Indigenous communities to take an active role in preserving their lands and resources while maintaining cultural practices that have sustained these ecosystems for centuries.

IPCAs not only provide legal protection for lands and biodiversity but also contribute to the social and economic well-being of Indigenous communities. These areas offer opportunities for economic development through eco-tourism, sustainable harvesting and cultural revitalization, creating a model of conservation that benefits both the environment and Indigenous people. The success of IPCAs in Canada has prompted other countries to consider similar models, illustrating how the recognition of Indigenous sovereignty can lead to more inclusive, effective and culturally sensitive conservation practices.

3.10 Participatory Governance Models: Empowering Indigenous Communities in Conservation

The legal recognition of Indigenous sovereignty has the potential to transform conservation law by creating more inclusive, participatory governance models. These models empower Indigenous communities to actively manage their territories, integrate traditional knowledge and influence legal frameworks that govern land use and environmental protection. Participatory governance in conservation involves the active engagement of local communities, particularly Indigenous peoples, in decision-making processes about resource management, land conservation and biodiversity protection. One of the key principles of participatory governance is that conservation policies should reflect the values and priorities of the communities directly affected by them. For example, the establishment of marine protected areas (MPAs) in the Pacific Islands has been informed by the traditional practices of local Indigenous peoples, who have long used sustainable fishing techniques and seasonal harvesting. These communities are now working alongside national governments to co-manage marine resources, ensuring that conservation strategies respect both ecological and cultural values [13]. By involving Indigenous communities in decision-making, these models foster greater local ownership and accountability, leading to more effective conservation outcomes.

At the international level, participatory governance models are increasingly supported by legal instruments such as the UN Declaration on the Rights of Indigenous Peoples (UNDRIP), which calls for the recognition of Indigenous peoples' right to self-determination and their participation in environmental decision-making processes. Such frameworks emphasize the importance of Indigenous sovereignty in shaping conservation policies that are not only environmentally sustainable but also culturally relevant.

3.11 Legal Recognition of Indigenous Sovereignty: A Global Trend

The recognition of Indigenous sovereignty in conservation law is part of a broader global trend toward legal pluralism, where multiple legal systems coexist and influence one another. Countries like New Zealand, Canada and Bolivia have led the way in integrating Indigenous governance into environmental law, setting an example for other nations to follow. As climate change and biodiversity loss continue to threaten ecosystems worldwide, the role of Indigenous knowledge and governance in conservation becomes even more critical. International environmental law, including agreements such as the Paris Agreement and the Convention on Biological Diversity (CBD), increasingly acknowledges the importance of Indigenous participation in environmental governance [14]. These agreements emphasize the need to integrate traditional ecological knowledge into global conservation strategies. By recognizing Indigenous sovereignty and legal rights, these frameworks support the implementation of conservation laws that are both effective and culturally appropriate.

The integration of Indigenous governance into national and international environmental laws offers a promising pathway toward achieving the Sustainable Development Goals (SDGs), particularly Goal 15 (Life on Land) and Goal 13 (Climate Action). By empowering Indigenous communities to manage and protect their lands, these legal frameworks help preserve biodiversity, mitigate climate change and promote the sustainable use of natural resources, benefiting both Indigenous peoples and the planet as a whole.

3.12 The Future of Indigenous Sovereignty in Conservation Law

The legal recognition of Indigenous sovereignty is a pivotal aspect of modern conservation law, providing a framework for sustainable land and resource management that respects both ecological integrity and cultural heritage. Landmark cases such as the Whanganui River in New Zealand and the creation of IPCAs in Canada demonstrate the positive impact of recognizing Indigenous governance in conservation efforts. As the world faces unprecedented environmental challenges, Indigenous knowledge systems offer valuable solutions grounded in centuries of experience.

The legal acknowledgment of Indigenous sovereignty not only advances environmental protection but also promotes social justice and reconciliation, creating a more inclusive and sustainable future for all.

3.13 Intersection of Cultural Beliefs and Legal Frameworks

A key feature of this chapter is its exploration of how cultural and spiritual beliefs intersect with conservation laws. It highlights examples like the Uluru-Kata Tjuta National Park in Australia, where the Anangu people's cultural values have led to legal measures prohibiting climbing Uluru and Bolivia's recognition of Pachamama (Mother Earth) as a legal entity. These cases reveal how integrating cultural narratives into legal systems enriches conservation efforts, creating laws that resonate with local communities and ensure their active participation in environmental stewardship. Cultural and spiritual beliefs have always been integral to the way Indigenous communities interact with their environment. In many cultures, nature is not simply a collection of resources to be exploited but is seen as a sacred entity deserving respect and protection. As global conservation efforts become more inclusive, the integration of these cultural narratives into legal frameworks is gaining importance. This chapter explores how such intersections of cultural beliefs and legal structures enrich conservation laws, making them more effective and relevant to the communities they serve. By considering cultural and spiritual values, these laws foster greater community participation in environmental stewardship. Examples like the Uluru-Kata Tjuta National Park in Australia [15] and Bolivia's recognition of Pachamama (Mother Earth) as a legal entity show how incorporating these beliefs into legal systems can create laws that are both culturally resonant and legally sound, ensuring more holistic and inclusive environmental protection.

3.14 Uluru-Kata Tjuta National Park: Protecting Sacred Sites Through Legal Measures

Uluru, one of Australia's most iconic landmarks, holds immense cultural and spiritual significance for the Anangu people, the traditional custodians of the land. Uluru's cultural value is deeply embedded in Anangu traditions, where it is considered a living, sacred being that holds stories and ancestral spirits. For decades, tourists climbed Uluru, disregarding its sacred status and the cultural beliefs of the Anangu people. This practice led to tensions between local Indigenous communities and the tourism industry. In 2017, following years of advocacy from the Anangu people and the Uluru-Kata Tjuta National Park Board of Management, which includes Anangu representation, the Australian government officially banned climbing Uluru [16]. This legal ban was not just a matter of tourism regulation but a direct reflection of the cultural and spiritual beliefs of the Anangu people, who view Uluru as a sacred site that should be respected. This decision marked a crucial intersection of cultural values and legal enforcement, aligning conservation law with Indigenous spirituality. The legal prohibition on climbing Uluru is a powerful example of how respecting cultural narratives within legal frameworks can enhance conservation efforts by ensuring that Indigenous peoples are active participants in decisions about their sacred sites. The law now protects not just the physical environment of Uluru but also its cultural and spiritual significance, demonstrating the value of integrating Indigenous beliefs into modern conservation legislation.

3.15 Bolivia's Recognition of Pachamama (Mother Earth) as a Legal Entity

Bolivia's approach to environmental protection offers another compelling example of how cultural beliefs can be embedded in legal systems to foster better conservation practices. In 2010, Bolivia passed the *Law of the Rights of Mother Earth*, which legally recognizes the rights of Pachamama—Mother Earth—as a living entity. The law is rooted in the Aymara and Quechua Indigenous cosmologies, which view the Earth not as a commodity but as a mother who sustains and nurtures all life. This legal framework is part of a broader movement in Bolivia to integrate Indigenous worldviews into national law, ensuring that the rights of nature are considered alongside the rights of human beings. The *Law of the Rights of Mother Earth* grants nature legal personhood, allowing ecosystems, species and natural entities to be represented in court and protected from exploitation [17]. This legal recognition of Pachamama reflects a profound cultural belief in the interconnectedness of all living things and the need for a reciprocal relationship between humans and nature. It acknowledges that environmental degradation is not just an ecological issue but a violation of spiritual and cultural values. By embedding these beliefs into the legal system, Bolivia has created a robust framework for environmental protection that resonates with the cultural values of its Indigenous communities. This intersection of spirituality and law ensures that the protection of nature is not just a matter of legal compliance but a cultural imperative. The law offers a model for other nations to follow, integrating Indigenous knowledge and worldviews into broader environmental governance.

3.16 Cultural Beliefs as Tools for Effective Environmental Governance

The integration of cultural beliefs into legal systems does not just benefit conservation efforts but also ensures that local communities are more invested in environmental governance. When laws reflect the spiritual and cultural values of Indigenous peoples, these communities are more likely to participate in the implementation and enforcement of conservation measures. This participatory approach has been shown to enhance the effectiveness of environmental protection by creating laws that are not only legally binding but culturally meaningful. For instance, in many Indigenous cultures, there is a belief in the sacredness of natural resources such as water, forests and wildlife. These beliefs often translate into practical stewardship practices, such as the sustainable management of forests, sacred groves and water bodies. By recognizing the legal rights of these resources and integrating cultural beliefs into environmental law, governments can create systems that prioritize sustainability and long-term environmental health. These laws help ensure that ecosystems are protected by those who have the deepest understanding of them and the greatest stake in their preservation. In the case of Uluru, for example, the law not only prohibits harmful practices like climbing but also promotes sustainable tourism that respects the spiritual and cultural significance of the site. Similarly, Bolivia's recognition of Pachamama brings the sacredness of nature into legal discourse, creating a framework for balancing economic development with environmental sustainability. These models demonstrate the practical value of aligning cultural beliefs with legal frameworks in the pursuit of effective environmental governance.

3.17 The Global Relevance of Cultural and Legal Integration

Globally, the integration of cultural beliefs into environmental law is becoming increasingly important as nations strive to address urgent environmental issues such as climate change, biodiversity loss and resource depletion. International instruments such as the United Nations Declaration on the Rights of Indigenous Peoples (UNDRIP) advocate for the recognition of Indigenous peoples' rights to govern their lands and resources according to their own cultural practices. By incorporating these rights into national legal systems, governments can strengthen conservation efforts and ensure that environmental laws are both culturally sensitive and legally sound.

The recognition of cultural and spiritual beliefs in conservation law is not just an Indigenous issue—it is a matter of global importance. As the world confronts ecological crises, integrating Indigenous perspectives into environmental governance provides invaluable insights into sustainable resource management. In many cases, Indigenous communities have been managing ecosystems for thousands of years, and their traditional knowledge is essential to addressing modern environmental challenges. By legally recognizing the cultural beliefs that underpin these practices, governments can create more effective and inclusive environmental laws that benefit both people and the planet.

3.18 A Holistic Approach to Conservation Law

The intersection of cultural beliefs and legal frameworks in conservation law represents a holistic approach to environmental stewardship, one that values both ecological and cultural sustainability. Cases like Uluru and Bolivia's recognition of Pachamama demonstrate the transformative potential of integrating Indigenous worldviews into modern legal systems. These examples show that when conservation laws resonate with local cultural values, they are more likely to be supported and successfully implemented. By embracing the cultural and spiritual beliefs of Indigenous peoples, legal frameworks can be strengthened, ensuring more effective, inclusive and sustainable conservation practices. As the world grapples with environmental crises, this approach offers a valuable pathway toward achieving long-term ecological resilience and social justice.

3.18.1 Addressing Global Challenges Through Legal Innovations

The chapter offers a forward-looking perspective by examining how conservation laws informed by Indigenous practices address pressing global challenges such as climate change, biodiversity loss and resource scarcity. It explores innovative legal mechanisms, such as Ecuador's Rights of Nature framework [18] and Australia's integration of Indigenous fire management practices to combat bushfires. These examples underscore the adaptability of Indigenous-inspired legal frameworks in mitigating contemporary environmental crises, making the chapter highly relevant to global sustainability agendas.

3.18.1.1 Indigenous Knowledge and Global Environmental Crises

In an era where climate change, biodiversity loss and resource scarcity are among the most urgent global challenges, Indigenous knowledge and practices offer critical insights into sustainable solutions. Indigenous communities have long managed their natural environments with a deep understanding of ecological balance and sustainability. Recognizing the value of this knowledge, many countries are beginning to integrate Indigenous wisdom into modern legal frameworks. These legal innovations not only contribute to effective conservation but also provide adaptive strategies to address the pressing environmental issues that threaten the planet. This analysis explores how legal systems, informed by Indigenous practices, can mitigate contemporary environmental crises and contribute to global sustainability efforts. It highlights specific legal mechanisms, such as Ecuador's Rights of Nature and Australia's integration of Indigenous fire management practices, showcasing how these frameworks can be adapted to address today's environmental challenges.

3.18.1.2 Ecuador's Rights of Nature: A Revolutionary Legal Framework

Ecuador's innovative approach to environmental law through the *Rights of Nature* framework is a landmark example of how Indigenous-inspired legal mechanisms can address global environmental challenges. Enshrined in Ecuador's 2008 Constitution, the Rights of Nature recognizes ecosystems, species and natural entities as legal persons with inherent rights, such as the right to exist, persist and regenerate [19]. This legal paradigm, rooted in Indigenous worldviews, particularly from the Andean cosmovision, acknowledges the interconnectedness of all life and the moral imperative to protect nature.

The *Rights of Nature* framework allows communities and organizations to file lawsuits on behalf of ecosystems, ensuring that environmental degradation is not just an ecological or economic issue, but a legal violation of nature's rights. This framework has proven particularly relevant in the context of climate change, as it empowers citizens to challenge environmentally destructive projects that threaten ecosystems and the climate. For example, Ecuadorian courts have used the Rights of Nature to halt the extraction of oil from the Yasuní National Park, one of the most biodiverse areas on Earth, protecting the land from exploitation and degradation.

The significance of Ecuador's *Rights of Nature* framework lies in its ability to shift the focus from nature as a resource to nature as a subject of legal protection. This legal approach supports global sustainability efforts by framing environmental protection as a human right that is inherently linked to the health of the planet. It offers a powerful tool to combat biodiversity loss and resource depletion, making it a model for other countries striving to integrate environmental justice into their legal systems.

3.18.1.3 Australia's Indigenous Fire Management: A Legal Strategy for Climate Resilience

Australia's adoption of Indigenous fire management practices represents another innovative legal response to contemporary environmental challenges, particularly in addressing the increasing frequency and intensity of bushfires exacerbated by climate change. Indigenous fire management, which has been practiced for thousands of years by Australian Aboriginal peoples, involves controlled, low-intensity burns that reduce the risk of large, catastrophic fires. These burns also promote biodiversity by preventing the accumulation of dry, combustible material, enhancing soil health and encouraging the regeneration of native plant species. In recent years, Australian policymakers have recognized the value of these traditional practices and have integrated them into national fire management strategies. This has led to legal recognition of Indigenous fire management techniques and the establishment of formal partnerships between government agencies and Indigenous communities. One notable example is the "Firesticks Alliance," which facilitates collaboration between

Indigenous fire practitioners and Australian state fire agencies [20]. This partnership helps to implement controlled burns in areas prone to large-scale fires, such as the vast bushland of northern Australia. By integrating Indigenous fire management practices into legal frameworks, Australia is addressing multiple global challenges, including climate change and biodiversity loss. These practices are not only reducing the severity of bushfires but also improving ecological resilience by maintaining the health of fire-dependent ecosystems. This model showcases how traditional knowledge can complement modern scientific practices, creating a more holistic approach to environmental management. The legal integration of these practices underscores the importance of honoring Indigenous knowledge in contemporary environmental law, offering a solution that is both sustainable and culturally appropriate.

3.19 Legal Recognition of Indigenous Knowledge in Global Environmental Governance

Indigenous legal innovations, such as Ecuador's *Rights of Nature* and Australia's Indigenous fire management practices, demonstrate how Indigenous knowledge can be a driving force in addressing global environmental issues. These legal frameworks provide a pathway for the integration of traditional ecological knowledge (TEK) into formal governance structures, bridging the gap between scientific and Indigenous approaches to environmental protection. In this way, legal recognition of Indigenous knowledge not only enhances conservation efforts but also empowers Indigenous communities to actively participate in environmental governance. For example, in the context of resource scarcity, Indigenous knowledge systems have long emphasized the sustainable management of natural resources through practices like agroforestry, rotational grazing and fishing. Legal frameworks that recognize and protect these practices ensure that they are passed down to future generations while also contributing to global efforts to mitigate resource depletion. By incorporating TEK into national and international legal structures, governments can implement policies that balance ecological health with human development needs, fostering sustainable livelihoods while preserving biodiversity.

3.20 The Role of Indigenous-Led Legal Mechanisms in Climate Change Mitigation

As climate change intensifies, Indigenous-led legal frameworks have an increasingly critical role to play in global climate adaptation and mitigation strategies. Many Indigenous communities, particularly those in the Global South, are at the forefront of climate change resilience, as they have lived in close connection with their environments for centuries. By integrating Indigenous knowledge into legal systems, countries can enhance their climate change response strategies, ensuring that mitigation efforts are culturally relevant and ecologically effective. One example of this is the establishment of Indigenous Protected and Conserved Areas (IPCAs) in Canada [21]. These areas, which are managed collaboratively by Indigenous communities and government agencies, represent a legally recognized framework for protecting large swaths of land from exploitation, deforestation and other environmental harms. IPCAs play a key role in climate change mitigation by preserving carbon-rich ecosystems like forests and wetlands, which act as vital carbon sinks. They also contribute to biodiversity conservation, ensuring that Indigenous communities continue to benefit from the land's resources in a sustainable manner.

IPCAs exemplify how Indigenous-led legal mechanisms can serve as powerful tools for addressing climate change, biodiversity loss and resource scarcity. By recognizing the rights of Indigenous communities to govern and manage their lands, these legal innovations ensure that conservation efforts are both ecologically effective and culturally grounded, contributing to the broader goals of global sustainability.

The legal innovations discussed in this analysis, Ecuador's *Rights of Nature*, Australia's Indigenous fire management practices and Canada's IPCAs demonstrate how Indigenous knowledge systems can be integrated into modern legal frameworks to address the most pressing global environmental challenges. These examples highlight the adaptability and effectiveness of Indigenous-inspired legal mechanisms in responding to climate change, biodiversity loss and resource scarcity. By recognizing the rights and governance structures of Indigenous peoples, legal systems can create more holistic and sustainable solutions to environmental issues, ensuring that the planet's ecological health is preserved for future generations. As the world confronts unprecedented environmental crises, the integration of Indigenous knowledge into legal frameworks offers a promising pathway for achieving global sustainability. Legal recognition of Indigenous governance not only strengthens conservation efforts but also empowers Indigenous communities to take an active role in shaping environmental policy. This inclusive approach to environmental law, which blends traditional knowledge with modern legal systems, offers a comprehensive and effective response to the complex challenges of the twenty-first century.

3.21 Alignment with International Protocols and SDGs

This chapter stands out by connecting Indigenous conservation practices to international legal instruments, conventions and the United Nations Sustainable Development Goals (SDGs). It discusses how Indigenous-led conservation aligns with targets such as SDG 13 (Climate Action), SDG 15 (Life on Land) and SDG 16 (Peace, Justice and Strong Institutions). By showcasing the integration of Indigenous perspectives in global agreements like the Convention on Biological Diversity (CBD) and the Paris Agreement, the chapter provides a roadmap for harmonizing local traditions with international environmental governance, appealing to readers interested in both localized and globalized legal dimensions of conservation. As the world grapples with pressing environmental challenges such as climate change, biodiversity loss and resource depletion, Indigenous knowledge systems offer invaluable insights into sustainable practices. These traditional conservation methods, rooted in millennia of interaction with local ecosystems, are increasingly being recognized in global environmental governance. This analysis explores how Indigenous-led conservation practices align with international legal frameworks, conventions and the United Nations Sustainable Development Goals (SDGs). By showcasing how Indigenous perspectives harmonize with global agreements like the Convention on Biological Diversity (CBD) and the Paris Agreement, the work highlights how local traditions can be integrated into international environmental governance. This approach not only underscores the significance of Indigenous knowledge in global conservation efforts but also presents a roadmap for aligning traditional practices with global sustainability agendas.

3.21.1 SDG 13: Climate Action and Indigenous Knowledge

One of the key challenges facing the world today is climate change and SDG 13, Climate Action aims to combat climate change and its impacts. Indigenous communities, particularly those living in ecologically sensitive areas, have long practiced climate-resilient strategies rooted in their deep understanding of local environments [22]. Indigenous fire management practices in Australia, for example, demonstrate a powerful way to reduce the risk of large-scale wildfires, which are increasingly exacerbated by climate change. These low-intensity controlled burns, developed over centuries of fire management, not only mitigate the immediate threat of wildfires but also help to regenerate ecosystems, preserve biodiversity and maintain carbon sinks, all of which contribute to climate adaptation and mitigation. The legal recognition of Indigenous fire management practices, as seen in Australia's integration of these methods into national bushfire management strategies, is a prime example of how Indigenous knowledge can contribute to SDG 13. These practices are not only a traditional form of climate adaptation but also demonstrate how local solutions can be scaled up to address global climate challenges. By aligning with the SDGs, this integration ensures that climate action is culturally sensitive, locally driven and scientifically informed, thereby providing an inclusive approach to climate resilience. Moreover, countries like Ecuador, which have legally enshrined the *Rights of Nature* into their constitution, represent a broader movement toward recognizing nature as a legal entity with rights that must be protected. Such measures, derived from Indigenous worldviews, address climate change by preventing large-scale environmental degradation and safeguarding ecosystems that play a crucial role in climate regulation.

3.21.2 SDG 15: Life on Land and Biodiversity Conservation

SDG 15 calls for the protection, restoration and sustainable use of terrestrial ecosystems, including the sustainable management of forests, combatting desertification, halting and reversing land degradation and halting biodiversity loss. Indigenous communities worldwide have long been stewards of the land, using sustainable practices that maintain biodiversity and ecosystem health. The recognition of Indigenous governance over protected areas, such as the establishment of Indigenous Protected and Conserved Areas (IPCAs) in Canada, exemplifies how Indigenous-led conservation efforts directly contribute to SDG 15 [23]. IPCAs represent a legal mechanism that empowers Indigenous communities to co-manage land in partnership with government agencies, blending traditional ecological knowledge with modern conservation science. These areas not only protect critical habitats but also preserve the cultural and spiritual connections that Indigenous peoples have with the land. By giving legal recognition to Indigenous land management practices, IPCAs contribute to the global conservation agenda by preventing deforestation, protecting biodiversity and ensuring that ecosystems are sustainably managed for future generations. Another example is the Bishnoi community in India, whose protection of local wildlife and trees is based on spiritual beliefs dating back to the fifteenth century. The legal recognition of certain trees and animal species in Rajasthan as protected species reflects the integration of Indigenous conservation practices into national environmental policies. By incorporating these practices into national conservation laws, the government supports the sustainable management of ecosystems and helps to meet the targets of SDG 15.

3.21.3 SDG 16: Peace, Justice and Strong Institutions

SDG 16 emphasizes the importance of peace, justice and strong institutions, which are critical for achieving sustainable development. One of the key components of SDG 16 is ensuring access to justice for all, particularly for marginalized and vulnerable communities, including Indigenous peoples. Legal recognition of Indigenous governance, including the recognition of the Whanganui River in New Zealand as a legal person, exemplifies how Indigenous communities are asserting their rights through legal frameworks that promote environmental justice. This legal innovation, which grants the Whanganui River personhood and protects its rights through both Indigenous and state-led governance, not only enhances environmental conservation but also reinforces Indigenous sovereignty and self-determination. Such legal frameworks recognize that the preservation of Indigenous cultures and ecosystems is inseparable from broader efforts to promote peace, justice and strong institutions [24]. When Indigenous communities are empowered to manage their natural resources and assert their rights, they contribute to building more inclusive and just legal systems, which is essential for achieving SDG 16.

3.21.4 Convention on Biological Diversity (CBD) and Indigenous Contributions

The Convention on Biological Diversity (CBD) is an international treaty that aims to conserve biological diversity, ensure sustainable use of its components and share the benefits arising from genetic resources fairly. Indigenous communities have long been key players in conserving biodiversity through traditional knowledge and sustainable resource management practices. The CBD explicitly acknowledges the role of Indigenous knowledge in biodiversity conservation, and its integration into national policies is essential for achieving the objectives of the convention.

For instance, the CBD's 2010 Nagoya Protocol on Access and Benefit-sharing (ABS) recognizes the rights of Indigenous peoples to benefit from the use of their traditional knowledge related to genetic resources [25]. This framework ensures that Indigenous communities are not only recognized as key stakeholders in biodiversity conservation but are also compensated for the use of their knowledge and resources. The integration of Indigenous practices into the CBD framework highlights the importance of collaboration between Indigenous peoples, governments and the international community in achieving biodiversity targets, directly aligning with SDG 15.

3.21.5 The Paris Agreement and Indigenous Climate Solutions

The Paris Agreement, an international treaty aimed at limiting global warming to below 2 °C, also benefits from the integration of Indigenous knowledge systems. Indigenous communities, who are often the most affected by climate change, offer valuable insights into climate adaptation and mitigation strategies [26]. For example, Indigenous knowledge of land management, water conservation and ecosystem restoration plays a critical role in building climate resilience. By recognizing Indigenous practices in national climate action plans (NDCs), countries can contribute more effectively to the goals of the Paris Agreement. Australia's incorporation of Indigenous fire management practices into national bushfire mitigation strategies is one such example of how Indigenous knowledge can contribute to the goals of the Paris Agreement. These practices are aligned with the agreement's emphasis on climate adaptation and resilience, making them an essential part of the global effort to combat climate change.

3.21.6 *Harmonizing Local Traditions with Global Legal Frameworks*

In today's legal and environmental landscape, aligning Indigenous conservation practices with international legal instruments and the SDGs offers a pathway to more inclusive, sustainable environmental governance. The integration of Indigenous knowledge into global frameworks like the Paris Agreement, the CBD and the SDGs demonstrates how local, traditional practices can address global environmental challenges. By recognizing and respecting Indigenous rights and knowledge, legal systems not only foster effective conservation but also contribute to achieving broader global sustainability goals. Indigenous-led legal innovations, such as Ecuador's *Rights of Nature*, Australia's fire management practices and Canada's IPCAs, offer practical examples of how Indigenous knowledge can be harmonized with international protocols to address climate change, biodiversity loss and other critical environmental issues. This chapter provides a roadmap for policymakers, legal scholars and conservationists interested in integrating local traditions with global environmental governance, ensuring that the world's ecosystems are protected for future generations. By blending historical insights, cultural narratives and pragmatic legal strategies, this chapter offers a multidimensional approach to understanding conservation practices, making it an essential contribution to discussions on sustainable development and environmental justice. Indigenous populations, with their deep-rooted knowledge of local ecosystems and sustainable resource management practices, have long been at the forefront of conservation efforts. From the sacred groves in India to the Dreamtime stories of Aboriginal Australia, cultural traditions have played a vital role in maintaining environmental harmony. This chapter investigates the intersection of culture and law, considering how traditional ecological knowledge (TEK) has been recognized and codified within national and international legal frameworks.

Through a comparative lens, the chapter reviews key pieces of legislation across the globe, including India's Forest Rights Act, 2006; and Biological Diversity Act, 2002; Australia's Native Title Act, 1993; the United States' Indian Self-Determination and Education Assistance Act and New Zealand's Te Urewera Act, 2014 [27]. These laws illustrate a global shift toward recognizing indigenous land rights and cultural practices as integral to biodiversity conservation. They empower indigenous communities to actively participate in managing their ancestral lands and natural resources, often through co-management arrangements that blend traditional ecological practices with scientific approaches. The work also explores the role of international conventions such as the Convention on Biological Diversity (CBD) and the UNESCO World Heritage Convention, which have increasingly acknowledged the importance of traditional knowledge and the rights of indigenous peoples in global conservation efforts. By emphasizing the legal protection of cultural landscapes, sacred sites and traditional resource use practices, these frameworks promote the integration of indigenous perspectives into formal conservation law. This provides a comprehensive analysis of how legal dimensions of conservation practices are shifting globally, focusing on the critical intersection of indigenous rights, cultural beliefs and environmental protection, ultimately fostering a more inclusive approach to safeguarding the planet's biodiversity. Cultural beliefs and practices profoundly shape human interaction with the environment. Legal frameworks across the globe increasingly integrate cultural dimensions to promote sustainable conservation. This analysis explores how legislation, informed by rituals, folklore and indigenous cosmologies, addresses biodiversity conservation, sustainable resource use and ecosystem protection.

3.22 Cultural Beliefs and the Environment: Rituals as Conservation Catalysts

Across the globe, rituals rooted in cultural and spiritual beliefs have become powerful tools for environmental conservation. In India, the practice of worshiping sacred groves small patches of forest dedicated to deities prevents deforestation and safeguards biodiversity. For instance, the Khasi tribes in Meghalaya regard groves as sanctuaries of spiritual and ecological importance, where cutting trees or hunting is taboo [28]. These practices, often passed down through generations, embody unwritten laws of conservation, preserving not only the flora and fauna but also the cultural identity of the community. Similarly, in Ghana, the veneration of sacred lagoons by local communities restricts fishing during specific seasons, allowing fish populations to regenerate and ensuring sustainable livelihoods.

3.23 Folklore as Environmental Stewardship

Folklore often serves as a repository of ecological wisdom, guiding communities on sustainable resource use. Aboriginal Australians' Dreamtime stories, which describe the origins of the land and its creatures, instill a sense of responsibility to care for the environment. These stories are not merely narratives but environmental codes, emphasizing respect for water bodies, forests and wildlife [29]. For example, tales about the Rainbow Serpent, a creator figure, teach communities to protect freshwater ecosystems, framing water as sacred. In Africa, the San people of the Kalahari Desert share myths that discourage overhunting and promote the conservation of waterholes, vital resources in arid landscapes. Legal systems, inspired by such folklore, can integrate traditional ecological practices into formal policies to reinforce conservation goals.

3.24 Indigenous Cosmologies and Legal Innovations

Indigenous cosmologies often view nature as an interconnected web of relationships, fostering a deep respect for the environment. This worldview has influenced groundbreaking legal frameworks like New Zealand's **Te Awa Tupua Act, 2017** [30], which grants the Whanganui River legal personhood. By recognizing the river as a living ancestor, the law incorporates Māori cosmology into national governance, ensuring its protection through a guardianship model. Similarly, Bolivia's **Law of the Rights of Mother Earth, 2010**, reflects Andean cosmology, granting nature the right to exist, regenerate and evolve. These laws demonstrate how indigenous spiritual perspectives can inspire innovative conservation approaches.

3.25 Biodiversity Conservation Through Cultural-Legal Synthesis

Laws that blend cultural practices with conservation principles strengthen biodiversity protection efforts. In the Philippines, the **Indigenous Peoples' Rights Act, 1997**, recognizes ancestral domains and traditional knowledge, enabling indigenous communities to co-manage protected areas like the Cordillera mountain ranges [31]. This integration ensures the sustainable use of resources while preserving cultural heritage. Similarly, India's **Biological Diversity Act, 2002**, emphasizes the role of local knowledge systems in managing biodiversity-rich areas, promoting access and benefit-sharing to empower indigenous populations.

3.26 Sustainable Resource Use and Ecosystem Protection

Legal frameworks informed by cultural beliefs address the challenge of balancing resource use and conservation. Kenya's **Wildlife Conservation and Management Act, 2013**, incorporates traditional community practices in managing wildlife corridors, reducing human-wildlife conflict while protecting endangered species [32]. In the United States, co-management agreements, such as those with Native American tribes for Yellowstone National Park, blend traditional ecological knowledge with modern science to manage ecosystems sustainably. These examples highlight how cultural dimensions can enrich legal approaches, fostering coexistence and long-term ecosystem health.

3.27 Harmonizing Culture and Law

Incorporating cultural beliefs into legal frameworks not only strengthens conservation but also preserves the identity and wisdom of indigenous communities. By protecting rituals, folklore and cosmologies, these laws create a more inclusive environmental governance system that honors the symbiotic relationship between humans and nature. This harmony is essential for addressing global ecological challenges, ensuring that future generations inherit both vibrant cultures and thriving ecosystems.

3.28 Legislative Protection for Indigenous Populations in India: A Detailed Analysis

India's legislative framework for indigenous populations, often referred to as Scheduled Tribes (STs) is deeply rooted in the country's Constitution and legal system. These laws aim to protect the cultural, social and environmental heritage of indigenous communities, particularly in the context of biodiversity conservation and natural resource management. Below is a comprehensive analysis of the key legislative measures that support these communities and their practices, including sacred groves and biodiversity protection (Table 3.1).

3.28.1 Constitutional Provisions

The Indian Constitution explicitly recognizes the unique status and vulnerabilities of Scheduled Tribes, embedding safeguards for their welfare [33]. **Article 244** provides for the administration of tribal areas through the Fifth Schedule (mainland India) and Sixth Schedule (northeastern states), enabling autonomy in governance. **Article 46** directs the state to promote the educational and economic interests of STs, ensuring protection from social injustice and exploitation. **Article 338A** establishes the National Commission for Scheduled Tribes (NCST) to monitor safeguards and address grievances.

3.28.2 The Forest Rights Act (FRA), 2006 in Brief

Objective, Recognizes and vests forest rights in forest-dwelling Scheduled Tribes and other traditional forest communities. **Key Provisions**, Individual and Community Rights: Grants individual land rights for agriculture and community rights to manage, protect and conserve forests [34]. **Cultural Recognition**, Protects areas of

Table 3.1 Legislative protection

Category	Details
Constitutional provisions	**Article 244**: Administration of tribal areas via the Fifth and Sixth Schedules
	Article 46: Promotion of educational and economic interests of Scheduled Tribes (STs)
	Article 338A: Establishes the National Commission for Scheduled Tribes (NCST) for grievance redressal
The Forest Rights Act (FRA), 2006	**Individual & community rights**: Grants land for agriculture and community forest management
	Cultural recognition: Protects sacred groves and promotes sustainable use
	Impact: Strengthens indigenous biodiversity conservation
Biological Diversity Act, 2002	**Access & benefit-sharing (ABS)**: Equitable sharing of biodiversity benefits
	People's biodiversity registers (PBRs): Foster community participation
	Impact: Recognizes indigenous contributions to conservation
Panchayats (Extension to Scheduled Areas) Act (PESA), 1996	**Decentralized governance**: Empowers Gram Sabhas for resource management
	Protection: Preserves land, culture and sacred groves
	Impact: Legal framework for community resource protection
Environment Protection Act, 1986	**Environmental impact assessments (EIAs)**: Safeguards biodiversity-rich tribal areas
	Impact: Indirectly supports tribal cultural ecosystems
Strengths	**Cultural sensitivity**: Respect for sacred groves and traditions
	Decentralization: Empowers local governance
	Integration of knowledge: Promotes traditional ecological practices
Challenges	**Bureaucratic hurdles**: Resistance limits implementation
	Development conflicts: Encroachment by industrial projects
	Awareness issues: Limited knowledge of rights among communities

cultural and religious significance, such as sacred groves, ensuring their sustainable use and preservation. **Empowerment**, Forest-dwelling communities gain a voice in forest management, reducing conflicts with the Forest Department. **Impact**, FRA strengthens indigenous claims over biodiversity-rich landscapes, reinforcing conservation through traditional knowledge and practices.

3.28.3 Biological Diversity Act, 2002

Objective, Protects India's biodiversity while recognizing the role of local and indigenous communities in conservation. **Key Provisions**, Access and Benefit-Sharing (ABS), Ensures that benefits derived from biodiversity use are shared equitably with communities contributing to its conservation. People's Biodiversity Registers (PBRs), Document traditional ecological knowledge and practices, fostering community participation. **Biodiversity Management Committees (BMCs)**, Local bodies responsible for managing biodiversity at the grassroots level [35]. Impact, The Act acknowledges the contribution of indigenous communities to biodiversity conservation, ensuring their participation and benefits.

3.28.4 The Panchayats (Extension to Scheduled Areas) Act (PESA), 1996

Objective, extends the 73rd Constitutional Amendment to Scheduled Areas, empowering Gram Sabhas (village assemblies) in decision-making. **Key Provisions**, Decentralizes governance by recognizing community control over natural resources.

Empowers indigenous communities to protect cultural and ecological heritage, including sacred groves. Restricts exploitation of resources without community consent [36]. **Impact**, PESA provides tribal communities with a legal framework to safeguard their land, culture and resources from external pressures.

3.28.5 The Environment Protection Act, 1986

Objective, Provides a framework for protecting the environment, indirectly supporting the preservation of culturally significant ecosystems like sacred groves. **Key Provisions**, Mandates environmental impact assessments (EIAs) for industrial projects in biodiversity-rich tribal areas [37]. Protects fragile ecosystems critical to indigenous communities' livelihoods and cultural practices. **Impact**, While not specific to indigenous populations, it indirectly safeguards ecosystems integral to their heritage.

3.28.6 *The Scheduled Tribes and Other Traditional Forest Dwellers (Recognition of Forest Rights) Act, 2006*

This Act, often referred to as the Forest Rights Act, overlaps with conservation objectives by recognizing community rights over forest resources, including minor forest produce. Allowing community-managed conservation strategies that align with cultural values. Cultural Sensitivity, Laws like FRA and PESA respect the cultural and spiritual significance of landscapes, such as sacred groves, to indigenous communities. Decentralization, empowering local communities through PESA and BMCs ensures participatory governance. Integration of Traditional Knowledge, The Biological Diversity Act promotes the use of indigenous ecological practices in conservation. Legal Recognition of Rights, Tribal communities' land, forest and cultural rights are legally recognized, reducing conflicts with external stakeholders.

Challenges in Implementation. Bureaucratic Hurdles, Implementation of laws like FRA faces resistance from traditional forest governance systems, limiting their reach.

Conflicts with Development Projects, Industrial development often encroaches on tribal lands despite legal protections.

Lack of Awareness: Indigenous communities are often unaware of their legal rights, limiting their ability to assert them. Insufficient Benefit-Sharing, The ABS provisions under the Biological Diversity Act are not uniformly implemented, leading to inequitable distribution of benefits.

3.29 Case Studies

3.29.1 *Niyamgiri Hills, Odisha*

The Dongria Kondh tribe successfully opposed bauxite mining in the Niyamgiri Hills, leveraging FRA and PESA to assert their cultural and environmental rights.

3.29.2 *Sacred Groves in Meghalaya*

Khasi communities use traditional laws and cultural practices to protect sacred groves, which are biodiversity hotspots.

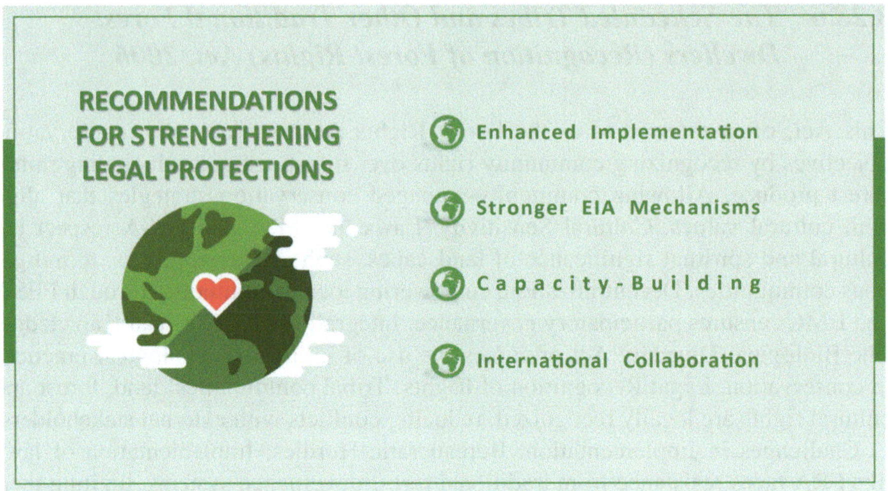

Fig. 3.2 Recommendations for strengthening legal protections

3.30 Recommendations for Strengthening Legal Protections

3.30.1 Enhanced Implementation

Strengthen grassroots capacity for implementing FRA and PESA through awareness campaigns and administrative support (Fig. 3.2).

3.30.2 Stronger EIA Mechanisms

Ensure stricter evaluation of projects impacting tribal lands and sacred ecosystems (Fig. 3.2).

3.30.3 Capacity-Building

Train local communities in legal and technical aspects of resource management (Fig. 3.2).

3.30.4 International Collaboration

Align domestic laws with global frameworks like the Convention on Biological Diversity to enhance resource and knowledge sharing (Fig. 3.2).

India's legislative efforts underscore the importance of cultural dimensions in conservation practices. Recognizing indigenous rights not only preserves biodiversity but also fosters sustainable development and social justice. For sacred groves and beyond, robust implementation and community empowerment remain key to achieving these goals.

3.31 Legislative Protection for Indigenous Populations in Australia: A Detailed Analysis

Australia's legal framework has evolved to recognize and protect the rights of its Indigenous populations, particularly Aboriginal and Torres Strait Islander peoples. These laws integrate traditional ecological knowledge with modern conservation efforts, promoting sustainable resource management and environmental stewardship. This analysis examines key legislation and its impact on the rights and cultural practices of Indigenous Australians (Table 3.2).

3.31.1 Constitutional Recognition and Challenges

Australia's Constitution initially ignored Indigenous Australians, but subsequent legal and political developments have sought to rectify this omission:

- **1967 Referendum**: Enabled the federal government to legislate on Indigenous issues and include them in the national census [38].
- **Uluru Statement from the Heart (2017)**: Called for constitutional recognition and a First Nations Voice to Parliament. While not yet legislated, it represents a crucial step in acknowledging Indigenous sovereignty [39].

3.31.2 Native Title Act, 1993

- **Objective**: Recognizes the traditional land rights of Aboriginal and Torres Strait Islander peoples, allowing them to claim ownership and use of ancestral lands [40].
- **Key Provisions**:
  - **Recognition of Native Title**: Confirms land rights under customary law where traditional connection can be proven.

Table 3.2 Legal frameworks and challenges for indigenous Australians

Aspect	Key details	Impact
Constitutional recognition	**1967 referendum**: Enabled legislation on Indigenous issues and inclusion in the census	Acknowledged Indigenous presence in national identity but requires further actions
	Uluru statement from the heart (2017): Called for constitutional recognition and First Nations Voice to Parliament	Yet to be legislated but symbolizes acknowledgment of Indigenous sovereignty
Native Title Act, 1993	**Objective**: Recognizes traditional land rights of aboriginal and Torres Strait Islander peoples	Restored land ownership; supported cultural and environmental practices
	Provisions: Recognition of native title, future acts regime, preservation of cultural practices	Enabled sustainable management of sacred sites like Uluru
EPBC Act, 1999	**Objective**: Protects environment and biodiversity with provisions for culturally significant sites	Empowers Indigenous-led conservation, recognizing sacred sites like Kakadu National Park
	Provisions: National heritage listing, indigenous protected areas, traditional knowledge inclusion	Indigenous communities manage over 50% of protected lands
Aboriginal Land Rights Act, 1976	**Objective**: Grants land ownership to aboriginal groups in the Northern Territory	Protected over 50% of NT lands; supported ecosystem conservation
	Provisions: Establishes land councils, recognizes sacred sites	Strengthened local governance for cultural and ecological preservation
Water rights and resource management	**Water Act, 2007**: Recognizes Indigenous water rights within the Murray-Darling Basin Plan	Promotes sustainable water use through Indigenous knowledge
Cultural heritage protection laws	**Objective**: Protects culturally significant sites from destruction or desecration	Prevents loss of sacred sites but requires stronger enforcement (e.g., Juukan Gorge incident)
	Provisions: State-based laws empower Indigenous management of heritage sites (e.g., QLD and VIC acts)	Preserves rock art and other significant cultural landmarks

(continued)

Table 3.2 (continued)

Aspect	Key details	Impact
Strengths of legal framework	Recognition of sovereignty, integration of traditional knowledge, cultural and environmental protection	Encourages Indigenous leadership in conservation and heritage protection
Challenges	High burden of proof for Native title claims, conflicts with industrial development, insufficient funding, lack of constitutional recognition	Limits full realization and enforcement of Indigenous rights

  - **Future Acts Regime**: Protects Native Title from being extinguished by future land use projects, requiring negotiation and compensation.
  - **Preservation of Cultural Practices**: Facilitates traditional ecological management, such as fire-stick farming.

- **Impact**:
  - Restored land ownership to Indigenous communities, allowing cultural and environmental practices to thrive.
  - Examples include the return of Uluru to the Anangu people, fostering a partnership for its sustainable management.

3.31.3 Environment Protection and Biodiversity Conservation Act, 1999 (EPBC Act) [41]

- **Objective**: Protects Australia's environment and biodiversity, with special provisions for culturally significant sites.
- **Key Provisions**:
  - **National Heritage Listing**: Protects Indigenous cultural sites of environmental importance, such as Kakadu National Park.
  - **Traditional Knowledge**: Encourages the incorporation of Indigenous ecological knowledge in environmental management.
  - **Indigenous Protected Areas (IPAs)**: Supports Indigenous-led conservation efforts, covering over 50% of Australia's protected lands.
- **Impact**:
  - Empowers Indigenous communities to lead conservation efforts.
  - Recognizes sacred sites, such as the Great Barrier Reef, which holds cultural significance for Torres Strait Islanders.

3.31.4 Aboriginal Land Rights (Northern Territory) Act, 1976

- **Objective**: Grants land ownership to Aboriginal groups in the Northern Territory, forming the foundation for land claim legislation across Australia [42].
- **Key Provisions**:
  - Establishes Land Councils to support Indigenous groups in managing their lands.
  - Recognizes sacred sites and prevents their exploitation.
- **Impact**:
  - Provided over 50% of the Northern Territory to Aboriginal groups.
  - Enabled communities to protect culturally significant ecosystems.

3.31.5 Water Rights and Natural Resource Management

- **Water Act, 2007**: Recognizes Indigenous rights to water, integrating cultural values into the Murray-Darling Basin Plan [43].
- **Impact**: Promotes the sustainable use of water resources by incorporating Indigenous knowledge of water management, critical for Australia's arid regions.

3.31.6 Cultural Heritage Protection Laws

- **Aboriginal and Torres Strait Islander Heritage Protection Act, 1984**: Safeguards culturally significant sites from destruction or desecration.
- **State-Based Legislation**:
  - Queensland's *Cultural Heritage Act, 2003* and Victoria's *Aboriginal Heritage Act, 2006* empower local Indigenous communities to manage and protect cultural sites [44].
- **Impact**:
  - Prevents the loss of sacred sites, such as rock art in the Kimberley region.
  - Highlights the need for stronger enforcement, as seen in the destruction of Juukan Gorge by mining operations in 2020.

3.31.7 *Strengths of Australia's Legal Framework*

1. **Recognition of Sovereignty**: Laws like the Native Title Act affirm Indigenous connections to land and culture.
2. **Integration of Traditional Knowledge**: Programs such as IPAs promote sustainable land management through Indigenous ecological practices.
3. **Cultural and Environmental Protection**: Legislation acknowledges the interdependence of cultural heritage and environmental conservation.

Challenges and Gaps in Implementation

1. **Proving Native Title**: The burden of proof remains high, requiring Indigenous groups to demonstrate continuous cultural connection to their lands.
2. **Conflicts with Development**: Mining and industrial projects often threaten Indigenous lands, as seen in the Juukan Gorge incident.
3. **Insufficient Funding**: Many Indigenous communities lack the resources to fully utilize legal protections.
4. **Lack of Constitutional Recognition**: The absence of formal constitutional recognition limits the enforceability of Indigenous rights.

3.32 Case Studies

Kakadu National Park: Managed jointly by the Mirarr people and the Australian government, Kakadu showcases successful integration of cultural and ecological conservation [45].

3.32.1 *A Joint Management Model of Cultural and Ecological Conservation*

Kakadu National Park, located in the Northern Territory of Australia, is one of the country's most significant protected areas, both ecologically and culturally. It is unique because of its joint management structure, which involves collaboration between the Mirarr people, the traditional owners of the land and the Australian government. This partnership is a model of how Indigenous knowledge and contemporary conservation efforts can be integrated to create a sustainable management system that benefits both cultural preservation and biodiversity conservation. Kakadu's success as a joint management area demonstrates the potential of combining Indigenous stewardship with modern conservation science to protect and maintain valuable ecosystems and cultural heritage.

3.32.2 *Historical Context and Traditional Knowledge of the Mirarr People*

The Mirarr people have lived in the region now known as Kakadu for thousands of years, holding an intricate understanding of the local ecosystems, flora, fauna and natural cycles. Their cultural practices, which include hunting, fishing and fire management, are deeply tied to the land and have been passed down through generations. These practices not only help preserve biodiversity but also maintain the health of the ecosystem. Historically, the Mirarr people, like many Indigenous communities, managed the land through a system of customary laws and traditions that were highly effective in maintaining the ecological balance of the region.

However, during the twentieth century, much of Kakadu's land was appropriated by the Australian government for mining and other development projects, leading to significant environmental degradation and cultural disruption. The history of land dispossession and the subsequent need for land rights and cultural recognition played a crucial role in the development of the joint management model that exists today.

3.32.3 *The Establishment of Joint Management*

Kakadu National Park was officially established in 1981, and the joint management agreement between the Mirarr people and the Australian government was formalized in 1991 through the Kakadu National Park Management Plan [46]. The agreement acknowledges the Mirarr people's role as traditional custodians of the land and their rights to participate in decision-making processes regarding the park's management. This legal recognition of the Mirarr people's rights, alongside the establishment of a governance framework, was critical in ensuring that both cultural and ecological values were prioritized in the park's conservation efforts. The joint management structure includes a board made up of representatives from both the Mirarr people and the Australian government, which oversees the park's governance. This system facilitates the sharing of knowledge and resources between the government and the Mirarr people, ensuring that cultural values are respected while also applying modern scientific techniques to ecological management.

3.32.4 *Cultural and Ecological Conservation: The Intersection*

The core strength of the joint management system in Kakadu lies in its ability to blend the cultural knowledge of the Mirarr people with modern ecological conservation strategies. The Mirarr people's traditional ecological knowledge (TEK), particularly their understanding of fire management, plant species and animal migration, is utilized to help maintain the park's biodiversity. For example, the practice of controlled burns, known as *fire-stick* farming has been integral in preventing larger, uncontrolled bushfires and promoting the regeneration of native vegetation [47]. This traditional method aligns with modern fire management techniques used to protect ecosystems in fire-prone areas. In addition, the Mirarr people contribute their knowledge of the park's wetlands, rivers and other natural features, which aids in water and land management practices. This integration of cultural and ecological knowledge helps protect the park's diverse ecosystems, which are home to a vast array of species, including the saltwater crocodile, several bird species and numerous plants that are of cultural significance to the Mirarr people.

3.32.5 Successes and Challenges of Joint Management

Kakadu National Park has been recognized internationally as a UNESCO World Heritage site due to its ecological significance and cultural heritage. The success of the joint management arrangement can be seen in the park's biodiversity conservation efforts and the strengthening of Indigenous cultural practices. The park's wetlands, for example, have been preserved through joint management practices that incorporate both scientific monitoring and traditional knowledge, helping maintain the health of the region's complex water systems [48]. Moreover, the park has become a model for Indigenous-led tourism, where the Mirarr people have been able to share their cultural heritage with visitors, providing a source of income and fostering cultural pride. This tourism model benefits from the deep connection that the Mirarr people have to the land, enriching visitors' understanding of the importance of conservation from a cultural perspective. However, challenges persist. The park's management is still subject to external pressures, including mining interests and the impacts of climate change. While the joint management framework ensures that the Mirarr people have a voice in decision-making, conflicts can arise when economic interests clash with conservation priorities. Furthermore, ensuring that Indigenous knowledge is adequately integrated into scientific research and that it is respected in legal and policy decisions remains an ongoing struggle.

3.32.6 A Model for the Future

Kakadu National Park exemplifies the potential for integrating Indigenous knowledge with modern conservation strategies through a joint management model. This collaboration has not only contributed to the preservation of Kakadu's ecological and cultural values but also empowered the Mirarr people to take an active role in managing their ancestral lands. The park's success provides valuable lessons for other regions and communities around the world, showcasing how Indigenous sovereignty and ecological sustainability can be harmonized. Moving forward, Kakadu stands as a testament to the power of collaborative conservation models that recognize the importance of both cultural and environmental stewardship. The park's ongoing management will continue to serve as a vital example of how legal frameworks can integrate Indigenous knowledge into global conservation efforts.

3.33 Rangers Programs

Indigenous ranger groups across Australia, such as the Wunambal Gaambera people in the Kimberley, use traditional fire management to prevent wildfires and protect biodiversity [49].

3.33.1 Indigenous Ranger Programs in Australia: Traditional Fire Management and Biodiversity Protection

Indigenous ranger programs have become a cornerstone of conservation efforts in Australia, blending traditional knowledge and modern scientific approaches. These programs empower Indigenous communities to manage their ancestral lands and protect biodiversity using time-honored practices such as traditional fire management [50]. One standout example is the Wunambal Gaambera people in the Kimberley region, who have successfully implemented traditional fire management to prevent wildfires and maintain ecosystem health. These programs not only foster environmental protection but also provide economic and cultural benefits to Indigenous communities, ensuring the intergenerational transmission of knowledge and stewardship practices.

3.33.2 Traditional Fire Management as a Conservation Tool

Traditional fire management, also known as "cool burning," is a central practice used by the Wunambal Gaambera people in the Kimberley. This method involves setting controlled, low-intensity fires during the cooler months to prevent the build-up of dense vegetation that can fuel destructive wildfires during the hotter months. The practice is deeply rooted in Indigenous ecological knowledge, which views fire as a tool for maintaining balance in the landscape. By controlling the timing, intensity and location of burns, the Wunambal Gaambera people manage the land in a way that promotes regeneration and biodiversity, while minimizing the risk of catastrophic fires that could devastate ecosystems. The key benefit of traditional fire management is its ability to reduce the severity of wildfires, which are increasingly becoming more frequent and intense due to climate change. By implementing regular low-intensity burns, Indigenous ranger groups like the Wunambal Gaambera can prevent large-scale, high-temperature fires that destroy habitats, disrupt biodiversity and pose risks to human life and property [51]. This practice not only protects the land but also ensures the continued availability of resources for local communities.

3.33.3 The Role of Indigenous Knowledge in Biodiversity Protection

Beyond wildfire prevention, traditional fire management is integral to the conservation of biodiversity in the Kimberley region. Many plant and animal species in the region are adapted to fire-prone environments, relying on periodic burns to regenerate or create new habitats. For example, certain plant species require fire to trigger the release of seeds, while animals like birds, reptiles and mammals benefit from the regrowth of vegetation that follows a burn. By using fire as a regenerative tool, the Wunambal Gaambera people maintain a healthy, diverse ecosystem that supports both cultural and ecological well-being. This biodiversity is crucial not only for local communities but also for the overall health of the landscape. The controlled burns help to maintain a mosaic of different habitats, promoting a variety of species and ensuring that the land continues to support the rich cultural and ecological resources upon which Indigenous communities depend.

3.33.4 Integration of Traditional Practices with Modern Conservation Approaches

The Wunambal Gaambera peoples' use of traditional fire management is not isolated from contemporary conservation efforts. Rather, it is an integrated approach that combines the knowledge of Indigenous elders with modern scientific research. These ranger programs, supported by initiatives such as the Australian Government's Indigenous Protected Areas (IPA) program, receive funding and resources to facilitate the implementation of traditional practices alongside modern ecological monitoring techniques. This integration ensures that conservation efforts are grounded in a deep understanding of local ecosystems while benefiting from the latest ecological research and technological advancements. For instance, modern fire management techniques, such as satellite technology and fire behavior modeling, are used to support the planning and monitoring of burns. These tools help determine the optimal timing and location of burns, enhancing the effectiveness of traditional fire management practices. The collaboration between Indigenous knowledge keepers and ecological scientists creates a holistic conservation model that respects cultural practices while ensuring the health of the ecosystem.

3.33.5 Cultural and Economic Benefits

Indigenous ranger programs also offer significant cultural and economic benefits to local communities. For the Wunambal Gaambera people, the ranger program serves as a vehicle for passing down traditional ecological knowledge to younger generations. In a time when many Indigenous practices risk being lost, these programs create opportunities for cultural revitalization and intergenerational knowledge transfer. Young people are trained as rangers, gaining practical skills in land management, conservation science and fire management while also learning about their cultural heritage. Economically, these programs provide employment opportunities in remote and rural areas, where jobs may be scarce. Rangers are often employed by both Indigenous organizations and government agencies, which fund the ranger programs to ensure the continuation of conservation work. These programs not only create jobs but also allow Indigenous communities to retain control over their lands and natural resources, providing economic self-sufficiency while also fostering cultural pride and autonomy.

3.33.6 Impact on the Kimberley Region's Biodiversity and Future Prospects

The Wunambal Gaambera peoples' ranger program has had a measurable impact on the biodiversity and ecological health of the Kimberley region. Through their traditional fire management, the Wunambal Gaambera have significantly reduced the occurrence of large-scale wildfires, thus protecting critical habitats and species. Their work has also been integral in the preservation of endangered species, such as the Northern Hairy-nosed Wombat, which relies on specific habitats that are carefully managed using traditional ecological practices [52]. Looking ahead, the success of Indigenous ranger programs like the Wunambal Gaambera's offers a promising model for expanding Indigenous-led conservation efforts across Australia and globally. These programs demonstrate that traditional knowledge, when combined with modern scientific tools, can provide effective solutions to some of the most pressing environmental challenges of our time, such as climate change, biodiversity loss and habitat degradation.

Indigenous ranger programs, particularly those led by the Wunambal Gaambera people, represent a successful fusion of traditional ecological knowledge and modern conservation practices. By using traditional fire management techniques, these programs not only help prevent wildfires but also protect biodiversity and ensure the health of the land. Furthermore, they empower Indigenous communities economically and culturally by providing employment opportunities and fostering cultural revitalization. As these programs continue to grow, they offer a valuable model for sustainable land management that integrates traditional wisdom with contemporary scientific practices, demonstrating the effectiveness of Indigenous-led conservation in addressing global environmental challenges.

3.34 Recommendations for Strengthening Indigenous Protections

3.34.1 Enhance Legal Frameworks

Amend the Native Title Act to reduce the burden of proof and expand protections against industrial exploitation.

3.34.2 Constitutional Recognition

Enact constitutional reforms to formally acknowledge Indigenous sovereignty and rights.

3.34.3 Expand Indigenous Protected Areas

Increase funding for IPAs, enabling more communities to lead conservation efforts.

3.34.4 Improve Consultation Processes

Strengthen mechanisms to ensure free, prior and informed consent for development projects affecting Indigenous lands.

Australia's legislative measures have significantly advanced Indigenous rights and environmental conservation. By integrating Aboriginal cosmologies and traditional practices into legal frameworks, these laws promote sustainable management and cultural preservation. However, ongoing challenges require legislative reform, better enforcement and greater investment to fully realize Indigenous sovereignty and ecological stewardship.

3.35 Australia: Aboriginal Cosmologies and Native Title

Cultural Practice: Aboriginal communities view land as sacred, interwoven with Dreamtime stories that govern resource use and conservation ethics.

Legislation, the Native Title Act, 1993 allows Aboriginal groups to claim rights over ancestral lands, enabling them to practice traditional ecological management [53]. Additionally, the Environment Protection and Biodiversity Conservation Act, 1999 includes provisions for culturally significant sites.

Impact: Legal recognition of Aboriginal knowledge systems has empowered communities to safeguard ecosystems through traditional fire management and sustainable practices.

3.36 Legislative Protection for Indigenous Populations in the United States: A Detailed Analysis

In the United States, Native American tribes are recognized as sovereign entities with inherent rights over their lands and resources. This legal recognition enables tribes to govern their territories, preserve cultural practices and contribute to environmental conservation [54]. The legislative framework combines federal laws, treaties and tribal self-governance initiatives, fostering a collaborative approach to resource management and cultural preservation.

3.37 Tribal Sovereignty: Foundations and Framework

Tribal sovereignty underpins Indigenous rights in the U.S., granting tribes authority over their lands, governance systems and cultural practices.

- **Doctrine of Tribal Sovereignty**: Affirmed by court cases like *Cherokee Nation v. Georgia (1831)*, recognizing tribes as "domestic dependent nations" [55].
- **Trust Relationship**: The U.S. federal government holds tribal lands in trust, with a fiduciary duty to protect Indigenous interests.

3.38 Key Federal Legislation Supporting Indigenous Rights

See Table 3.3.

Table 3.3 Key federal legislation

Act	Objective	Key provisions	Impact
Indian Self-Determination and Education Assistance Act (ISDEAA), 1975	Promotes tribal autonomy by allowing tribes to manage federal programs on education, health and natural resources	• Enables tribes to enter self-determination contracts with federal agencies like the Bureau of Indian Affairs (BIA) and U.S. Forest Service • Supports integration of traditional ecological knowledge (TEK) in environmental management	Empowers tribes to independently manage resources, fostering culturally sensitive conservation strategies
National Historic Preservation Act (NHPA), 1966	Protects cultural heritage sites, including those of significance to Native American tribes	• Establishes the Tribal Historic Preservation Officer (THPO) role, enabling tribes to oversee heritage sites on their lands • Requires federal agencies to consult tribes on projects affecting sacred sites	Preserves culturally significant landscapes, such as the Bears Ears National Monument, holding spiritual importance for multiple tribes
Native American Graves Protection and Repatriation Act (NAGPRA), 1990	Ensures the return of ancestral remains and sacred artifacts to tribes		Protects burial grounds and strengthens cultural identity by returning significant cultural items to tribal communities
Clean Water Act (CWA), 1972 & Clean Air Act (CAA), 1963	Allows tribes to establish water and air quality standards on their lands, recognizing Indigenous environmental management		Enhances tribal capacity to address pollution and protect natural resources

3.38.1 Indian Self-Determination and Education Assistance Act (ISDEAA), 1975

- **Objective**: Promotes tribal autonomy by allowing tribes to manage federal programs on education, health and natural resources.
- **Key Provisions**:

  - Enables tribes to enter self-determination contracts with federal agencies like the Bureau of Indian Affairs (BIA) and the U.S. Forest Service.
  - Supports the integration of traditional ecological knowledge (TEK) in environmental management.

- **Impact**: Empowers tribes to independently manage resources, fostering culturally sensitive conservation strategies [56].

3.38.2 National Historic Preservation Act (NHPA), 1966

- **Objective**: Protects cultural heritage sites, including those of significance to Native American tribes [57].
- **Key Provisions**:
  - Establishes the Tribal Historic Preservation Officer (THPO) role, enabling tribes to oversee heritage sites on their lands.
  - Requires federal agencies to consult tribes on projects affecting sacred sites.
- **Impact**: Preserves culturally significant landscapes, such as the Bears Ears National Monument, which holds spiritual importance for multiple tribes.

3.38.3 Native American Graves Protection and Repatriation Act (NAGPRA), 1990

- **Objective**: Ensures the return of ancestral remains and sacred artifacts to tribes.
- **Impact**: Protects burial grounds and strengthens cultural identity by returning significant cultural items to tribal communities [58].

3.38.4 Clean Water Act (CWA), 1972 & Clean Air Act (CAA), 1963

- **Provisions for Tribes**: Allows tribes to establish water and air quality standards on their lands, recognizing Indigenous environmental management [59].
- **Impact**: Enhances tribal capacity to address pollution and protect natural resources.

3.39 Co-management of Natural Resources

3.39.1 Yellowstone National Park (and Other Federal Lands)

- **Co-Management Agreements**: Tribes collaborate with federal agencies to manage resources using both traditional and scientific methods.
- **Key Example**: The Nez Perce tribe's role in managing bison in Yellowstone National Park [60].
- **Impact**: Protects wildlife while upholding Indigenous practices, such as subsistence hunting and controlled burns.

3.39.2 Alaska Native Claims Settlement Act (ANCSA), 1971

- **Objective**: Granted land and monetary compensation to Alaska Native corporations, enabling them to manage resources.
- **Impact**: Promoted tribal stewardship over vast ecosystems, balancing development with conservation [61].

3.40 Sacred Lands and Environmental Justice

3.40.1 Bears Ears National Monument

- **Cultural Significance**: Sacred to the Hopi, Zuni, Ute and Navajo tribes.
- **Legal Recognition**: President Obama designated it as a national monument in 2016, incorporating Indigenous co-management [62].
- **Challenges**: Subsequent reductions under the Trump administration sparked lawsuits, emphasizing the tension between conservation and political interests.
- **Current Status**: Restored by President Biden in 2021, reaffirming Indigenous voices in land management.

3.40.2 Environmental Justice Framework

- **Executive Order 12,898 (1994)**: Acknowledges the disproportionate environmental burdens on Indigenous and minority communities, mandating agencies to consider tribal impacts in decision-making [63].

3.41 Integration of Traditional Ecological Knowledge (TEK)

- **What is TEK?** A body of knowledge, practices and beliefs developed by Indigenous peoples through interactions with their environment.
- **Applications**:
  - Controlled burns by tribes like the Karuk in California to prevent wildfires.
  - Sustainable fisheries management by the Lummi Nation in the Pacific Northwest.
- **Legislative Support**: TEK is increasingly incorporated into federal conservation programs, enhancing biodiversity and climate resilience.

3.42 Case Studies: Success and Challenges

3.42.1 Success Stories

3.42.1.1 Salmon Restoration

The Yakama Nation's leadership in restoring salmon populations in the Columbia River showcases the effective blend of TEK and science [64].

3.42.1.2 Coastal Resilience

The Chugach Alaska Corporation integrates traditional knowledge in managing marine ecosystems, benefiting biodiversity and local economies [65].

3.42.2 Ongoing Challenges

3.42.2.1 Pipeline Projects

Tribes like the Standing Rock Sioux oppose projects like the Dakota Access Pipeline, citing threats to water resources and sacred lands [60].

3.42.2.2 Jurisdictional Conflicts

Overlapping state, federal and tribal authorities can complicate resource management.

3.43 Strengths of U.S. Legislative Framework

3.43.1 Recognition of Sovereignty

Laws like ISDEAA and NHPA empower tribes to manage their resources and protect cultural heritage.

3.43.2 Incorporation of TEK

Enhances conservation outcomes by valuing Indigenous knowledge systems.

3.43.3 Environmental Justice

Ensures tribal perspectives are included in federal decision-making processes.

3.44 Recommendations for Strengthening Protections

3.44.1 Stronger Enforcement Mechanisms

Enhance the enforcement of laws like NHPA to prevent desecration of sacred sites.

3.44.2 Expanded Funding

Provide resources for tribal capacity-building in resource management and environmental advocacy.

3.44.3 Enhanced Co-management

Broaden co-management agreements to cover more federal lands and waters.

3.44.4 Climate Change Adaptation

Support tribal-led climate resilience initiatives, incorporating TEK for sustainable solutions.

The United States has made significant strides in protecting Indigenous rights and integrating cultural practices into environmental conservation. However, challenges like jurisdictional disputes, underfunding and environmental injustices persist. Strengthening legislative frameworks and fostering collaborative governance will be crucial in ensuring that Native American tribes continue to thrive as stewards of their ancestral lands and natural resources.

3.45 United States: Tribal Sovereignty and Environmental Management

Cultural Practice, Native American tribes often view natural resources as integral to cultural identity, leading to practices such as controlled burns and wildlife protection.

Legislation, The Indian Self-Determination and Education Assistance Act, 1975 and co-management agreements like those for Yellowstone National Park, allow tribes to integrate traditional knowledge into environmental management. The National Historic Preservation Act, 1966 also protects culturally significant natural sites.

Impact, Legal frameworks ensure that tribal perspectives shape conservation strategies, blending traditional practices with scientific approaches.

3.46 Legislative Protection for Indigenous Populations in Brazil: A Detailed Analysis

Brazil is home to a diverse array of Indigenous communities, many of whom inhabit the Amazon rainforest, a critical global ecosystem [66]. These communities rely on traditional knowledge and practices to live sustainably while protecting biodiversity. The Brazilian Constitution and associated laws have recognized Indigenous rights and their role in conservation, but challenges in enforcement and political resistance have hampered their effectiveness.

3.46.1 Legal Framework for Indigenous Rights in Brazil

3.46.1.1 The Brazilian Constitution of 1988

The 1988 Constitution marks a pivotal moment in recognizing Indigenous rights, emphasizing their cultural autonomy and territorial protections [67].

- **Key Provisions**:
  - **Article 231**:

    Recognizes Indigenous peoples' rights to their traditional lands, stating these are "inalienable and indisposable."
    Mandates that Indigenous lands must be demarcated by the federal government.
  - **Article 232**:

    Empowers Indigenous groups to legally defend their rights in Brazilian courts.
- **Cultural Rights**: The Constitution upholds Indigenous peoples' cultural heritage and their role in safeguarding the environment.

3.46.1.2 Indigenous and Tribal Peoples Convention (ILO Convention 169)

- **Ratification**: Brazil ratified this international treaty in 2002 [68].
- **Provisions**:
  - Protects Indigenous land rights and cultural identity.
  - Mandates free, prior and informed consent (FPIC) before projects affecting Indigenous lands.

3.46.1.3 Statute of the Indigenous Peoples (Statute 6.001, 1973)

- Provides a legal framework for the protection and promotion of Indigenous rights, although it predates the progressive changes of the 1988 Constitution [69].

3.46.1.4 Environmental Laws

- **Forest Code (2012)**: Establishes legal protections for native vegetation, requiring landowners to conserve a percentage of forests, especially in the Amazon [70].
- **National System of Conservation Units (SNUC, 2000)**: Includes Indigenous territories within conservation areas, recognizing their role as guardians of biodiversity [71].

3.46.2 Role of Indigenous Territories in Conservation

- **Extent**: Indigenous territories cover over 13% of Brazil's land, primarily in the Amazon.
- **Conservation Impact**:
  - Studies show that deforestation rates in Indigenous territories are significantly lower compared to other areas.
  - Traditional ecological knowledge (TEK) promotes sustainable use of resources and biodiversity protection.

Examples of Indigenous-Led Conservation:

- **Kayapo Tribe**: Protect millions of hectares of rainforest using TEK and alliances with NGOs.
- **Yanomami Territory**: One of the largest protected Indigenous areas, preserving critical ecosystems in the Amazon.

3.46.3 Challenges in Enforcement

3.46.3.1 Land Demarcation

- **Progress**: As of 2023, over 700 Indigenous territories have been demarcated [72].
- **Challenges**:
  - Lengthy and bureaucratic processes delay demarcation, leaving communities vulnerable to land invasions.
  - Political resistance, particularly under administrations prioritizing industrial and agricultural expansion, has stalled new demarcations.

3.46.3.2 Illegal Activities

- **Deforestation and Mining**:
  - **Impact**: Over 20% of Amazon deforestation occurs in Indigenous territories, driven by illegal logging, mining and cattle ranching [73].
  - **Key Example**: Illegal gold mining in the Yanomami territory has led to environmental degradation and health crises.
- **Weak Enforcement**: Environmental agencies like IBAMA face budget cuts and political interference, weakening their ability to combat these activities [74].

3.46.3.3 Industrial and Agricultural Expansion

- **Bolsonaro Administration (2019–2022)**:
  - Rolled back environmental protections and weakened Indigenous rights, favoring agribusiness and infrastructure projects.
  - Proposed legislation sought to open Indigenous lands to mining and energy projects without their consent [75].
- **Lula Administration (2023–present)**:
  - Promised to strengthen Indigenous rights and combat deforestation but faces significant opposition from powerful agribusiness lobbies [76].

3.46.4 Judicial Interventions and Advocacy

- **Supreme Federal Court (STF)**:
  - Key decisions have upheld Indigenous land rights, including blocking legislation that sought to limit land demarcations based on the "timeframe thesis" (*marco temporal*), which argued that tribes could only claim lands they occupied in 1988 [77].
- **Indigenous Advocacy Groups**:
  - Organizations like APIB (Articulation of Indigenous Peoples of Brazil) play a crucial role in mobilizing resistance against rights violations and environmental exploitation [78].

3.46.5 International Recognition and Support

- **Amazon Fund**: Supported by countries like Norway and Germany, the fund promotes sustainable development and Indigenous-led conservation in the Amazon.
- **UNDRIP (United Nations Declaration on the Rights of Indigenous Peoples)**: While non-binding, it provides an international framework advocating for Indigenous rights, influencing Brazil's policies and advocacy efforts.

Fig. 3.3 Recommendations for strengthening indigenous rights

3.46.6 Recommendations for Strengthening Indigenous Rights

3.46.6.1 Accelerate Land Demarcation

Streamline bureaucratic processes and ensure adequate funding for demarcation efforts (Fig. 3.3).

3.46.6.2 Enhance Enforcement Mechanisms

Strengthen agencies like IBAMA and FUNAI (National Foundation for Indigenous Peoples) to combat illegal activities effectively (Fig. 3.3) [68].

3.46.6.3 Protect Indigenous Leaders

Address threats and violence against Indigenous activists, who face increasing attacks from illegal loggers and miners (Fig. 3.3).

3.46.6.4 Support Sustainable Livelihoods

Invest in eco-friendly initiatives that provide economic benefits to Indigenous communities, reducing dependence on harmful activities (Fig. 3.3).

3.46.6.5 Promote Indigenous Participation

Ensure Indigenous representation in decision-making bodies at local, national and international levels (Fig. 3.3).

Brazil's legislative framework recognizes the critical role of Indigenous communities in conserving the Amazon and preserving cultural heritage. However, persistent challenges in enforcement, political resistance and economic pressures undermine these protections. Strengthening legal mechanisms, ensuring adequate funding and empowering Indigenous leadership are essential steps to secure both Indigenous rights and the ecological future of the Amazon rainforest.

3.46.7 Brazil: Indigenous Land Rights and the Amazon

Cultural Practice, Amazonian tribes rely on folklore and cosmologies that emphasize living in harmony with nature. Legislation, the Brazilian Constitution of 1988 recognizes indigenous rights to traditional lands and protects these areas under environmental laws. However, enforcement remains a challenge amidst increasing deforestation and industrial pressure. Impact, legal provisions have supported indigenous-led conservation but require stronger implementation mechanisms to combat exploitation.

3.47 Legislative Protection for Indigenous Populations in New Zealand: A Detailed Analysis

New Zealand is home to the Māori, the indigenous people whose cosmology and cultural practices are deeply entwined with the natural world. Māori views of nature go beyond ecological management; they are grounded in a spiritual and ancestral connection to the land, water and all living beings. This worldview has shaped New Zealand's evolving legal landscape, particularly regarding the rights of nature and the protection of Māori cultural and environmental interests [79]. Notably, the country has pioneered groundbreaking legal reforms that recognize natural entities as legal persons, incorporating Māori cosmological beliefs into national law.

3.47.1 Māori Cosmology and Environmental Stewardship

Māori cosmology (or *Te Ao Māori*) sees the natural world as a living, interconnected entity. Rivers, forests, mountains and other natural features are regarded as ancestors (*tipuna*), whose well-being is intrinsically linked to the Māori people's identity, culture and spiritual practices. Central to this belief is the concept of *kaitiakitanga*, or guardianship, which emphasizes an ethical duty to protect and preserve the environment for future generations. This worldview fosters an ethic of care, with Māori communities actively engaging in environmental management through practices such as controlled burning, fishing regulations and sustainable farming [80]. However, for these practices to be effective, legal recognition of their cultural and spiritual connection to nature is essential.

3.47.2 Key Legislation Protecting Māori Interests and Recognizing the Legal Personhood of Nature

Over the past few decades, New Zealand has made significant strides in legally recognizing Māori perspectives and their role in environmental conservation, especially through the concept of *legal personhood* for natural features.

3.47.2.1 The Te Urewera Act, 2014

- **Cultural Context**: The Te Urewera region is sacred to the Tūhoe iwi (tribe), who consider the forest to be an ancestral entity. For centuries, the Māori have protected it through sustainable land use practices rooted in their worldview [81].
- **Legal Impact**:
  - The **Te Urewera Act** formally granted **Te Urewera** (a large forested area in the North Island) the status of a **legal person**.
  - This was a groundbreaking law that recognized the forest as a living entity with its own rights, allowing it to be represented in court, making decisions for its protection.
  - The Act also created the **Te Urewera Board**, consisting of both Tūhoe representatives and government officials, who manage the land in line with both Māori cultural values and legal frameworks.
  - **Key Provisions**:

    The forest is now regarded as a legal person with rights, duties and responsibilities, much like a corporation or individual.

    This status ensures the forest's protection and management in line with Tūhoe values, including maintaining the ecosystem and fostering sustainable practices.

3.47.2.2 The Te Awa Tupua Act, 2017 [82]

- **Cultural Context**: The **Whanganui River** is an essential part of Māori cosmology, considered an ancestor by the iwi of the region. The Māori people view themselves as descendants of the river, with a deep spiritual, physical and cultural connection to it.
- **Legal Impact**:
  - The **Te Awa Tupua Act** granted the **Whanganui River** the legal status of a **person**, marking another landmark achievement in New Zealand's legal recognition of the rights of nature.
  - The law legally recognized the river's personhood, allowing it to be represented in legal matters and providing for its protection according to Māori values.
  - **Key Provisions**:

    The river is now a "legal entity" and has rights, including the right to be protected and maintained.

    A **guardianship arrangement** was established, involving both Māori (the Whanganui iwi) and the New Zealand government, to ensure the river's care and to make decisions regarding its management.

    This arrangement ensures that decisions about the river's use, such as for hydroelectricity or other industrial purposes, must align with the river's health and Māori values.

3.47.2.3 Treaty of Waitangi (Te Tiriti o Waitangi), 1840

- **Historical Context**: The Treaty of Waitangi was signed between the British Crown and Māori chiefs in 1840, establishing a formal relationship and recognizing Māori rights to land, resources and self-governance [83].
- **Modern Relevance**:
  - The **Treaty of Waitangi** is still central to Māori legal rights today. In the context of environmental law, it has been invoked to ensure that Māori have a say in how natural resources are managed and protected.
  - The Treaty continues to influence environmental governance, especially in the recognition of Māori customs, practices and values in the management of natural resources.

3.47.3 Impact and Global Implications of Legal Personhood for Nature

The legal personhood status granted to Te Urewera and the Whanganui River is innovative, not only within New Zealand but globally. These laws bridge cultural beliefs with legal frameworks, creating a model that intertwines human rights, environmental protection and cultural integrity.

Key Impacts:

- **Cultural Preservation**: By legally recognizing the spiritual and ancestral significance of natural features, these laws ensure the continuation of Māori cultural practices and identity.
- **Enhanced Stewardship**: The **Te Urewera Act** and the **Te Awa Tupua Act** have provided a legal framework for Māori stewardship over their ancestral lands and waters, ensuring that Māori values and traditional ecological knowledge shape conservation practices.
- **Legal Precedents**: These laws set legal precedents for other nations seeking to recognize the rights of nature or integrate Indigenous knowledge systems into environmental governance.
- **International Attention**: Countries around the world, including those with Indigenous populations, have looked to New Zealand's innovative legal reforms as a model for environmental conservation and Indigenous rights.

Challenges:

- **Enforcement and Implementation**: While these laws are revolutionary, their implementation requires ongoing efforts from both government bodies and Māori communities to ensure that the rights of Te Urewera and the Whanganui River are protected in practice.
- **Commercial Interests**: Balancing the interests of commercial development with the rights of nature and Indigenous peoples remains a challenge. For example, the implementation of the Te Awa Tupua Act has required careful negotiations to balance development needs with the river's environmental health.

3.47.4 Broader Implications for Conservation and Indigenous Rights

The recognition of legal personhood for Te Urewera and the Whanganui River offers a **new paradigm** for integrating Indigenous worldviews into environmental law. These legal reforms present a holistic approach that values both ecological integrity and the cultural connection between Indigenous peoples and the land.

Global Models:

- **Other Countries**: New Zealand's approach is being discussed as a model in other countries with significant Indigenous populations, such as Canada, Australia and the United States, for integrating Indigenous legal traditions with national legal systems.

- **Future Developments**: The success of these initiatives may pave the way for further legal recognition of nature's rights globally, contributing to a broader movement to protect ecosystems as entities in their own right.

New Zealand's legislative framework, particularly the **Te Urewera Act** and **Te Awa Tupua Act**, represents a bold and innovative integration of Māori cultural values into the legal system. By granting legal personhood to nature, these laws not only protect the environment but also respect and affirm Māori cultural and spiritual relationships with the land and waters. These reforms create a model for other nations to explore as they seek to balance Indigenous rights with environmental conservation, fostering a deeper, more sustainable relationship with the natural world.

3.47.5 New Zealand: Māori Cosmology and Legal Personhood of Nature

Cultural Practice, Māori cosmology views rivers and mountains as ancestors, fostering an ethic of care and stewardship. Legislation, The Te Urewera Act, 2014 and Te Awa Tupua Act, 2017, grant legal personhood to the Te Urewera forest and Whanganui River, respectively. This status allows them to be represented legally, ensuring their protection in line with Māori values. Impact, These groundbreaking laws integrate cultural beliefs into legal frameworks, offering innovative models for global conservation.

3.48 Legislative Protection for Indigenous Populations in Africa: A Detailed Analysis

Across Africa, indigenous communities have long been the custodians of vast and biodiverse ecosystems. In many African societies, environmental stewardship is intricately linked to cultural beliefs, traditional knowledge and practices, such as folklore, taboos and rituals. These practices have historically regulated the use of natural resources and contributed to the preservation of biodiversity. However, colonial history and modern economic pressures have often undermined indigenous governance systems, leading to the marginalization of indigenous peoples and their conservation practices. In recent decades, African governments have started to recognize the importance of integrating indigenous knowledge into formal conservation efforts, particularly through legislation that empowers local communities to manage and benefit from wildlife and natural resources [84]. This shift toward community-based conservation (CBC) is aimed at fostering a balance between protecting biodiversity and respecting cultural traditions.

3.48.1 Cultural Practices and Folklore in African Conservation

Many African societies have deep-rooted cultural practices that help preserve biodiversity, and these practices are often embedded in **folklore**, **taboos** and **rituals**. These traditions have been passed down through generations and are seen as sacred responsibilities to protect natural resources. For example:

- **Taboos**: Many indigenous groups have taboos that prohibit hunting certain species, cutting specific trees, or over-harvesting resources during certain times of the year. These taboos are deeply integrated into the social and spiritual lives of the communities.
- **Rituals**: Certain species of animals, trees, or even water sources are believed to be inhabited by spirits or ancestors, which are revered through ritual practices. The protection of these sacred sites or species is therefore a communal effort that ensures their survival.
- **Traditional Ecological Knowledge (TEK)**: Indigenous communities possess a wealth of knowledge about the local ecosystems, including species behaviors, plant cycles and sustainable resource management methods. This knowledge is passed down orally and helps in managing resources in a sustainable manner, such as rotational hunting and farming systems or setting aside "conservation areas" within territories.

However, despite the ecological wisdom embedded in these practices, indigenous communities have often been sidelined by modern conservation policies, which are typically top-down and neglect local traditions.

3.48.2 Legislative Protection and Community-Based Conservation (CBC)

Legislation in Africa is increasingly recognizing the rights and contributions of indigenous and local communities to conservation. Community-based conservation laws seek to formalize indigenous roles in conservation and ensure that local communities can manage natural resources sustainably while benefiting from them economically.

3.48.2.1 Kenya: Wildlife Conservation and Management Act, 2013

- **Cultural Context**: In Kenya, traditional land tenure systems and community-based conservation practices are integral to many indigenous communities, especially among pastoralist groups like the Maasai. These communities have historically managed vast tracts of land for both grazing and wildlife conservation [85].
- **Legal Framework**: The **Wildlife Conservation and Management Act, 2013**, was established to enhance the management and protection of Kenya's wildlife and promote community involvement in conservation. The Act:
  - Recognizes **community conservancies** as legal entities that can manage wildlife and benefit from eco-tourism activities.
  - Enables local communities to establish wildlife sanctuaries and protected areas, fostering wildlife conservation while promoting sustainable land use.
  - Ensures that communities directly benefit from the revenue generated from wildlife, including tourism fees and resource use rights.
  - Provides incentives for communities to conserve wildlife by offering access to tourism and eco-friendly enterprises.
- **Impact**: The **Wildlife Conservation and Management Act** has helped empower indigenous communities by involving them in wildlife management decisions, thus aligning conservation goals with local economic interests. For example, Maasai communities have successfully managed wildlife conservancies, ensuring the survival of elephants and other species while protecting their cultural practices and way of life.

3.48.2.2 South Africa: Community-Based Natural Resource Management (CBNRM) Laws

- **Cultural Context**: Indigenous communities in South Africa, such as the Khoisan and Xhosa, have cultural practices that prioritize environmental stewardship [86]. Historically, their lands were taken away under colonial and apartheid laws, but there has been a push to return land and empower indigenous groups in recent years.
- **Legal Framework**: The South African government has implemented several policies and legal frameworks that aim to integrate indigenous communities into conservation efforts:
  - The **National Environmental Management Act (NEMA), 1998** and its associated policies promote **Community-Based Natural Resource Management (CBNRM)** programs, which empower local communities to manage natural resources while promoting conservation goals.

- South Africa has also implemented the **Biodiversity Act, 2004**, which provides for the involvement of indigenous communities in the conservation of biological diversity. This includes the recognition of **traditional knowledge** and its integration into formal conservation practices.
- The **Environmental Conservation Act** and the **Biodiversity Stewardship Program** allow for indigenous communities to play a significant role in the management of protected areas and biodiversity hotspots, often through partnerships with national parks and conservation agencies.

- **Impact**: These laws have allowed indigenous communities to regain control over their ancestral lands and participate in decision-making processes related to conservation. Additionally, they enable communities to benefit economically through eco-tourism, sustainable agriculture and wildlife management practices, all while preserving their cultural traditions.

3.48.2.3 Other African Nations

Several other African countries have also adopted legal frameworks that integrate indigenous communities into conservation, including:

- **Tanzania**: The **Wildlife Conservation Act, 2009**, provides legal recognition of community-based conservation areas, allowing communities to manage wildlife in collaboration with the government [87].
- **Namibia**: **Namibia's Communal Land Reform Act (2002)** empowers indigenous communities to manage natural resources, including wildlife and to establish conservancies, which contribute to conservation and tourism.
- **Botswana**: The **Botswana Wildlife Conservation and National Parks Act** has provisions that recognize community-managed areas, where local communities can benefit from wildlife conservation and eco-tourism activities.

3.48.3 Challenges and Opportunities

While legislative advances have provided opportunities for indigenous communities to engage in conservation, several challenges remain:

3.48.3.1 Enforcement and Implementation

- Despite legal recognition, the actual implementation of community-based conservation laws is often hindered by limited resources, weak governance structures and political resistance. Many local communities continue to face encroachment by commercial interests, such as large-scale agriculture or mining, which threaten traditional conservation practices.

3.48.3.2 Conflicts with Commercial Interests

- In some cases, the integration of indigenous communities into formal conservation systems has led to conflicts with private companies or government interests, particularly in relation to land rights. For example, tourism ventures may prioritize commercial objectives over community needs, undermining the benefits of conservation for local populations.

3.48.3.3 Marginalization of Indigenous Knowledge

- While some legal frameworks recognize indigenous knowledge, there remains a risk of it being sidelined in favor of "scientific" conservation models that do not take into account the holistic, culturally embedded practices of indigenous communities. There is a need for better integration of traditional ecological knowledge into the formal conservation sector.

In Africa, legislation has made significant strides toward recognizing and incorporating indigenous knowledge and practices into environmental conservation efforts. Laws such as Kenya's **Wildlife Conservation and Management Act, 2013** and South Africa's **CBNRM framework** empower local communities to manage their natural resources, integrating cultural traditions with biodiversity protection. These laws have demonstrated that community-based conservation can be effective in preserving ecosystems while promoting socioeconomic benefits for local populations. However, challenges remain in ensuring equitable implementation and balancing indigenous practices with modern conservation needs. Nonetheless, Africa's legal innovations provide a model for the global recognition of indigenous rights in environmental governance.

3.48.4 Africa: Folklore and Community-Based Conservation

Cultural Practice, Many African societies embed environmental stewardship in folklore, with taboos and rituals prohibiting the overuse of resources. **Legislation**, Countries like Kenya and South Africa have implemented community-based conservation laws, such as the Wildlife Conservation and Management Act, 2013, which empower local communities to manage and benefit from wildlife resources. **Impact**, These laws preserve biodiversity while respecting cultural traditions, promoting coexistence between humans and wildlife.

3.49 Detailed Analysis of Global Legislative Protection for Indigenous Populations in Conservation

Indigenous communities around the world have long been the stewards of vast and biodiverse landscapes. Their cultural practices, traditional knowledge and close relationship with the environment have contributed significantly to the preservation of ecosystems and biodiversity. However, historical colonization, land dispossession and exclusion from decision-making processes have marginalized indigenous peoples in global conservation frameworks. In response, several international conventions and treaties have evolved to recognize and protect the rights of indigenous populations, acknowledging their integral role in sustainable environmental management. These global initiatives emphasize the integration of cultural, spiritual and environmental dimensions into formal conservation practices, helping to ensure the sustainability of both biodiversity and indigenous cultures.

3.49.1 Convention on Biological Diversity (CBD)

The **Convention on Biological Diversity (CBD)**, adopted in 1992, is one of the most significant global frameworks for biodiversity protection [88]. The CBD recognizes the importance of traditional knowledge, innovations and practices of indigenous communities in the sustainable use and conservation of biodiversity.

Key Provisions:

- **Article 8(j)**: The CBD explicitly acknowledges the role of indigenous peoples in biodiversity conservation through **Article 8(j)**, which calls for the "respect, preservation and maintenance" of traditional knowledge, innovations and practices that contribute to biodiversity conservation. This article also promotes the fair and equitable sharing of benefits arising from the use of such knowledge.
- **Access and Benefit-Sharing (ABS)**: The **Nagoya Protocol (2010)** [89], an additional agreement under the CBD, addresses the fair and equitable sharing of benefits from the use of genetic resources and traditional knowledge. The protocol emphasizes the need for **free, prior and informed consent (FPIC)** from indigenous communities before the use of their traditional knowledge or genetic resources.
- **Recognition of Indigenous Rights**: The CBD encourages parties to implement measures to protect the rights of indigenous communities, including land rights and cultural practices that contribute to biodiversity conservation.

The CBD provides an international legal framework for the recognition and protection of indigenous knowledge and cultural practices, enabling indigenous communities to participate in global efforts to conserve biodiversity. By recognizing the value of traditional ecological knowledge (TEK), the CBD helps to bridge the gap between indigenous wisdom and scientific approaches to conservation. However, the implementation of these provisions remains challenging, as it requires the active engagement of states, proper safeguards and mechanisms to ensure indigenous participation in decision-making processes.

3.49.2 UNESCO World Heritage Convention

The **UNESCO World Heritage Convention (1972)** [90] is another important global treaty that bridges cultural and environmental conservation. The convention aims to protect sites of **outstanding universal value**, recognizing their significance both in terms of cultural and environmental heritage.

Key Provisions:

- **Cultural and Natural Heritage**: The convention distinguishes between **cultural heritage** (e.g., monuments, groups of buildings, or sites of historical or cultural significance) and **natural heritage** (e.g., landscapes, geological formations and biodiversity hotspots). It also recognizes that many heritage sites embody both cultural and natural values, particularly those associated with indigenous communities.
- **Cultural Landscapes**: The concept of **cultural landscapes** was introduced to recognize areas where the interaction of people with their environment has created enduring and unique ecosystems. These landscapes, shaped by indigenous knowledge, practices and stewardship, are eligible for World Heritage status.
- **Inclusion of Indigenous Perspectives**: While the World Heritage Convention has traditionally focused on environmental and cultural preservation, more recent efforts have integrated indigenous voices in the identification, nomination and management of World Heritage sites. Many World Heritage sites have been designated due to their spiritual, cultural and ecological significance to indigenous communities.

The **World Heritage Convention** has helped preserve culturally significant natural sites by recognizing their dual importance to both environmental conservation and cultural heritage. Sites such as **Uluru-Kata Tjuta National Park** in Australia [15], **the Whanganui River** in New Zealand and **the Serengeti** in Tanzania have received World Heritage status, with indigenous communities playing key roles in their management. However, challenges remain in ensuring the full participation and representation of indigenous peoples in the governance of these sites, as well as in addressing potential conflicts between conservation goals and indigenous land rights.

3.49.3 International Labour Organization (ILO) Convention No. 169

The **ILO Convention No. 169**, adopted in 1989, is the first international legal instrument dedicated to protecting the rights of indigenous and tribal peoples. It has been instrumental in promoting indigenous rights across a variety of sectors, including environmental conservation [91].

Key Provisions:

- **Indigenous Land Rights**: The convention asserts that indigenous peoples have the right to own, use and control the land and resources they have traditionally occupied or used. This includes recognition of **land tenure rights**, which are crucial for the sustainable management of natural resources.
- **Consultation and Consent**: The convention emphasizes the importance of consulting indigenous communities in matters that affect their lands and resources, including conservation and environmental management. It also affirms their right to **free, prior and informed consent (FPIC)**.
- **Cultural Rights**: ILO 169 recognizes the cultural rights of indigenous peoples, affirming that their traditions, languages and spiritual practices should be respected in the context of environmental conservation.

Impact:

ILO Convention No. 169 has played a pivotal role in recognizing the rights of indigenous people in the context of development and environmental protection [92]. It encourages the recognition of indigenous governance systems and promotes the integration of traditional ecological knowledge into national and international conservation frameworks. However, the convention is not universally ratified, limiting its global impact.

3.49.4 UN Declaration on the Rights of Indigenous Peoples (UNDRIP)

The **United Nations Declaration on the Rights of Indigenous Peoples (UNDRIP)**, adopted in 2007 [93], is a landmark international document that affirms the individual and collective rights of indigenous peoples. While not legally binding, it has been widely endorsed and serves as a guiding framework for the protection of indigenous rights worldwide.

Key Provisions:

- **Land and Resource Rights**: UNDRIP emphasizes the right of indigenous peoples to **own, use and manage their traditional lands and resources**. This includes rights over biodiversity-rich areas that are essential for global conservation efforts.
- **Traditional Knowledge**: The declaration recognizes the value of **traditional knowledge**, particularly in biodiversity conservation and climate change mitigation. It urges states to protect and promote indigenous peoples' knowledge, cultures and practices, ensuring their inclusion in environmental management frameworks.
- **Self-Determination**: UNDRIP upholds the right of indigenous peoples to determine their own priorities for development, which includes control over conservation practices and the management of their natural resources.

Impact:

UNDRIP has provided a global platform for the recognition of indigenous peoples' rights, including their environmental and cultural rights. It has influenced national policies and helped indigenous groups advocate for their inclusion in conservation decisions. However, the declaration's non-binding nature means that its implementation depends on the political will of states.

3.49.5 Convention on International Trade in Endangered Species of Wild Fauna and Flora (CITES)

Protection of Indigenous Rights in Wildlife Conservation

The **CITES** treaty, established in 1973 [94], aims to ensure that international trade in wild animals and plants does not threaten their survival. While primarily focused on species conservation, it recognizes the importance of **community involvement** in wildlife protection.

Key Provisions:

- **Sustainable Use of Resources**: CITES supports the sustainable use of wildlife resources by indigenous communities, particularly in cases where traditional practices can ensure species conservation.
- **Community Involvement**: Indigenous communities are encouraged to engage in sustainable wildlife management practices and in some cases, communities are granted permits for the trade of certain species under regulated conditions, provided that these practices do not harm biodiversity.

Impact:

CITES has helped facilitate the legal trade of wildlife products from indigenous communities, ensuring that it is done sustainably and ethically. It has promoted the integration of indigenous communities into global conservation efforts by recognizing their traditional knowledge and practices.

Global initiatives such as the **Convention on Biological Diversity (CBD), UNESCO World Heritage Convention, ILO Convention No. 169, UNDRIP** and **CITES** have made significant strides in recognizing the role of indigenous communities in conservation. These treaties acknowledge the deep connection between indigenous peoples and their environments, integrating cultural values, traditional knowledge and spiritual practices into conservation frameworks. While these global initiatives provide an important legal foundation for the protection of indigenous rights, challenges remain in terms of enforcement, equitable benefit-sharing and ensuring the full participation of indigenous peoples in decision-making processes. Nonetheless, these frameworks represent a progressive shift toward more inclusive and culturally sensitive conservation policies on the global stage.

3.50 Global Initiatives: Cultural Integration in Conservation Treaties

The Convention on Biological Diversity (CBD) recognizes traditional knowledge and encourages its use in biodiversity conservation.

The UNESCO World Heritage Convention protects culturally significant natural sites, recognizing their dual cultural and environmental importance.

Impact: These frameworks foster international collaboration in integrating cultural dimensions into conservation practices.

3.50.1 Challenges and Opportunities

Challenges, Conflicts between cultural practices and modern conservation goals. Inequitable implementation of laws favoring industrial interests over cultural preservation. Marginalization of indigenous voices in policymaking. Opportunities, strengthening legal recognition of traditional ecological knowledge. Promoting co-management frameworks between governments and local communities. Using cultural narratives to foster public support for conservation initiatives. Legal frameworks that incorporate cultural dimensions offer promising pathways to sustainable conservation. By respecting indigenous cosmologies, rituals and folklore, such laws not only preserve biodiversity but also empower communities to play a central role in environmental stewardship. Global efforts must continue to balance cultural values with ecological imperatives, ensuring equitable and inclusive conservation practices.

Conclusion

Indigenous communities across the globe share a profound connection with their natural environment, a relationship that is deeply interwoven with their cultural, spiritual and social identities. This intricate bond has given rise to ethnoecological paradigms, a form of traditional ecological knowledge that serves as the foundation for many customary laws. However, religious beliefs, often manifesting as cultural norms, can sometimes create barriers to the development and evolution of these laws. This analysis explores the dynamics of ethnoecological paradigms within indigenous environmental law narratives, focusing on their symbiotic wisdom and the challenges posed by conflicting cultural norms. Ethnoecology refers to the way indigenous people perceive and manage their ecosystems through culturally rooted knowledge systems. These paradigms emphasize the interdependence between humans and nature, advocating sustainable practices long before the advent of modern environmental movements. For instance, rotational farming, sacred groves and seasonal hunting restrictions are not mere practices but codified forms of customary laws that reflect deep ecological insights. Religious beliefs often serve as the moral compass of a community, influencing its legal frameworks and societal norms. Among indigenous communities, spiritual connections to nature frequently underpin customary laws. For example, the belief in sacred landscapes or totemic species reinforces the conservation of biodiversity. However, when religious beliefs become rigid or are interpreted in ways that conflict with adaptive environmental needs, they can hinder the evolution of these laws. For instance: **Rigid Ritual Practices**, certain rituals may mandate the use of rare natural resources, leading to unsustainable exploitation. **Gender-Based Restrictions**, Cultural taboos often exclude women from participating in environmental decision-making, despite their pivotal roles in resource management. **Resistance to Modernization**, Religious conservatism can resist the integration of scientific insights into traditional practices, creating gaps in addressing contemporary ecological challenges.

Symbiosis in Indigenous Environmental Law, despite these challenges, indigenous environmental laws exhibit a remarkable ability to harmonize spiritual beliefs with ecological imperatives. This symbiosis can be seen in: **Sacred Landscapes**: Many communities designate forests, rivers, or mountains as sacred, thereby protecting these ecosystems from exploitation. **Seasonal Calendars**, the alignment of agricultural and fishing activities with lunar or solar cycles ensures resource regeneration. **Community-Centric Governance**, decision-making processes often involve collective wisdom, reducing the risk of overexploitation and fostering accountability. **The Khasi Tribe of Northeast India**, their belief in sacred groves has preserved biodiversity hotspots for centuries. However, pressures from modernization and shifting religious practices challenge these traditional norms. **The San People of Southern Africa, t**he San's tracking and hunting laws, rooted in spiritual respect for prey, exemplify sustainable resource use. Yet, colonial and modern religious influences have disrupted their traditional governance. Navigating the Barriers, addressing the barriers posed by cultural norms requires a nuanced approach that respects indigenous sovereignty while promoting adaptability. Key strategies include,

inclusive Dialogues, engaging diverse community members, including women and youth, ensures a more holistic understanding of environmental challenges. **Integrating Scientific Knowledge**: Bridging traditional wisdom with scientific insights can enhance the resilience of customary laws. **Legal Recognition**: Strengthening the legal status of indigenous environmental laws at national and international levels can provide protective frameworks against external pressures.

The symbiotic wisdom inherent in ethnoecological paradigms offers invaluable lessons for global environmental governance. While religious beliefs and cultural norms may pose challenges, they also enrich the narrative by embedding ethical dimensions into environmental law. However, it is an undisputed fact that there is a constant tug of war between customary laws and statutory laws. In the twenty-first century, this dynamic has brought the issue of inclusivity into sharp focus. Statutory laws, often derived from colonial or modern state structures, may undermine or marginalize customary laws, eroding the sovereignty and agency of indigenous communities. The tension between these two frameworks reflects deeper questions about power, representation and justice. Customary laws are rooted in collective memory and cultural specificity, while statutory laws often claim universality and formal authority. Bridging this divide requires genuine inclusivity—an approach that respects indigenous traditions while ensuring that they adapt to changing ecological and social realities. By fostering mutual respect and integration between these legal systems, humanity can achieve a more equitable and sustainable future, honoring the diverse voices and wisdom that have long safeguarded our planet.

Audience-Centric Relevance

This book is meticulously designed to cater to a diverse audience, reflecting the interdisciplinary nature of environmental challenges and their solutions:

Academics and Researchers, Scholars in law, anthropology, sociology and environmental studies will find this book an invaluable resource. It provides a rich repository of case studies and theoretical insights that bridge the gap between disciplines, offering a deeper understanding of the interplay between cultural beliefs, legal systems and sustainability.

Policymakers and Activists, Policymakers grappling with the complexities of implementing sustainable practices will benefit from the book's evidence-based analysis. It offers actionable insights into how laws informed by indigenous knowledge can lead to more effective and equitable environmental policies. Activists, too, will gain inspiration and strategic guidance from the success stories of indigenous communities resisting ecological degradation.

Global Citizens, For those passionate about the future of the planet, this book serves as a call to action. By shedding light on the lived experiences of indigenous communities and their contributions to environmental stewardship, it fosters a sense of shared responsibility and encourages a shift toward more inclusive and sustainable practices.

Ethnoecological Paradigms and Global Environmental Governance

The book underscores the global relevance of ethnoecological paradigms in addressing environmental challenges. It aligns Indigenous conservation practices with international legal instruments, such as the Convention on Biological Diversity (CBD) and the United Nations Sustainable Development Goals (SDGs). By doing so, it highlights how local traditions can inform global strategies, creating a unified approach to sustainability. For example, the integration of traditional fire management practices by Indigenous ranger groups in Australia into national bushfire mitigation strategies demonstrates the adaptability of indigenous knowledge in addressing contemporary crises. Similarly, the emphasis on participatory governance models, as seen in the management of Indigenous Protected Areas (IPAs), offers a template for harmonizing local and global conservation efforts.

A Path Forward: Legal and Ethical Dimensions of Sustainability

One of the book's core messages is the need to rethink environmental governance through an ethical lens. It argues for the inclusion of cultural values and indigenous wisdom in legal and policy frameworks, advocating for a paradigm shift from anthropocentric to ecocentric models. This shift is not merely theoretical but has practical implications for achieving global sustainability goals. The recognition of Indigenous sovereignty, as seen in initiatives like Canada's IPCAs, demonstrates how legal acknowledgment of Indigenous governance can enhance conservation outcomes. By empowering Indigenous communities to manage their lands, these frameworks not only protect biodiversity but also uphold cultural heritage and social justice.

A Call to Action

Symbiotic Wisdom: Exploring Ethnoecological Paradigms within Indigenous Environmental Law Narratives is more than a book; it is a movement toward a more inclusive and sustainable future. By bridging ethnoecological paradigms, legal frameworks and global ideologies, it offers a comprehensive understanding of the challenges and opportunities in environmental governance. It calls on readers, academics, policymakers, activists and global citizens alike to embrace a more holistic perspective on sustainability, one that honors the wisdom of Indigenous communities and the power of environmental laws. Through its interdisciplinary approach, this book not only illuminates the critical role of Indigenous knowledge and legal frameworks in conservation but also inspires a collective commitment to protecting our planet for generations to come. By weaving together cultural, legal and ecological narratives, it provides a roadmap for achieving environmental sustainability in an increasingly interconnected world.

References

1. Sengar, B. (2023). Fracturing and formation of cultural spaces of Florida Seminole: From settlements to reservation. In B. Sengar & A. M. E. Adjoumani (Eds.), *Indigenous societies in the post-colonial world*. Springer. https://doi.org/10.1007/978-981-19-8722-9_3
2. Sarmokadam, P. V., & George, A. N. (2024). Traditional knowledge and bio economy. In L. K. Panicker, P. Nelliyat, & O. V. Oommen (Eds.), *Biodiversity and business*. Springer. https://doi.org/10.1007/978-3-031-71674-4_24
3. Patwardhan, A., Ghate, P., Mhaskar, M., et al. (2021). Cultural dimensions of sacred forests in the Western Ghats Biodiversity Hot Spot, Southern India and its implications for biodiversity protection. *International Journal of Anthropology and Ethnology, 5*, 12. https://doi.org/10.1186/s41257-021-00053-6
4. Malaihollo, M. (2023). On due diligence and the rights of indigenous peoples in international law: What a Māori world view can offer. *Netherlands International Law Review, 70*, 65–86. https://doi.org/10.1007/s40802-023-00233-5
5. Petryshen, W., Ciccantell, P. S., & Langford, T. (2024). The Elk Valley, Canada. In M. Hendryx (Eds.), *Sustainable development and rural public health*. Sustainable Development Goals Series. Springer. https://doi.org/10.1007/978-3-031-62509-1_5
6. Muñoz Prudencio, L. S. (2024). Animals and the law in Bolivia. In F. Dalpane & M. Baideldinova (Eds.), *Animal law worldwide*. T.M.C. Asser Press, The Hague. https://doi.org/10.1007/978-94-6265-643-7_2
7. Colangelo, S. A., & André, A. (2023). Environmental justice before U.S. courts. In G. Antonelli, et al. (Eds.), *Environmental law before the courts*. Springer. https://doi.org/10.1007/978-3-031-41527-2_3
8. .Genetic diversity goals and targets have improved, but remain insufficient for clear implementation of the post-2020 global biodiversity framework. *Conservation Genetics, 24*, 181–191. https://doi.org/10.1007/s10592-022-01492-0
9. Pickett, S. T. A., Simone, A.T., Anderson, P., et al. (2024). The relational shift in urban ecology: From place and structures to multiple modes of coproduction for positive urban futures. *Ambio, 53*, 845–870. https://doi.org/10.1007/s13280-024-02001-y
10. Xie, J., Li, H., Furuya, K., et al. (2024). Participatory intention and behavior in green cultural heritage conservation: An application of the extended theory of planned behavior. *Heritage Science, 12*, 299. https://doi.org/10.1186/s40494-024-01407-x
11. Mührel, J. (2024). Rights of nature in liberal legal systems. In *Rights of nature in liberal legal systems and international law*. Springer. https://doi.org/10.1007/978-3-031-69059-4_8
12. Kwon, K., Gunton, T., Rutherford, M., et al. (2024). Setting tiered management triggers using a values-based approach in an indigenous-led cumulative effects management system. *Environmental Management*. https://doi.org/10.1007/s00267-024-02075-0
13. Nursey-Bray, M. (2023). Building collaborative models for change: Engaging indigenous people and country into in socially just conservation. In C. Baldwin & S. van Bommel (Eds.), *Rural development for sustainable social-ecological systems*. Palgrave Studies in Environmental Sustainability. Palgrave Macmillan. https://doi.org/10.1007/978-3-031-34225-7_12
14. Ekardt, F., Günther, P., Hagemann, K., et al. (2023). Legally binding and ambitious biodiversity protection under the CBD, the global biodiversity framework and human rights law. *Environmental Sciences Europe, 35*, 80. https://doi.org/10.1186/s12302-023-00786-5
15. (2020). Uluru-Kata Tjuta National Park, Australia. In A. Chen, Y. Ng, E. Zhang, & M. Tian (Eds.), *Dictionary of Geotourism*. Springer. https://doi.org/10.1007/978-981-13-2538-0_2633
16. Tuyen, Q. D. (2023). Introduction—Jalan Nao. In *Heritage conservation and tourism development at Cham sacred sites in Vietnam*. Global Vietnam: Across Time, Space and Community. Springer. https://doi.org/10.1007/978-981-99-3350-1_1
17. Thakur, A. (2024). Why nature deserves a seat at the table: A case study on nature's personhood. *Jindal Global Law Review*. https://doi.org/10.1007/s41020-024-00247-x

18. Rivas-Echeverría, F., Ramos, L., Gil-Osuna, B., et al. (2024). Automating case assessment in Ecuador's legal system: A web-based application for COIP consultation. *International Journal of Information and Technology, 16*, 2901–2913. https://doi.org/10.1007/s41870-024-01891-1
19. Fernanda Miño Puga, M. (2023). Cinema and Ecuador's Buen Vivir: Negotiating coloniality in the community. In *Ecuadorian cinema for the 21st century*. Palgrave Macmillan. https://doi.org/10.1007/978-3-031-40989-9_6
20. Nikolakis, W., Ross, R. M., & Steffensen, V. (2024). How bureaucracies interact with Indigenous Fire Stewardship (IFS): A conceptual framework. *Fire Ecology, 20*, 79. https://doi.org/10.1186/s42408-024-00303-w
21. Dudley, N. (2024). What does the global biodiversity framework mean for protected and conserved areas?. In N. Finneran, D. Hewlett, & R. Clarke (Eds.), *Managing protected areas*. Palgrave Macmillan. https://doi.org/10.1007/978-3-031-40783-3_2
22. Singh, A., Pope, F. D., Radcliffe, J., et al. (2024). Delivering sustainable climate action: reframing the sustainable development goals. *NPJ Climate Action, 3*, 110. https://doi.org/10.1038/s44168-024-00194-2
23. Lehmann, I. (2023). Inspiration from the Kunming-Montreal global biodiversity framework for SDG 15. *International Environmental Agreements, 23*, 207–214. https://doi.org/10.1007/s10784-023-09608-8
24. Küfeoğlu, S. (2022). SDG-16: Peace, justice and strong institutions. In *Emerging technologies*. Sustainable Development Goals Series. Springer. https://doi.org/10.1007/978-3-031-07127-0_18
25. Nelliyat, P. (2024). Access and Benefit Sharing (ABS) potential estimation: Methodology and empirical results. In L. K. Panicker, P. Nelliyat, & O. V. Oommen (Eds.), *Biodiversity and business*. Springer. https://doi.org/10.1007/978-3-031-71674-4_17
26. Zhang, M. Z., Han, Y., Xu, Z., et al. (2024). Bias-corrected NESM3 global dataset for dynamical downscaling under 1.5 °C and 2 °C global warming scenarios. *Scientific Data, 11*, 399 (2024). https://doi.org/10.1038/s41597-024-03224-0
27. Szöllősi-Cira, L. (2022). New Zealand's nuclear-free policy. In *New Zealand's global responsibility*. Palgrave Macmillan. https://doi.org/10.1007/978-981-16-7349-8_4
28. Albert, S., Porter, J., & Green, J. (2023). The Nongai Dawai Khasi healers of Meghalaya—A tribal understanding of the human potential. In S. Reddy, N. Guite, & B. Subedi (Eds.), *Ethnomedicine and tribal healing practices in India*. People, Cultures and Societies: Exploring and Documenting Diversities. Springer. https://doi.org/10.1007/978-981-19-4286-0_10
29. Kaushal, N. (2023). The role of Indian culture in enlightening the notions of environmental stewardship and sustainable living mechanism. In S. Dhiman (Ed.), *Sustainable development and environmental stewardship*. Springer. https://doi.org/10.1007/978-3-031-28885-2_5
30. Thakur, A. (2024). Why nature deserves a seat at the table: A case study on nature's personhood. *Jindal Global Law Review, 15*, 671–691. https://doi.org/10.1007/s41020-024-00247-x
31. da Silva, E. C., Guerrero-Moreno, M. A., Oliveira, F. A., et al. (2024). The importance of traditional communities in biodiversity conservation. *Biodiversity and Conservation*. https://doi.org/10.1007/s10531-024-02999-3
32. Didarali, Z., Kuiper, T., Brink, C. W., et al. (2022). Awareness of environmental legislation as a deterrent for wildlife crime: A case with Masaai pastoralists, poison use and the Kenya Wildlife Act. *Ambio, 51*, 1632–1642. https://doi.org/10.1007/s13280-021-01695-8
33. Shah, J. (2024). Getting a grip on green—Indian cities and the promise of sustainability, resilience, inclusion. In M. H. P. Müller (Ed.), *Indien im 21. Jahrhundert – Auf dem Weg zur postindustriellen Ökonomie. Ökonomien und Gesellschaften im Wandel*. Springer Gabler. https://doi.org/10.1007/978-3-658-43014-6_17
34. Kumar, K. (2024). Forest rights Act 2006 and the question of traditional knowledge: A legal framework for forest management in India. In S. C. Rai & P. K. Mishra (Eds.), *Sacred landscapes, indigenous knowledge and ethno-culture in natural resource management*. Advances in Geographical and Environmental Sciences. Springer. https://doi.org/10.1007/978-981-97-4206-6_10

35. Odong, N. A. (2024). Reconciling the incongruence between the Cartagena protocol on biosafety to the convention on biological diversity and the GATT/WTO rules. *International Environmental Agreements, 24*, 497–513. https://doi.org/10.1007/s10784-024-09649-7
36. Gulzar, S., Haas, N., & Pasquale, B. (2023). Does political affirmative action work and for whom? Theory and evidence on India's scheduled areas. In A. Deshpande (Ed.), *Handbook on economics of discrimination and affirmative action*. Springer. https://doi.org/10.1007/978-981-19-4166-5_51
37. Ho, C. W. L., & Caals, K. (2024). How the EU AI act seeks to establish an epistemic environment of trust. *Asian Bioethics Review, 16*, 345–372. https://doi.org/10.1007/s41649-024-00304-6
38. Mann, J. (2023). The redefinition of citizenship in Australia, 1950s–1970s. In J. Mann (Ed.), *Citizenship in transnational perspective*. Politics of Citizenship and Migration. Palgrave Macmillan. https://doi.org/10.1007/978-3-031-34358-2_4
39. Harris, B. (2024). The voice to parliament. In Indigenous peoples and constitutional reform in Australia. Springer. https://doi.org/10.1007/978-981-99-7121-3_8
40. Matter-Seibel, S. (2024). Syncretic translations: Indigenizing the Bible and rewriting Biblical stories in Native North American literature. In S. Dievenkorn & S. Levin (Eds.), *[Re]Gained in translation II: Bibles, histories and struggles for identity*. TRANSÜD. Arbeiten zur Theorie und Praxis des Übersetzens und Dolmetschens (Vol. 134). Frank & Timme. https://doi.org/10.57088/978-3-7329-9175-4_16
41. Mummery, J., & Mummery, J. (2023). Overcoming segregation problematics for environmentally accountable and transformative policy in a changing climate: The case of Australia's EPBC Act. In B. Edmondson (Ed.), *Sustainability transformations, social transitions and environmental accountabilities*. Palgrave Studies in Environmental Transformation, Transition and Accountability. Palgrave Macmillan. https://doi.org/10.1007/978-3-031-18268-6_7
42. Cubillo, B., Brimblecombe, J., & Stacey, N. (2024). The representation of Aboriginal health and wellbeing values within coastal marine and fisheries policies of the Northern Territory of Australia. *Maritime Studies, 23*, 27. https://doi.org/10.1007/s40152-024-00370-4
43. Jacob, D. E., Nelson, I. U., & Izah, S. C. (2024). Indigenous water management strategies in the global South. In S. C. Izah, M. C. Ogwu, A. Loukas, & H. Hamidifar (Eds.), *Water crises and sustainable management in the global South*. Springer. https://doi.org/10.1007/978-981-97-4966-9_16
44. Keith, K. (2023). Insights from community development for strengthening landcare in Queensland. In C. Baldwin & S. van Bommel (Eds.), *Rural development for sustainable social-ecological systems*. Palgrave Studies in Environmental Sustainability. Palgrave Macmillan. https://doi.org/10.1007/978-3-031-34225-7_9
45. Feary, S. A., Eastburn, D., Sam, N., & Kennedy, J. (2012). Western Pacific. In J. Parrotta & R. Trosper (Eds.), *Traditional forest-related knowledge. world forests* (Vol. 12). Springer. https://doi.org/10.1007/978-94-007-2144-9_11
46. Valentim, H. I. L., Feio, M. J., & Almeida, S. F. P. (2024). Fluvial protected areas as a strategy to preserve riverine ecosystems—A review. *Biodiversity and Conservation, 33*, 439–462. https://doi.org/10.1007/s10531-023-02774-w
47. Andersen, A. N. (1996). Fire ecology and management. In C. M. Finlayson & I. Von Oertzen (Eds.), *Landscape and vegetation ecology of the Kakadu Region, Northern Australia. Geobotany* (Vol. 23). Springer. https://doi.org/10.1007/978-94-009-0133-9_9
48. May, S. K., & Tacon, P. S. C. (2020). Kakadu National Park: Rock art. In C. Smith (Ed.), *Encyclopedia of global archaeology*. Springer. https://doi.org/10.1007/978-3-030-30018-0_2241
49. McCaul, J. (2023). Caring for country as deliberative policymaking. In N. Moodie & S. Maddison (Eds.), *Public policy and indigenous futures*. Indigenous-Settler Relations in Australia and the World (Vol 4). Springer. https://doi.org/10.1007/978-981-19-9319-0_4
50. Croker, A. R., Woods, J., & Kountouris, Y. (2023). Changing fire regimes in East and Southern Africa's savanna-protected areas: Opportunities and challenges for indigenous-led savanna burning emissions abatement schemes. *Fire Ecology, 19*, 63. https://doi.org/10.1186/s42408-023-00215-1

51. Dobbs, R. J., Davies, C. L., Walker, M. L., et al. (2016). Collaborative research partnerships inform monitoring and management of aquatic ecosystems by Indigenous rangers. *Reviews in Fish Biology and Fisheries, 26*, 711–725. https://doi.org/10.1007/s11160-015-9401-2
52. Baird, I. G., Ziegler, A. D., Fearnside, P. M., et al. (2024). Ruin-of-the-rivers? A global review of run-of-the-river dams. *Environmental Management.* https://doi.org/10.1007/s00267-024-02062-5
53. Rofe, M. W., & Hepburn, D. J. (2024). Acts of ongoing repression? Aboriginal cultural heritage and landscape protection in postcolonial Australia. In M. Ripmeester &M. W. Rofe (Eds.), *Global iconoclasm: Contesting "official" mnemonic landscapes.* RaumFragen: Stadt—Region—Landschaft. Springer VS. https://doi.org/10.1007/978-3-658-43691-9_8
54. Maxcy-Brown, J., Capone, D., & Elliott, M. A. (2023). Characterizing the nature and extent of access to unsafely managed sanitation in the United States. *Nature Water, 1*, 915–928. https://doi.org/10.1038/s44221-023-00157-7
55. Corbett, E. (2023). Destruction by territorial expulsion: The cherokee removal. In K. W. Gray (Ed.), Global encyclopedia of territorial rights. Springer. https://doi.org/10.1007/978-3-319-68846-6_525-2
56. Cullen, T., & Toedt, M. (2020). Public health informatics and the American Indian/Alaska native populations: Improving community health despite challenges. In J. Magnuson, & B. Dixon (Eds.), *Public health informatics and information systems.* Health Informatics. Springer. https://doi.org/10.1007/978-3-030-41215-9_22
57. National Historic Preservation Act. (2020). *Encyclopedic dictionary of archaeology.* Springer. https://doi.org/10.1007/978-3-030-58292-0_140065
58. Jiménez, M. J. O. (2023). Restitution of indigenous cultural objects in Latin America. In C. A. M. Jedlicki, N. Oosterman, & R. Christofoletti (Eds.), *Colonial heritage, power and contestation.* The Latin American Studies Book Series. Springer. https://doi.org/10.1007/978-3-031-37748-8_8
59. Elrod, A. A. (2023). The EPA and its regulations. In R. Brinkmann (Ed.), *The Palgrave handbook of global sustainability.* Palgrave Macmillan. https://doi.org/10.1007/978-3-031-01949-4_119
60. Johansen, B. E. (2023). Alberta's moonscape: If this sounds apocalyptic, it is. In *Resource devastation on native American lands.* Springer. https://doi.org/10.1007/978-3-031-21896-5_7
61. Bennett, M. M. (2023). Gravel grabs: The rocky foundations of indigenous geologic power in the Arctic. *Ambio, 52*, 1184–1197. https://doi.org/10.1007/s13280-023-01862-z
62. Weber, J. (2024). Canyon de Chelly National monument and the vanishing Navajo Meridian. In J. Weber & S. Sultana (Eds.), *The changing geography of national parks and protected areas.* Palgrave Macmillan. https://doi.org/10.1007/978-3-031-74653-6_9
63. Cabello, M., Hyland, M., & Marantz, N. (2023). From state of the practice to state of the art: Improving equity analysis in regional transportation plans. *Transportation.* https://doi.org/10.1007/s11116-023-10439-4
64. McGinnis, M., Woolley, J., & Gamman, J. (1999). Bioregional conflict resolution: Rebuilding community in watershed planning and organizing. *Environmental Management, 24*, 1–12. https://doi.org/10.1007/s002679900210
65. Paxton, J. (1989). United States of America. In J. Paxton (Ed.), *The statesman's year-book.* Palgrave Macmillan. https://doi.org/10.1057/9780230271180_175
66. Polidoro, M., & de Oliveira, D. C. (2024). Prevalence and spatial autocorrelation of tuberculosis in indigenous people in Brazil, 2002–2022. *Journal of Racial and Ethnic Health Disparities.* https://doi.org/10.1007/s40615-024-01924-2
67. da Silva, A. R. F., & Codeço, R. R. (2024). Brazilian CFIA: Evolution towards the traditional?. In N. Monebhurrun, C. Olarte-Bácares, & M. A. Velásquez-Ruiz (Eds.), *International investment law and arbitration from a Latin American perspective.* International Law and the Global South. Springer. https://doi.org/10.1007/978-3-031-49382-9_2
68. Dreher, C. (2024). Assessing the application of consultation and indigenous peoples' protocols. In *A legal assessment of the efficacy of consultation with indigenous peoples.* Springer. https://doi.org/10.1007/978-3-031-50539-3_5

69. Monteiro, G. F. A., Yeung, L. L. T., Caleman, S. M. Q., et al. (2019). Indigenous land demarcation conflicts in Brazil: Has the Supreme Court's decision brought (in)stability? *European Journal of Law and Economics, 48*, 267–290. https://doi.org/10.1007/s10657-019-09628-3
70. Chiavari, J., Lopes, C. L., & de Alcantara Machado, L. (2023). The Brazilian forest code: The challenges of legal implementation. In N. Søndergaard, C. D. de Sá, & A. F. Barros-Platiau (Eds.), *Sustainability challenges of Brazilian agriculture*. Environment & Policy (Vol. 64). Springer. https://doi.org/10.1007/978-3-031-29853-0_15
71. Rodrigues, F. B., Alexandre, R. J. R., Pena, S. A., et al. (2024). Conservation gaps for Brazilian bats, limited protection across conservation units and the importance of the indigenous lands. *Science and Reports, 14*, 23183. https://doi.org/10.1038/s41598-024-74369-6
72. de Langavant, B. H. C. (2024). Cross-cultural interactions, indigenous agency and resistance in the borderlands of the Upper Paraguay Basin. In P. S. León & B. H. C. de Langavant (Eds.), *Resistance in the Iberian worlds from the fifteenth to the eighteenth century*. Palgrave Macmillan. https://doi.org/10.1007/978-3-031-63406-2_14
73. Ribeiro, J. M. P., Maculan, G., de Ávila, B. O., et al. (2025). Deforestation by production displacement: Expansion of cropland and cattle ranching on Amazon Forest. *Environment, Development and Sustainability*. https://doi.org/10.1007/s10668-024-05917-3
74. Winkler, H., Lecocq, F., Lofgren, H., et al. (2022). Examples of shifting development pathways: Lessons on how to enable broader, deeper and faster climate action. *Clim Action, 1*, 27. https://doi.org/10.1007/s44168-022-00026-1
75. Trajber Waisbich, L. (2024). Mobilising international embeddedness to resist radical policy change and dismantling: The case of Brazil under Jair Bolsonaro (2019–2022). *Policy Sciences, 57*, 145–169. https://doi.org/10.1007/s11077-023-09519-0
76. Mezzanotti, G., & Løland, O. J. (2024). From religious populism to civil religion: A discourse analysis of Bolsonaro's and Lula's inaugural and victory speeches. *International Journal of Latin American Religions, 8*, 279–304. https://doi.org/10.1007/s41603-023-00214-9
77. IFI/Plenum Data Company. (1997). Abstracts of documents in this supplement. In *Political science abstracts*. Springer. https://doi.org/10.1007/978-1-4615-5971-9_1
78. Guimarães, S. (2024). The pandemic, mining violence and the case of the Sanöma/Yanomami people. *The Journal of Medical Humanities*. https://doi.org/10.1007/s10912-024-09905-6
79. (2023). New Zealand. In *The Statesman's Yearbook 2024.*. Palgrave Macmillan. https://doi.org/10.1057/978-1-349-96076-7_135
80. Davies, C., Timu-Parata, C., Stairmand, J., et al. (2022). A kia ora, a wave and a smile: An urban marae-led response to COVID-19, a case study in Manaakitanga. *International Journal of Equity in Health, 21*, 70. https://doi.org/10.1186/s12939-022-01667-8
81. Bader-Plabst, K. (2024). Aotearoa—Neuseeland. In: Natur als Rechtssubjekt. Springer. https://doi.org/10.1007/978-3-658-44120-3_3
82. de Froideville, S. M., & Bowling, R. (2022). Te Awa Tupua: An exemplary environmental law?. In J. Gacek & R. Jochelson (Eds.), *Green criminology and the law*. Palgrave Studies in Green Criminology. Palgrave Macmillan. https://doi.org/10.1007/978-3-030-82412-9_12
83. Burns, C., Hetaraka, M., & Jones, A. T. (2024). Tiriti o Waitangi: The treaty of Waitangi, principles and other representations. *New Zealand Journal of Educational Studies, 59*, 15–29. https://doi.org/10.1007/s40841-024-00312-y
84. Gbadegesin, O. A., & Gbadamosi SAN, O. A. (2024). Indigenous ecological knowledge: A transformative approach to biodiversity legislation in Nigeria. *Environmental Management, 74*, 317–331. https://doi.org/10.1007/s00267-024-01994-2
85. Lesorogol, C., & Lesorogol, P. (2024). Community-based wildlife conservation on Pastoral Lands in Kenya: A new logic of production with implications for the future of pastoralism. *Human Ecology, 52*, 15–29. https://doi.org/10.1007/s10745-024-00482-9
86. Rivera, A., Bovey, M., Torres, C., et al. (2024). Community-based natural resource management in Roatan: Strengths and challenges. *Ambio, 53*, 1864–1878. https://doi.org/10.1007/s13280-024-02065-w
87. Kegamba, J. J., Sangha, K. K., Wurm, P. A., et al. (2024). The influence of conservation policies and legislations on communities in Tanzania. *Biodiversity and Conservation, 33*, 3147–3170. https://doi.org/10.1007/s10531-024-02906-w

88. Kim, Y., Tanaka, K., & Perrings, C. (2023). The impact of international conservation agreements on protected areas: Empirical findings from the convention on biological diversity using causal inference. *Environmental Management, 72*, 203–218. https://doi.org/10.1007/s00267-023-01818-9
89. Zheng, X. (2023). The Nagoya protocol and international human rights law. In *The complementarity between the Nagoya protocol and human rights*. Sustainable Development Goals Series. Springer. https://doi.org/10.1007/978-981-99-3513-0_1
90. Cadotte, M. W., Alabbasi, M., Akib, S., et al. (2024). Gauging the threat of invasive species to UNESCO world heritage sites relative to other anthropogenic threats. *Biological Invasions, 26*, 3959–3973. https://doi.org/10.1007/s10530-024-03424-0
91. Hahs, J. (2022). The ILO beyond Philadelphia. In F. Nullmeier, D. González de Reufels, & H. Obinger (Eds.), *International impacts on social policy*. Global Dynamics of Social Policy. Palgrave Macmillan. https://doi.org/10.1007/978-3-030-86645-7_14
92. Kyllönen, K. M., Kirchner, S., Poelzer, G., et al. (2024). Indigenous rights, social media and protest movements in Sápmi. *Mineral Economics*. https://doi.org/10.1007/s13563-024-00445-y
93. Challender, D. W. S., Cremona, P. J., Malsch, K., et al. (2023). Identifying species likely threatened by international trade on the IUCN Red List can inform CITES trade measures. *Nature Ecology and Evolution, 7*, 1211–1220. https://doi.org/10.1038/s41559-023-02115-8
94. Goyes, D. R. (2024). National legislative adoption of international wildlife law after treaty ratification. *Crime, Law and Social Change, 81*, 143–162. https://doi.org/10.1007/s10611-023-10117-7

MIX
Papier aus verantwortungsvollen Quellen
Paper from responsible sources
FSC® C105338

If you have any concerns about our products,
you can contact us on
ProductSafety@springernature.com

In case Publisher is established outside the EU,
the EU authorized representative is:
Springer Nature Customer Service Center GmbH
Europaplatz 3, 69115 Heidelberg, Germany

Printed by Libri Plureos GmbH
in Hamburg, Germany